Infamous
Manhattan

Infamous Manhattan

A Colorful Walking Tour of New York's Most Notorious Crime Sites

ANDREW ROTH

A CITADEL PRESS BOOK
Published by Carol Publishing Group

A Citadel Press Book
Published by Carol Publishing Group
Citadel Press is a registered trademark of Carol Communications, Inc.
Editorial Offices: 600 Madison Avenue, New York, N.Y. 10022
Sales and Distribution Offices: 120 Enterprise Avenue, Secaucus, N.J. 07094
In Canada: Canadian Manda Group, One Atlantic Avenue, Suite 105,
    Toronto, Ontario M6K 3E7
Queries regarding rights and permissions should be addressed to
Carol Publishing Group, 600 Madison Avenue, New York, N.Y. 10022

Carol Publishing Group Books are available at special discounts for bulk purchases,
sales promotion, fund-raising, or educational purposes. Special editions can be created
to specifications. For details, contact: Special Sales Department, Carol Publishing
Group, 120 Enterprise Avenue, Secaucus, N.J. 07094.

MANUFACTURED IN THE UNITED STATES OF AMERICA

10 9 8 7 6 5 4 3 2 1

Library of Congress Cataloging-in-Publication Data
Roth, Andrew, 1958–
    Infamous Manhattan : a colorful walking tour of New York's most
notorious crime sites / Andrew Roth.
        p. cm.
    "A Citadel Press book"
    ISBN 0–8065–1701–8 (pbk.)
    1. Crime—New York—Manhattan (N.Y.) 2. Criminals—New York—
    Manhattan (N.Y.) 3. Criminals—Homes and haunts—New York—
    Manhattan (N.Y.) 4. Manhattan (New York, N.Y.)—Description and
    travel. I. Title.
HV6795.M32R67   1995
364.9747′1—dc20   95–9372
                                                                       CIP

To Anni,
who stole my heart

Contents

Preface

"What a task we have here undertaken! To penetrate beneath the
thick veil of night and lay bare the fearful mysteries of darkness in the
metropolis—the festivities of prostitution, the orgies of pauperism, the
haunts of theft and murder, the scenes of drunkenness and beastly
debauch, and all the sad realities that go to make up the lower
stratum—the underground story—of life in New York!"

—*New York By Gas-Light*, 1850

New York is famous for many things, but it is infamous for its crime.
It is the thing that people think of first when they think of New
York. Guidebooks to the city invariably contain dire warnings on
crime and safety, parents fret over their city-bound children, and residents of every other locality in the country shake their heads in
wonder over the very idea that anyone can live there at all.

The great quantity of bad behavior in New York has given this city
not only a fearful reputation, however, but also a deep and fascinating criminal heritage. Yet it is the architecture, the art galleries, the
museums, the theaters, and the restaurants that get all the attention.
Guidebooks and walking tours neglect the rich history of wrongdoing and offer residents and visitors nothing to ogle besides cast-iron
dormers, crenulated quoins, and museumed Vermeers.

Infamous Manhattan is a manual to the monuments and landmarks of New York that are not set in stone or steel, but are nevertheless an intrinsic part of the city: the famous, curious, and colorful
crimes and villains of immoral, illegal, licentious, fascinating Manhattan. Arranged in walking tours, it brings readers to the thresholds—quite literally—of hundreds of Manhattan crimes and criminals
past and present, well-known, notable, and undeservedly obscure.

Infamous Manhattan covers the entire span of New York criminal
history, from New Amsterdam's very first murder in 1638 to the
World Trade Center conspiracy trial of 1995. It details a huge range
of illegal and questionable activity, from murder (represented here in
many varieties) to robberies to drug dealing to plain slander.

The crimes that made Manhattan famous are here, of course, but
there is a great deal more. Forging the city's criminal history into

walking tours has, curiously, freed me to point out places and incidents that a more conventional case book or history might ignore. So you'll find within the neglected Anthony Hintz murder, the inspiration for Budd Schulberg's "On the Waterfront"; the office of Madame Van Buskirk, an infamous nineteenth-century abortionist; a biography of pioneering Tong hitman Sing Dock; and criminal minutiae that has to my knowledge appeared in no other book, such as the site of the first recorded Mafia hit, English murderer Dr. Crippen's New York connection, and the spot where exotic dancer Little Egypt met her untimely death.

And there's another unexpected advantage to the book's topographical approach. Manhattan's methodical march of settlement northward means that the tours unfold more or less chronologically. The first stop of the first tour, in fact, is New Amsterdam's first recorded murder. Thus, with some exceptions and excursions, *Infamous Manhattan* also forms a loose narrative history of crime in Manhattan.

While the book concentrates on revealing specific incidents, it also sketches the scope and development of crime in New York. Various stops provide springboards for brief discussions of, for example, the rise and fall of several red-light districts, the crimes of New Amsterdam's first settlers, the history of gambling, racketeering in the garment district, the Black Hand, and other practices and trends.

Each chapter covers one or several distinct neighborhoods. Short histories of local crime introduce each chapter. The walking tours follow; each should take about two to three hours to complete, depending upon your gait and gawk (the Broadway tour may be a bit longer). For those too tired—or too timid—to embark on the walks, *Infamous Manhattan* should be engaging even in the comfort and safety of home.

Every chapter also contains off-tour sites (labeled "Also Infamous"); short biographies (called "Mug Shots") culled from the gallery of New York fiends, heroes, and victims; and lists of criminal trivia and superlatives. The last chapter is a unique guide to bars and restaurants where readers can drink and dine along with the ghosts of New York crimes past.

The choice of incidents and personalities was determined to some extent by geography, and not every part of the city is covered. Thus some famous Manhattan sins and sinners are left out; this is inevitable in any book of New York crime that hopes to be portable. The Upper West Side and Harlem (and Washington Heights and Inwood) are not included: their relatively late settlement means that notable crimes have not accumulated in sufficient numbers for convenient walking. Perhaps by the next edition. There should be, anyway, enough murder and mayhem here to satisfy every aficionado of crime and every resident, visitor, and devotee of this inimitable, if occasionally unwholesome, island.

Acknowledgments

Many people have contributed to this book. For their help with research I would like to thank the staffs of the peerless New York Public Library, the library and print division of the New York Historical Society, the print division of the Museum of the City of New York (especially Terry Ariano), the Municipal Archives of the City of New York, and the photo library of the New York Post (especially Steve Abrams and Gretchen Viehmann). I received invaluable suggestions, answers, criticisms, or moral support from Jane Alpert, Jacques Bagio, Paige Beaver, John Castellucci, Kevin Cote, Jay Decker, Mark Dery, Helen Duffy, Janet Dunson, Santiago Fittipaldi, Al Fried, Margaret Hadleigh-West, Jenna Weissman Joselit, Lindy Judge, Daniel Levine, Dirk Lindemann, Jeremy McLaughlin, Margot Mifflin, William Newman, John Ponder, Lisa Ramaci, Art Raveson, Dina Silva, Tom Starace, Steve Vincent, Mark Zucker and Penny Zucker and I thank them all for helping to make this a better book.

My thanks also go to: the Berlin design firm of LindemannBagios, which produced the maps with consummate skill; my agent, Laurie Fox, whose energetic efforts helped to make this book a reality; and my editor, Kevin McDonough, for his guidance and assistance.

The support of my family was essential and I thank my parents and brothers for their enthusiasm and suggestions throughout this project.

The invaluable and unstinting contributions of Jay Sullivan deserve more than simple thanks. Throughout the years of researching and writing, elations and disappointments, Jay has always been there, to offer editorial assistance, suggestions, encouragement, or sometimes just a whiskey and soda. This book would have been impossible without him.

Without the support and love of Anni Klose, writing this book would not only have been impossible, but meaningless.

" . . . such various attempts to rob and so many Robberies actually committed, having of late been very frequent, within the circuits of this City, both Day and Night, it is become hazardous for any person to walk in the latter."

—John Holt,
1762

"Destructive rascality stalks at large in our streets and public places, at all times of the day and night, with none to make it afraid . . . ."

—*The Commercial*,
1840

"New York, in fact, is surfeited with murder. It is a commonplace of the day's news; it has ceased to attract attention. Men are stabbed or shot down or blackjacked, not secretly, but in the open, crowded streets at midday, for little or no cause. Life has become cheaper in New York than in the wildest of Western mining-camps."

—*Harper's Weekly*,
1908

" . . . the conditions of our streets have gotten much more dangerous and for you to feel comfortable walking home tonight you are going to need to see police officers."

—Rudolph W. Giuliani,
1993

Infamous
Manhattan

1

Broadway, Union Square, Gramercy Park

A Criminal Sketch of Lower Broadway

Broadway was originally a narrow Indian trail on the crest of a low ridge on a forested, wilderness island. The handful of soldiers, settlers, traders, and refugees who came here from Holland in 1625 built a small fort at the foot of Broadway, where the Custom House now stands, and expanded the Indian trail. By 1647, when Peter Stuyvesant became governor, there were about 800 residents in New Amsterdam, as the Dutch then called New York, and the trail had become known as Breedweg and served as the main street of the scrappy community.

Crime in Broadway's Dutch infancy was, like the street itself, quite modest. There was a bit of petty thievery, a good lot of public drunkenness, some brawling, and a healthy and unstoppable stream of cursing and blaspheming. The city fathers blamed much of this gracelessness on the wine jug and the tavern, and one of the first laws promulgated by Dutch Director General Peter Stuyvesant upon his arrival attempted to regulate the settlement's grog shops, as " . . . we have observed and remarked the insolence of some of our inhabitants, who are in the habit of getting drunk, of quarreling, fighting, and of smiting each other . . . ."

There were fewer than four taverns in the area around what is now Bowling Green Park, and the large, open intersection between these taverns must have been an enticing spot for drunken revelry and might easily be considered New York's first crime zone. A brawl in front of Abraham Pietersen's tavern, just above the northeast corner of Broadway and Beaver Street, in the early morning of July 22, 1648, resulted in the stabbing and death of Gerrit Slomp. And

1

Broadway, Union Square, and Gramercy Park

End here

East 22nd
East 21st
East 20th
East 19th
East 18th
East 17th
East 16th
East 15th
East 14th

Fifth Avenue
Broadway
Irving Place
Gram Pa
Union Square
Fourth Ave.

32
30 31
29
28
27
26
25

East 13th
East 12th
East 11th
East 10th
East 9th
East 8th
Waverly Place
Astor Place
East 4th
Great Jones
Bond
Bleecker
Houston
Prince
Spring
Broome

Washington Square Park
West 4th
West 3rd
Bleecker

24
23
22
21
20
19
18
17
16

West Broadway
Broadway
Lafayette
Wooster
Greene
Mercer
Howard
Canal

Canal
Lispenard
Franklin Place
Franklin
Leonard
Worth
Thomas
Duane
Chambers
Murray
City Hall Park
Fulton
Dey
Cortland
Liberty
Cedar
Thames
Rector
Exchange Alley
Morris
Battery Place
Custom House
Whitehall
Battery Park

West Broadway
Church
Broadway
Broad
World Trade Center

15
14
13
12
11
10
9
8
7
6
5
4
3
2
1

Continue at bottom of other map

Start here

Schout (Sheriff) Cornelius van Tienhoven reported to the Common Council in 1654 " . . . that not long since very indecent and disgraceful things had been perpetrated, on the Broadway in this City by certain women." Unfortunately, the Schout fails to provide a detailed description.

Despite this auspicious start, however, Broadway, throughout the seventeenth and eighteenth centuries, under both the Dutch and English, was never much of a locus of crime, especially compared to the rough dock neighborhoods and the poorer and denser blocks around Pearl, Stone, and Beaver Streets. Broadway grew instead into a prosperous neighborhood of fine homes and expensive shops set peaceably on the wide, airy boulevard.

Still, the locale did not remain completely undisturbed, and complaints were occasionally noted, mostly burglaries. An item in the *New York Journal or General Advertiser* of July 20, 1769 records an early Broadway crime, fairly typical in type and size:

> On Tuesday evening was examined and committed to gaol a Man who has called himself Hamilton and says he is a Sailor, who confessed that he had in his Possession and sold to Different Persons the three Damask covers off the Cushions, and three Prayer Books, lately stolen out of St. Paul's Church in the city.

A veritable crime wave hit the neighborhood when John and Elizabeth Dowers established a tavern at Broadway and Robinson Street (now Park Place). This indefatigable couple were indicted no less than seven times between 1765 and 1766 for thievery and keeping a disorderly house.

The British occupation of the city and the several succeeding years proved to be a lawless period. A particularly modern-sounding incident took place in August 1778 when Peter Ball, walking down Broadway at eleven at night, was attacked by five men who robbed him of everything from cash to shoes and threatened to kill him if he called for help.

But things really didn't get going on Broadway for another half century or so, and it was not until the appearance of the grand hotels that it became really suitable for thieves, prostitutes, con men, and others in the fraternity (and sorority) of vice. Millionaire real estate baron John Jacob Astor built the first luxury hotel on Broadway, the Astor House, in 1836. By 1854 there were over twenty huge, sumptuous, and very popular hotels on the street, pushing out the last of the flinty residents and fostering a population of travelers and revelers far away from the confines and conscience of home. These hotels fostered the growth nearby of theaters, saloons, and dance halls. And these establishments provided, in turn, a fertile soil for a rapid flowering of brothels, houses of assignation, gambling dens, and the like, creating an extensive, prosperous, and surprisingly open red-light district in what is now SoHo (see p. 128).

The city responded by organizing the celebrated Broadway Squad, thirty or so of New York's tallest and handsomest police officers. But they did little in the way of crime-fighting: their main task was to control traffic on the congested street and impress tourists. The squad's lack of real muscle made them the object of local jokes.

By the 1870s, Broadway Squad or no, the neighborhood was getting seamy. Journalist and popular historian Herbert Asbury noted that " . . . one of the notorious places of the city was the Thieves' Exchange in the Eighth Ward, near Broadway and Houston Street, where criminals and their fences met each night and dickered openly over their beer and whiskey for jewelry and other loot." The corner of Broadway and Broome Street was a well-known hangout for pimps.

Because of the growth of such unpleasantness, fashionable sinning began a move uptown, along with the hotels and theaters, to the neighborhood around 23rd Street. Lower Broadway, becoming commercial, slowly darkened. By the 1890s, a writer, thinking back on old nighttime revelries, could lament that, "It is silent and abandoned after eight o'clock. One is almost startled by its solitude."

This solitude and abandonment remain. A commercial district breeds commercial crimes, and, with only a few exceptions visited on this tour, colorful crimes have taken up elsewhere.

Stalking Lower Broadway _____

> Nearest subway: Bowling Green 4 & 5
> Nearest bus lines: M 6; M 9; M 10; X 25

Start in front of the steps of the Custom House, which occupies the site of Fort Amsterdam, the small, wooden fortress laid out by the Dutch in 1625.

1 The first stop on our first tour is, serendipitously, the site of the first recorded murder in New Amsterdam. It happened, just about where you now stand, in the late afternoon of May 15, 1638. This was only twelve years after the arrival of Peter Minuit and his fabled purchase of Manhattan Island. The European population of the outpost was something around five hundred hardy souls. Beyond Wall Street there was nothing but wilderness.

An eyewitness account, a sworn statement from one Thomas Hall, describes in detail this prime homicide:

> . . . while he, the deponent, was standing at the gate of Fort Amsterdam, he saw Gerrit Jansen, gunner, come to said fort with a drawn knife in his hand and, following him, Jan Gysbertsen from Rotterdam, also with a drawn knife. Being come outside the gate of the fort, Gerrit Jansen above named spoke: "If I must stand, I will stand," and immediately, one striking at the other, Jan Gysbertsen wounded said Gerrit Jansen in his head, who fell over some palisades that lay there and said: "The devil shall take you for this," at the same time approaching Jan Gysbertsen. Jan Gysbertsen aforesaid thereupon made a pass at Gerrit Jansen and hit him in the left breast, so that he staggered a little; nevertheless, in turning around, Gerrit aforesaid hit Jan from behind in his buttock. Further, as Gerrit could not do any more on account of his wounds, Jan Gysbertsen asked him if he, Gerrit Jansen, wanted any more. Whereupon he gave for answer that he had enough, not going forth and coming within the gate of Fort Amsterdam, he fell to the ground and was dead.

Gysbertsen immediately skipped town. Several months later he was sentenced *in absentia* to death, but there is no evidence that he was ever seen again.

A curious incident occurred three years later, involving the second murder in New Amsterdam. Nine African slaves were convicted of killing Jan Premero, another slave, in a brawl, but, for economy's sake—nine able-bodied slaves being a bit much to lose in one afternoon—the Common Council, the city government, decided that the prisoners should draw lots, "whereupon," the council minutes relate, "the lot fell by God's Providence on *Manuel Gerrit, the Giant*, who was accordingly sentenced to be hanged by the neck until dead as an example to all such malefactors." Gerrit evidently came by his nickname honestly, for as soon as he stepped off the scaffold, erected by the fort here, the two halters around his neck broke under his weight. Cries of mercy quickly went up from the crowd, and Gerrit was saved, as he was chosen, by God's Providence.

Take a few steps north to Bowling Green, a center of revolutionary violence and treason during late Colonial times.

❷ An early spark of the American Revolution was ignited in the greenery of this small park. Led by the Sons of Liberty, a militant pro-independence group, a dramatic riot erupted here on November 1, 1765, in protest of the British law that first raised the cry of "no taxation without representation"—the hated Stamp Act. A crowd hanged an effigy of the governor in City Hall Park, and then

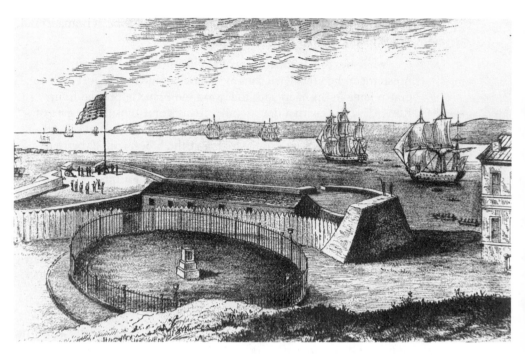

A de-Georged Bowling Green Park in 1776 (at right, the Kennedy mansion).

marched down Broadway to the fort. Reported the *New-York Post-Boy:*

> After they had shown many insults to the effigy, they retired from the fort gate to the Bowling Green, the palisadoes [*sic*] of which they instantly tore away, marched with the gallows, &c. into the middle of the Green, (still under the muzzles of the fort guns), where with the palisades and planks of the fort fence, and a chaise and two sleighs, taken from the Governor's coach-house, they soon reared a large pile of wood round the whole, to which setting fire, it soon kindled a great flame, and reduced the coach, gallows, man, devil, and all to ashes.

There was more treason here a decade later, on July 9, 1776, when a ragtag mob of radicals destroyed a statue of their sovereign, King George III, that stood in the middle of the Green. It's said that the statue was melted down into bullets that killed four hundred British soldiers during the War for Independence.

3 To the west of the small park, 1 Broadway stands on the lot where the Kennedy mansion could once be found. It was so fine that the British expropriated it when they occupied the city from 1776 to 1783, and it served as the headquarters for redcoats General Sir William Howe and Sir Henry Clinton. Inside the Kennedy mansion, Clinton worked out the nefarious plan for that great American traitor Benedict Arnold to deliver West Point to the British. Arnold later lived next door at 3 Broadway, the north end of the present building.

Walk up three blocks to the northwest corner of Rector Street and Broadway, where the Arcade Building (71 Broadway) stood in the late nineteenth century.

4 On December 4, 1891, a number of local wage workers were out for a noon hour of fresh air in Trinity Churchyard. At 12:21 PM their lunch was interrupted by the blast of an immense explosion—it was heard two and a half miles away—which showered them with splinters of glass and wood and surrounded them in a white cloud of dust and plaster. Those who turned their heads in the direction of the Arcade Building witnessed the startling sight of a body shooting from a second-story window and landing, amid a billow of brick and plaster, in the middle of Rector Street.

The unfortunate missile was Benjamin F. Norton, the secretary of the well-known and much-hated, financier and money manipulator Russell Sage, whose office was poor Norton's launching pad. The crusty Sage, was, in that age of tycoons and robber barons, Wall Street's richest man, and its most despised. Sage ran no railroads or steamship lines. He made his millions by relentless and crafty stock trading, guileful buying and selling, and steely bargaining. The contemporary attitude toward the man was summed up by biographer Paul Sarnoff: "It was said of 'Mr. Sage' that he was a miser, a cruel, heartless usurer, a manipulator, a corruptor of politicians and the judiciary. It was charged that he was a plunderer, a wrecker, a despoiler of both the corporate treasuries he commandeered and the unwitting shareholders he gulled. Many maintained with grim certainty that he possessed no human feelings, that he was a 'charitable bankrupt' and that he seemingly endlessly sang only one song: 'money, money, my money.' "

A half-hour before the explosion, a messenger entered the anteroom of the financier's office and asked for Mr. Sage. Nothing too unusual, and though the messenger was unfamiliar he attracted no special attention. He carried a small black satchel and offered a business card with the name H. D. Wilson; he said he was on a confidential mission from John D. Rockefeller. When the normally secretive Sage appeared, enticed out of his office by the Rockefeller name, the messenger, without a word, handed him a letter. It read:

> Give me $1,200,000 at once or I shall drop this bag which contains ten pounds of dynamite and you and all the occupants of this building will be killed. Will you give me the money? Yes or No?

There are two versions of what happened next. One goes like this: Sage carefully read the note and then began to inch his way toward the door of his office.

"Where are you going?" screamed the messenger.

"To my vault, Sir. Surely you don't think I keep such an amount about my office?"

"I don't trust you!" the man shrieked, drawing a pistol from his coat and aiming it at his bag of dynamite.

"If you don't trust me, how can I trust you?" replied Sage, who then dived head first for the doorway.

That is the Sage version. The second version is the Laidlaw version:

As Sage read the note, the front door opened and William Laidlaw, Jr., a broker's clerk from a neighboring firm, walked in. The old man, beaming, greeted Laidlaw with an enthusiastic clasp on the shoulder and a fervent handshake, which enabled him to step neatly behind the clerk and, using him as a shield, make a jump for his office door.

Whichever version you choose—and they were both dragged through the courts for many years in a series of celebrated trials after Laidlaw sued the financier for injuries (the clerk eventually lost)—the immediate result was the same. The messenger fired his pistol into the satchel; a huge explosion shattered the office and Norton, who was also in the anteroom, took flight.

Sage, miraculously, was only shaken and scratched. Laidlaw had severed an artery but did not require hospitalization.

The messenger was blown to bits, with the curious exception of his head, which was found amidst the rubble neatly severed and intact. The clue that led to his identification, though, was not this extremity but a single pants button, stolen from the scene by an enterprising, if somewhat unethical, reporter. He traced it to a tailor in Boston, who found it belonged to his customer Henry L. Norcross, a young note broker in that city. It turned out that the unbalanced Norcross had invented a device he thought would revolutionize the operation of elevated railroads, but, as often happens with such visionaries, the world refused to listen. Constantly rebuffed in his search for start-up capital, he was driven to extraordinary measures. Found in his safe at home was a note that read: " 'Dear Mother: I am going to New York to get $1,200,000. If successful, I shall return. If not I shall kill myself.' (signed) Henry L. Norcross."

Walk a block up to 115 Broadway, where the City Hotel, New York's most prestigious hostelry in the early nineteenth century, once stood.

5 Judge Joseph Force Crater (see p. 122) is New York's most famous vanished jurist, but he was not the first. That distinction belongs to

Justice John Lansing Jr., in his day a much more prominent and noted legalist than Crater. He was, in fact, one of the young republic's leading public figures. Lansing was born in Albany in 1754 and became a lawyer twenty-one years later, but most of his career was spent in public office. He was a member of the New York Assembly, took a seat in Congress under the Articles of Confederation, served as mayor of Albany, and was appointed chief justice of the New York Supreme Court. In 1787 he represented New York (along with Alexander Hamilton) at the Constitutional Convention.

At the age of seventy-five Lansing's public career had ended, but he still practiced law, and occasionally traveled into the city on business. Such an occasion arose on December 12, 1829, when the judge put up here at the City Hotel. He left the hotel at 5:00, tottering, most likely, for he was an old man, past the spot where you now stand. He was to post a letter to Albany, and then meet a friend. Instead, he vanished. His family advertised for him: "When last seen he was dressed in black and had powdered hair." But even with this distinctive costume and coiffure, he failed to attract anyone's notice. No one responded to the advertisement, no word or sign of the man arose, and the Judge has remained forever lost. Journalist and politician Thurlow Weed claimed, years afterwards, that he had been given evidence that Lansing had been murdered. But because the murderer's descendants were now wealthy (indeed, wealthy because of the murder) and held positions of public trust, he would not, he said, reveal the perpetrator's name. A tidbit like that makes the mystery all the more titillating. On the other hand, it is reported that descendants of Lansing investigated Thurlow's story and found it had no basis in fact. Another, more plausible report states that he died in a brothel and his family secretly removed his body to avoid scandal. Better an unsolved mystery than an unchaste history, evidently.

ALSO INFAMOUS

The blocks behind St. Paul's Chapel, where the World Trade Center now rises, were, in the late eighteenth century, a favored locale for prostitutes and brothels. Patrick M'Robert, visiting New York in 1774, reported that "Above 500 ladies of pleasure keep lodgings contiguous within the consecrated liberties of St. Paul's. This part of the city belongs to the church, and has thence obtained the name of the *Holy Ground*." A soldier stationed in the city during the Revolutionary War wrote that the prostitutes here "not only destroy men by sickness, but they sometimes inhumanly murder them; . . . since Monday last two Men were found inhumanly Murthered [*sic*] & concealed, besides one who was castrated in a barbarous manner."

Walk up another block to the northwest corner of Broadway and Cedar.
Pause and look to your left, where you'll see the huge twin towers of the
World Trade Center looming above you. This landmark was the target,
on February 26, 1993, of one of the worst terrorist bombings the country
has ever experienced.

6 The toe of Manhattan contains perhaps the greatest concentration of
capitalist strength in the world. Because of this, it has long been an
irresistible target for bomb-laden radicals and reactionaries of one ilk
or another, from the mysterious author of the Wall Street Bombing
of 1920 (see p.66) to '60s radical Sam Melville (see p. 234) to the
Fuerzas Armadas de Liberación Nacional (FALN) in the '70s (see p.
282).

Those responsible for the World Trade Center bombing of February 26, 1993, however, are in another class altogether. They attempted not just a symbolic strike against U.S. capitalism, but tried
to literally close it down.

The World Trade Center is a city within the city. A full 10 percent
of the financial district's office space is contained in the trade center.
It houses stores, restaurants, a police station and jail, and offices of
many of the most important government agencies and financial companies. Fifty thousand people work here; 80,000 visit the two towers
every day.

The bomb, placed in an underground garage beneath the center's
foundation, was intended to bring one tower crashing into the other,
an event that would have disabled Manhattan, brought an end to
this economic linchpin, and killed tens of thousands of people. The
prospect is chilling to consider.

The actual damage was slighter but startling nevertheless: the immense bomb, 1,500 pounds of explosive paste composed of urea and
nitric and sulfuric acids packed into the back of a van, blew a hole in
the subbasement five stories deep, killed six people, and injured
thousands.

It disabled the tower's infrastructure entirely—knocking out the
electricity, water supply, and the backup power system—and caused
half a billion dollars worth of property damage. The FBI later said
the bomb was "the largest by weight and by damage of any impro-
vised explosive device that we've seen since the inception of forensic
explosive identification."

Tens of thousands of workers had to make their way to safety on
the ground through dark, smoke-filled stairwells, some of them
walking for four hours and down 100 flights. Thirty-seven people
were plucked off the roof by helicopter. Thousands were treated for
smoke inhalation, shock, and other injuries.

Police expecting a hard search for sophisticated terrorists (the short list included Serbian nationalists, Bosnian militants, and Iraqi President Saddam Hussein) were surprised when, within the week, they nabbed a suspect who appeared to be considerably more of an amateur.

At about 2 P.M. February 26, some two hours after the blast, Mohammed Salameh went to a Jersey City Ryder truck rental agency to report that the yellow van he had recently rented had been stolen from a supermarket parking lot. He asked for his $400 deposit back. The clerk refused, telling him he needed a police report. He returned several days later, without a report, and pleaded for his deposit. He was again refused.

By that time, investigators had pulled a mangled piece of iron car frame from the bomb site with an identification number, and traced it to the yellow van from the Jersey City agency. There they heard the story of the persistent customer. Won't you please, the FBI suggested to the clerk, call Mr. Salameh and tell him his deposit is waiting? Incredibly, Salameh returned.

The arrest of Salameh soon led police to three others, Nidal Ayyad, Mahmud Abouhalima, and Ahmad Ajaj. Two other indicted suspects, Ramzi Ahmed Yousef (said to be the real brains behind the operation) and Abdul Rahman Yasin, slipped away.

The plot appeared to be quite low-tech. The group spent months assembling chemicals in a rented garage space in New Jersey and then mixing the explosives in plastic garbage cans. The explosive paste, mixed with old newspapers, was poured into four cardboard boxes. Four containers of nitroglycerin were attached to blasting caps with twenty-foot fuses.

On February 26, Salameh, with Yousef beside him, drove the rented, loaded van into Manhattan, followed by Abouhalima driving a blue Lincoln. They pulled into the World Trade Center's public parking garage on level B-2 and parked on a ramp near an outer wall where they hoped the bomb would knock out the building's foundation. They lit the four fuses with a disposable cigarette lighter and departed in the Lincoln. At 12:18 P.M. the van exploded.

The resulting trial—a lengthy affair of technical and circumstantial evidence that was so dull even the judge was said to have fallen asleep at one point—resulted in the convictions of the four defendants. On March 4, 1994, they were sentenced to the unusual terms of 240 years each. In February, 1995, Ramzi Ahmed Yousef was captured in Pakistan and brought back to the U.S. to face charges for his role, said to be a major one, in the bombing.

A motive for the attack, never made explicit during the trial, became evident later when the government indicted a group of twelve others, several with connections to the World Trade Center defendants, with conspiracy to bomb the United Nations headquarters, the FBI headquarters, and the Holland and Lincoln Tunnels as part of an urban *jihad* directed against the "infidel" United States.

The group was allegedly inspired by an Islamic religious leader, Sheik Omar Abdel Rahman, said to espouse a virulent and violent form of Islamic fundamentalism. Rahman, from Egypt, established himself in New Jersey after his acquittal in his native country on charges of complicity in the 1981 assassination of President Anwar el-Sadat. Several of the accused men—and several of the convicted World Trade bombers—worshipped at a Jersey City mosque where Rahman regularly preached. The government maintains that the World Trade Center bombing was the opening salvo of the group's religious war.

One of the indicted conspirators was Sayyid Nosair, already incarcerated for charges stemming from the assassination of Rabbi Meir Kahane (see p. 249). On October 1, 1995, the defendants were convicted on 48 of the 50 charges.

Keep walking up Broadway and cross into City Hall Park at Murray Street.

❼ Here we reach a principal spot in the city's criminal history.

Throughout most of the eighteenth century and much of the nineteenth century, City Hall Park was the nucleus of crime and punishment in New York City. At one time or another during those years court, prison, police headquarters, and hanging ground were all located on this green triangle.

As early as 1725, resolutions from the Common Council directed that gallows be erected "at the usual place of execution on the Commons." In 1784, an odd-looking gallows—usually described as "the Chinese Pagoda"—was put up where the East Wing of City Hall now stands. Officially called "The Execution House," it was something of an all-purpose complex, including a gallows, whipping-post, and stocks. Francis Higgins, hanged in 1784 for highway robbery, was apparently the first involuntary occupant of the Pagoda. Not all felons were executed here though; especially popular, or unpopular, criminals were brought to the far outskirts of town to avoid unruly crowds, and so in 1816 Ishmael Frazer (condemned for arson) and Diana Silleck (convicted of murder) were hanged at the intersection of Bleecker and Mercer Streets, and murderer James Johnson was hanged at Second Avenue and 13th Street in 1824 (see p. 219). Roosevelt Island and Ellis Island were favorite gallows sites as well, so much so that the venerated entry point for Europe's huddled masses was once known as Gibbet Island. In 1834, public executions were outlawed.

The first real jail in the city (previously prisoners were confined in rooms in the old City Hall) was the "New Gaol" (also called "Debtors' Prison" or sometimes "The Provost"), built in 1757–59 to the east of where City Hall (which didn't appear until 1811) now stands. Just twenty years later the need arose for another place of incarceration, and so in 1775, on the west side of City Hall, the "Bridewell" was built. During the Revolution the British made use of both jails, and it was in the New Gaol that the well-known English villain Provost Marshal Cunningham ruled, abusing his prisoners and dispensing cursory justice on Gallows Hill, located at present-day Centre and Pearl Streets. The New Gaol was renovated in 1830 to serve as a public records depository, and lasted until 1903; the Bridewell came down in 1838.

Walk around and in back of City Hall. The long history of municipal corruption and crime is dramatically marked—and literally set in stone—in the New York County Courthouse, more familiarly known as the Tweed Courthouse.

8 The political scandals of New York City commenced almost as soon as the community itself. Political appointments made in Amsterdam and London were often motivated by favoritism or nepotism, and the Dutch and English administrators of the city were rarely noted for their competence. Especially venal officials included Director General Wooter Van Twiller (1633–38), an alcoholic incompetent who appropriated thousands of acres of West India Company land for himself; Governor Benjamin Fletcher (1692–97), of whom a colonist wrote that "To recount all his arts of squeezing money both out of the publick and private purses would make a volume instead of a letter . . . ."; Governor Edward Hyde, Lord Cornbury (1702–08), considered the most unscrupulous of all the colonial governors for his monstrous graft; Governor William Cosby (1732–36) who openly took bribes and sold government positions; and Governor George Clinton (1743–53), another drinker who accumulated £80,000 during his term.

In 1838 Samuel Swartwout, the collector for the Custom House in New York, embezzled $1.25 million—the first public official to pass the million dollar mark—and left the country. The Board of Aldermen in the 1850s was so notorious for graft and corruption that they earned the nickname "The Forty Thieves." One member was William Tweed.

Tweed was born in New York in 1823. After his apprenticeship with "The Forty Thieves," Tweed went on to a stint in Congress, an appointment on the Board of Education, and membership on the

Grandparent of the tombs: New York's first lock-up, the New Goal.

Board of Supervisors. By 1863, Tweed was both head of Tammany Hall, the primary political machine in the city, and chairman of the New York County Democratic party, positions that made him the preeminent powerbroker in the city. Firmly installed as "Boss" Tweed, he and his cohorts, "the elegant" Oakey Hall, "Slippery Dick" Connolly, and Peter "Brains" Sweeny, plundered and pillaged the city from 1866 to 1871.

"The House That Tweed Built" now stands as an imposing monument to New York City's most famous and inimitable political crook. When completed, the courthouse—slated to cost $250,000—had run up a bill of some $13 million. The padded expenses, of which the Tweed Ring reportedly took 65 percent, included $1.5 million for plumbing and gaslight fixtures; $2.87 million for plastering; and $5.7 million for furniture, carpets, and shades. The brooms cost $41,190. Cuspidors were a bargain at $190 each. The stationery for the building was supplied by a firm owned by Tweed. The marble was supplied by a quarry owned by Tweed. There were at least five dead men listed on the payroll.

Revelations of their jobbery in the press led to the ring's downfall and the arrest of Tweed in 1871. While serving a sentence in the Ludlow Street jail, he effected a thrilling escape (obviously with inside help) and made it all the way to Spain before being traced and returned to New York. He died in his cell on April 12, 1878.

Once the very personification of machine politics and municipal corruption, Boss Tweed has found a soft spot in the heart of the city, and the Tweed Courthouse, once threatened with demolition, is now a fondly considered landmark.

Walk west on Chambers Street to the northwest corner of Broadway and Chambers and the site of the celebrated Colt-Adams case.

9 John Colt was the unknown brother of the very famous Samuel Colt, the inventor of the revolver and a rich and well-connected New Yorker. Brother John, however, toiled in obscurity as an accountant and teacher of penmanship in a second-story office here at the northwest corner of Chambers and Broadway, in a building preceding the present one. He intended to become famous by writing a tome on bookkeeping, a long shot at best. As it happened, Colt gained his notoriety in a rather more dramatic way. On a number of counts, not limited to murder, Colt's case became one of the most interesting and infamous of the nineteenth century.

For his publishing needs, Colt contracted with one of the city's best printers, Samuel Adams, but at an early point a misunderstanding developed over $50 that Adams thought was owed to him. The printer decided to drop by Colt's office—on September 17, 1841— to wrangle over the bill. As one account of the case delicately put it, "the different opinions held by the two about the debt led to ill feeling." More specifically, Colt picked up a hammer from his desk and bashed in his printer's head.

The bookkeeper then took a walk through City Hall Park to mull things over. Rather than going to the authorities, where he at least had a chance to plead self-defense, he decided the best thing to do was to keep quiet, clean up, and box the body for shipment to New Orleans. Conveniently, suspiciously even, he had just the right crate sitting in his office, and with a little maneuvering, Samuel Adams was packed. Colt's confession, taken down shortly after his arrest, describes the proceedings in morbid, absorbing detail:

> After several efforts I succeeded in raising the body to a chair, then to the top of the box, and, turning it around a little, let it into the box as easy as I could, back downward, with head raised. The head, knees, and feet were still a little out, but by reaching down to the bottom of the box, and pulling the body a little towards me, I readily pushed the head and feet in. The knees still projected, and I had to stand upon them with all my weight before I could get them down.

Colt had the crate brought down to Maiden Lane and put into the hold of the next ship going to New Orleans, the *Kalamazoo*. The cumbersome box was addressed to "R. P. Gross of St. Louis," care of "Mr. Gray, New Orleans"—unimaginative pseudonyms for a would-be writer.

Adams was quickly missed, and Colt easily found, and within a week the bookkeeper had been arrested and confessed, claiming self-defense. The jury brought in a verdict of murder in the first degree.

The trial was the talk of the town, but the subsequent adventures of the convicted man attracted even more attention. During his incarceration, which, due to his brother's wealth and connections, he passed in comparative luxury, he was visited regularly by his lover, Caroline Henshaw. They decided to marry on the very day appointed for his execution, November 18, 1842. Dr. George Anthon, the rector of St. Mark's-in-the-Bowery, performed the ceremony. Brother Samuel and John Howard Payne, author of "Home Sweet Home," were witnesses. The ceremony was nearly as long as the marriage: the couple were given one hour together in Colt's cell.

Near four o'clock, when all was ready for the official killing, came more surprises. Jailers fetching Colt for his appointment found him dead on his prison-cell cot, a knife upright in his chest—a suicide! And—yet more excitement—at the same time the entire jail was set into a panic by a fire in the cupola, and there was much confusion until the blaze was put out. It was a trying day for the New York City criminal justice system. As the *New York Herald* excitedly reported the next day, "The death of Adams, and the circumstances attending that fatal deed, can only be paralleled by the trial, sentence, and awful suicide of Colt. The history of the case cannot be equalled in its horror by that of any criminal trial on record."

The unexpected events of the day gave rise to a rumor, repeated still in accounts of the trial, that the fire was deliberately set by confederates of Colt as a distraction while they substituted another body in his cell and helped the condemned man escape. Quite a lot of subterfuge and precise coordination if true. And just who was the poor fellow murdered by Colt's helpful friends? Anyway, we have the Right Reverend Anthon's word that the body in the cell was indeed Colt's. He is believed to be buried in Anthon's church, St. Mark's-in-the-Bowery.

Walk up two blocks to Thomas Street, which was not laid out until the late nineteenth century. Prior to that there was a large square here enclosed by Duane, Worth (then Anthony), and Church Streets, which formed the bucolic grounds of New York Hospital from 1773 to 1870, and the setting, in 1788, of the Doctor's Riot.

10 In the eighteenth century, it was illegal to perform autopsies except under certain very restricted conditions, such as if the body was that of an executed criminal. This was considered by the medical profession an ignorant, unenlightened prejudice and an obstacle to the progress of science, and medical schools ignored it as much as possible and got their corpses as they pleased. A little cottage industry developed: unsavory people, dubbed "resurrectionists," would dig up freshly buried bodies and bring them to a hospital, where eager young interns would plunge into them with no questions asked.

In the late 1780s there were dark rumors that New York Hospital was encouraging this ungodly unearthing, and supposedly a number of violated graves had been found. On April 13, 1788, as a group of young boys were playing in the rear of the medical building, a waggish intern rattled an amputated arm out of a window and yelled, "It's your mother's!" An unfortunate jest, as the mother of one of the boys had recently died, and the father, upon hurrying to his wife's grave, found it plundered.

Or so the story goes, perhaps embellished a tad during two hundred years of retelling. What is certain, however, is that a mob of anywhere from four hundred to five thousand citizens occupied the hospital that day and forced the medical students to flee in terror to the safety of the jail. Rioting continued the next day and the introduction of the militia resulted in gunfire that left three rioters dead. The medical students, after a petrifying two days in the jailhouse surrounded by an angry mob, eventually regained their school.

Here we take a brief excursion off of Broadway. Go left on Thomas Street and walk three blocks to 86 Thomas Street and one of the landmarks of New York criminal history, the site of the city's first sensational, and sensationalized, murder, that of the unfortunate prostitute Helen Jewett. The address was then 41 Thomas Street.

11 The crimson volume of murder has no bloodier page than the one whereon is written the brutal butchery of the lovely Helen Jewett by her lover, Richard P. Robinson, which occurred in this city on the night of the 11th of April, 1836. It was a most damnable crime, and created a tremendous sensation. The comeliness and intellect of the fair but frail Helen, her remarkable career since first she embarked upon the treacherous sea of passion, and the tragic fate that overtook her while yet the bloom was on her cheek and the fire was in her eye, combined to interest every one in the case, and made it the talk of the street, the store, the hotel, and the club.

So gushed Charles Sutton, superintendent of the Tombs prison, in his 1874 account of the case.

"Bronzed like an antique statue": the body of Helen Jewett.

Sutton called Helen Jewett "the acknowledged queen of the promenade," who "swept like a silken meteor through Broadway." She was born Dorcas Doyen in Augusta, Maine in 1813 and made her way to New York, already a professional, at the age of eighteen. Chroniclers agree that she was beautiful, vivacious, and well educated. Her *boudoir* was stocked with the works of Byron, Scott, Dryden, Pope, Homer, Shakespeare, and Irving. Like many another wage earner, she worked her way up the ladder, plying her craft first at a Mrs. Post's in Howard Street, then at Mrs. Ann Weldon's bagnio at 55 Leonard Street, then at the prominent *Palais de Duchesse Berri* on Duane Street. She ended up at the sumptuous pleasure house of Mrs. Rosina Townsend at 41 Thomas Street. Mrs. Townsend's place was described by a contemporary as ". . . the centre of attraction for all the roistering spirits of town. The profusion of extravagance of the celebrated Aspasia, ministered to by Pericles, the greatest ornament of Athens, was not greater than was nightly seen during the summer season at the hotel in Thomas street."

Jewett had been carrying on a torrid and nonprofessional affair with Richard P. Robinson, a young jeweler's assistant and tireless roisterer. While making the rounds of dance halls and brothels, usually beneath a flowing cape and flamboyant hat, he used the alias of "Frank Rivers." At some point Robinson, according to the prosecution, decided to put an end to his affair with Jewett in an abrupt and permanent manner. Some say he was set on marrying his employer's daughter, and that Jewett was inconvenient. Or that Jewett knew a little too much about a previous girlfriend of Robinson's, who had died under mysterious circumstances. A day or two before the murder, he visited the Broadway pharmacy of a Dr. Chabert, for some reason known as the "Fire King," and tried to buy arsenic, unsuccessfully. So Robinson settled on sturdier means and stole a hatchet from his workplace.

On the fateful night of April 11, Robinson tied the handle of the hatchet to a tassel on his cape, and so concealing the murder weapon, set off for an appointment with "the queen of the promenade."

Mrs. Townsend recalled at Robinson's trial that he arrived at her brothel at nine or half-after, and that at eleven Jewett called for a bottle of champagne to be brought to her chambers. Delivering the bubbly, the landlady saw Robinson lying on the bed, with his head on his arm and his face to the wall. At three in the morning Mrs. Townsend was awakened by a late-arriving customer and saw a lamp belonging to Jewett on a table by the back door of the house, which was uncustomarily unlocked. Returning the lamp to her employee's room, she opened the door to a cascade of black smoke and found the bedsheets—and Jewett's body—aflame. Fire was not the cause of death, Mrs. Townsend was quick to see: rather, Jewett's forehead was riven and the young woman dead from a blow inflicted by a heavy and sharp instrument.

James Gordon Bennett, editor of the year-old *New York Herald*, described the body, which he saw the next day:

> The countenance was calm and passionless—not the slightest appearance of emotion was there. An arm lay over her bosom; the other was inverted and hanging over her head. The left side, down to the waist, where the fire had touched, was bronzed like an antique statue. For a few moments I was lost in admiration at the extraordinary sight—a beautiful female corpse, that surpassed the finest statue of antiquity. I was recalled to her horrid destiny by seeing the dreadful bloody gashes on the right temple, which must have caused instantaneous dissolution.

Evidence and testimony indicated that Robinson had fled through the backyard, and, in clambering over several fences, managed to lose both his cape and hatchet. The city watch (no police in that era), found him hours later at home, apparently asleep in bed. Informed of his lover's murder, he commented laconically, "This is a bad business."

The trial was a sensation. For five days the courtroom, and the streets around it, was packed, and the proceedings were several times delayed because of overcrowding. Thousands milled around in City Hall Park to hear the latest word. Public sympathy was overwhelmingly behind the dashing Robinson. Young blades came to the trial sporting the glazed cap that he favored, which became known as the "Frank Rivers Cap." Also in fashion was the "Robinson Cloak," modeled on the garment the young man wore while bar- and brothel-hopping. The evidence against Robinson seemed solid: Mrs. Townsend told of receiving him and seeing him in Jewett's room, other witnesses placed him at the scene, the hatchet and the cloak were traced back to him, the attempt to buy poison described.

Robinson's defense was simple and direct. A friend, Robert Furlong, was produced, who swore that the prisoner was smoking "segars" with him that night. And he wore a frock coat, not a cape, and a cap, not a tall hat. And they didn't part until a quarter after ten, and he was sure because they had compared watches. That this witness was bribed and perjured himself was assumed even at the time, as it was assumed that corruption had stolen into the jury room, for despite overwhelming evidence to the contrary, the twelve men quickly brought in a verdict of not guilty. Cheering erupted in the courtroom.

Concludes Sutton: "Thus ended the famous trial, than which there has been no more interesting one in the history of our courts. The curtain came down upon the stage, the footlights were out, the play was over. Robinson, the murderer, walked forth into the sunlight, while poor Helen, the lovely, fair, frail, misguided girl, rested in her grave."

Robinson went to Texas, where he died two years later. The appropriate moral touch was added to the case two weeks after the trial when Robert Furlong, the defense witness, committed suicide by leaping into the Hudson.

MUG SHOTS

JACOB HAYS
New York's First Detective

Prior to the passage of the Municipal Police Act in 1844, which first established an organized police department, New York functioned with a long-antiquated and outclassed watch system. To a great extent, the city relied on one man for its investigative and detective work: High Constable Jacob Hays, the most notable police officer of his day. "For about forty years subsequent to the beginning of the century," reported early police historian Augustine Costello, "he was the head and front, and guiding spirit of the police of this city; in fact Jacob Hays was a police force all by himself. He, personally, and often unaided, ran down criminals, suppressed riots, and in addition to his functions as High Constable, he originated and organized a detective department, of which he himself was the central figure and the one-man power."

The tireless Hays was born in 1772 in Bedford, New York, and appointed High Constable in 1802. Until his death nearly fifty years later, he was reappointed High Constable by every incoming Mayor. The office was abolished when his tenure ended.

He was the main instrument in solving several of the most famous cases of his time, including the 1831 robbery of the City Bank (see p. 66), and the notorious 1827 Holdgate forgery case, in which hotel owner Timothy B. Redmond, a dead ringer for forger James Holdgate, was perilously close to the gallows before Hays dramatically established his innocence by hauling the real article into the courtroom.

It's said that Hays invented that venerable police procedure, "the third degree," but that is probably an exaggeration. The legend arises out of his role in the John Johnson murder case (see p. 219). Johnson was arrested by the High Constable and taken to the Rotunda in City Hall Park, where the body of the slain sailor James Murray was lying beneath a sheet. With Johnson at his side, Hays whipped the sheet from the corpse and in a stentorian voice demanded, "Look upon the body—have you ever seen that man before?"

"Yes, Mr. Hays, I murdered him," the stunned Johnson said. A little psychological pressure, yes, but physical abuse was evidently not Hays' style.

Hays died at seventy-eight. His portrait once hung in the Governor's Room in City Hall but he no longer seems to rate.

Turn back and take a left on West Broadway; pause for a moment at Leonard Street, and look to your right toward Broadway.

12 About the middle of the block, on the south side, is the site of the "Leonard Street Robbery" of October 24, 1921, pulled off by the (briefly) legendary master criminal Gerald Chapman, and the largest theft in American history up to that date.

On that night postal driver Frank Haveranck was hauling a load of mail along his usual route, driving uptown on Broadway, when he noticed a touring car gaining on him from behind. Slowing down to let the car pass, Haveranck discovered with alarm that one of the occupants had jumped on his running board and was pointing a .38 in his direction. He heard a command: "Slow down and turn left here." He turned the truck into Leonard Street and approached a streetlight, where the robber told him to pull over. "Do it the way you would a routine pickup." The touring car pulled up behind and another figure emerged from the car into the streetlight's cast.

The robber on the running board was Gerald Chapman, an incorrigible but very dapper criminal with a long prison record for burglary and robbery. The second thief was Ivan Dahl Von Teller, better known as Dutch Anderson, an upper-class European who was a swindler and forger and aristocratic charmer. The pair had become friends and partners in prison, Chapman showing Anderson the ins and outs of thievery and Anderson returning the favor by teaching Chapman the finer points of style. Chapman, who grew up in a poor Irish neighborhood in Brooklyn, spent hours catching up on his education and practicing an English accent. He emerged from prison Gatsby-like—a self-created, refined, cultured gentleman crook. Upon his release he meticulously planned this mail truck robbery.

Haveranck was forced to open the mail truck and the two robbers skillfully sifted through the mail pouches, pulling out only those with registered mail. They threw four pouches into their car (driven by a third accomplice, Charlie Loerber) and took off, driving right past the corner where you're now standing and taking a left down West Broadway. It was not until they reached a hideout on Long Island that they realized they had pulled off the largest haul ever: $2,643,720 in bonds, securities, and traveler's checks and over $375,000 in real green cash. The police quickly ascertained the identities of the culprits, but were unable to track them down. We'll leave them hiding a little longer: The manner of their escape, and their subsequent escapades, will be uncovered a little further along on this tour.

Proceed another block up West Broadway to Franklin Street.

13 Excluding perhaps in some very exhaustive history of the theater, you are likely to come across a mention of the once-popular musical comedy *Florodora* only in the context of two notorious twentieth-century killings. One is the Stanford White shooting, still a strong contender for New York's most famous murder (see p. 163). The other, earlier, killing, is the Nan Patterson case, a shooting that took place here at the intersection of Franklin Street and West Broadway, on June 4, 1904.

The Patterson version had Young awkwardly shooting
himself on his left side with a gun held in his right hand.

Patterson was the *Florodora* connection: she had a minor part in
the play as a member of the road company. While on her way to perform in California, she met Francis Thomas Young, better known as
Caesar Young, a wealthy gambler, bookie, race-horse owner, and
blade. Nan and Caesar commenced a romance in 1902, although
Young had been married a good decade at the time.

For two years the pair carried on an open affair, appearing at the
track and on the town together, Young lavishing money on his
young mistress and promising to divorce his wife.

Meanwhile, Margaret Becker Young was trying desperately to get
her man back, and finally, in the summer of 1904, had cajoled him
into a trip to Europe for a few months, away from the distractions of
Nan. The Youngs were booked on the liner *Germanic*, leaving from
West Fulton Street at nine-thirty the morning of June 4. Just before
seven that morning, declaring an urgent need for a shave and a new
hat, Young left his wife in bed in their hotel room in the uptown St.
Paul. He took a hansom cab to Columbus Circle where he had

The prosecution's version claimed that when Patterson
threatened suicide, Young grabbed the gun and was shot.

arranged a rendezvous with Patterson. Nan squeezed in and the cab
headed downtown toward Fulton Street. At the Fifth Avenue Hotel
Young ordered the cab to a halt and ran into Knox's hat store for a
new topper. At Bleecker Street and West Broadway the two dashed
into a saloon for a few drinks (this was about eight in the morning,
remember) before continuing on their way southward. Young never
did get his shave. As the hansom cab rattled through this intersection
a shot rang out. Some moments later—and the length of those moments were a matter of much courtroom debate—the cabby lifted
the trap in the roof of the cab and heard Patterson screaming. Caesar Young died as the cab hurried to the Hudson Street Hospital.

The State claimed Patterson had pulled out a revolver and shot Young. Patterson claimed Young had pulled out a revolver and shot himself. Inconveniently for her version, the path of the fatal bullet went downward from just below Young's shoulder to the top of his lung, a difficult way to self-destruct. In addition, the revolver was found in Young's coat pocket, another neat trick for a suicide.

Other facts, though, seem to corroborate Patterson's version. Powder marks were found on Young's right hand; none were found on his lover's hands. The young woman was, by several accounts, genuinely hysterical when taken from the cab, crying over and over, "Oh, Caesar, Caesar, what have you done!" And why would Patterson shoot her sole—and lavish—source of support?

The papers went all out on this juicy story, drawn irresistibly to the steamy mixture of adultery, high living, a wronged woman, and mysterious goings-on in a closet-sized hansom cab. When they ran out of things to say about developments in the courtroom, editors resorted to reporting on Patterson's many marriage proposals and printing portions of her execrable jailhouse poems. The public was no less enthusiastic. Reported the *New York Times*: "When court was opened yesterday morning the rush for admission was so great that in less than five minutes it was necessary to close the doors, and until midnight last night the Criminal Courts Building was invested with great throngs of the curious who blocked the streets and refused to move. . . . At three o'clock the street in front of the building was packed from curb to curb."

Patterson went through three trials. The first was halted after the death of a juror; the following two ended in deadlocked juries. The prosecution, unwisely, had committed itself to securing a conviction for first degree murder, too difficult for a case with so many uncertainties. Patterson was freed on May 12, 1905, to great celebration. After a very brief return to the stage—her acting was reportedly even worse than her poetry—she sank back into obscurity.

What really happened in the hansom cab? The likeliest explanation is that Patterson, desperate at the prospect of losing Young, cooked up a scheme to wave a pistol about and threaten suicide if Young left her. She could show the extent of her love for the gambler and at the same time put more than a little bit of pressure on him. Young, presumably, tried to grab the gun away from her and was shot in the tussle.

For a more recent case, go right on Franklin back toward Broadway, but pause at Franklin Place, the lonely site of a rather gruesome part of what came to be called the CBS Murders.

14 In the early morning of April 13, 1982, the body of Margaret Barbera was found in the driveway to your right, dead from a single bullet wound in the head. The evening before, three employees of CBS were murdered on Pier 92, on the Hudson River by 52nd Street, by the same assailant. The murders shocked the city and instigated a massive manhunt for what was clearly a hired killer.

Barbera had worked for the Candor Diamond Company, an anything but forthright concern set up by Irwin and Madeleine Margolies for the purpose of bilking their financial backers through a complex scheme of fictitious diamond sales and faked sales invoices. It was fraud on a massive scale, with the Margolies hauling in, over the course of a year and a half, around $5.5 million. Barbera was their bookkeeper and a hardworking confederate who kept the several books—some accurate, some wholly fallacious—needed to conduct the scam. Around the summer of 1981, the financing bank began to get suspicious of Candor and called in the FBI to investigate. Soon the sordid scheme began to fray. With the heat on, Barbera struck a deal with the Feds to exchange testimony for leniency. If convicted, Irwin Margolies would probably have gotten just a handful of years. But unaccountably, he crossed the divide that usually separates the white-collared criminal from his scruffier compatriots: he settled on murder, and hired an amateur hit man, Donald Nash, to silence his bookkeeper. Margolies also wanted Barbera's coworker and lover, Jenny Soo Chin, assassinated. On January 7, 1982, Chin's car was discovered near the Lincoln Tunnel, the seat bloodstained and a .22 shell casing on the floor. Her body was never found.

Nash stalked Barbera for several months, striking that April night as she retrieved her car from a parking lot on Pier 92. As she fumbled to put her key in the car door lock—a lock that Nash had jammed with a wooden toothpick—he walked up behind her and placed a single .22 bullet through her head. He dragged her body to his van, parked beside. Three CBS employees, Leo Kuranski, Robert Schulz, and Edward Benford, also returning to their cars, saw the commotion and went to help. Nash, in a panic, chased them across the parking lot as they turned heel and tried to escape, shooting and killing all three. Confused and unnerved, he sped away, and happened upon this deserted spot before you to deposit Barbera.

The shocking assassinations put the case on the front page and mobilized the full strength of the NYPD. A massive manhunt was launched, and the FBI called in. Nash was not hard to find: He had left a broad trail of phone calls, shell casings, and the like, and within a week was captured in Kentucky, heading south. He was convicted of four counts of second-degree murder for his work on April 12 and of conspiracy to commit the murder of Jenny Soo Chin. He was sentenced to a minimum of 100 years. Irwin Margolies was sentenced to two consecutive sentences of twenty-five years to life for the murders of his two employees. That time was to be served after the twenty-eight years he was handed for the Candor fraud, the longest sentence ever given for a white-collar crime in New York. Madeleine Margolies served three years for tax evasion, and is now presumably living on the ill-gotten money and diamonds the couple carefully stashed away before trial.

Continue back to Broadway and up to Canal.

15 In the nineteenth century a small hotel popular with the business class, the Brandreth House, stood in the triangular intersection formed by Broadway, Canal, and Lispenard. On July 23, 1859, it provided the backdrop for a Victorian tragedy which has unfortunately dropped into obscurity. The participants were the beautiful Virginia Stewart, her lover Robert C. MacDonald, a cotton broker from North Carolina, and, as chronicler Charles Sutton put it, "rum, rage and jealousy—grim triumvirate." It seems they enjoyed an idyllic relationship in North Carolina until MacDonald took to the bottle and became a sloppy and unpalatable drunk. Stewart fled north to New York, but MacDonald followed, catching up with her here on the steps of the hotel.

"I am told you are living with another man—is that so?" he cried. Stewart said nothing, giving him only a contemptuous glance. A bad move, it appears, for MacDonald drew a Colt revolver, bounded up the steps, and shot her in the head at almost point-blank range. The murderer then turned the weapon on himself, but his gun was wrestled away by a witness before he could fire again. Still, he was not denied his dramatic exit, for, while awaiting trial in the Tombs prison, he managed to procure a bottle of Muir's Elixir of Opium and toss back a fatal dose. Incidentally, it's said that the proprietor of the hotel, Doc Brandreth, sold narcotics and spent a great deal of his time out of town, in Sing Sing prison.

Walk up four blocks and pause between Broome and Spring where the grand and luxurious St. Nicholas Hotel once stood on the west side of Broadway. A section of it remains, faded and disheveled, at 521–523 Broadway.

16 An admittedly small milestone in the history of crime, the last recorded case of the fatal use of a sword-cane, occurred at this spot on August 2, 1854. Dr. Robert H. Graham, after a rambunctious night on the town, was careening through the halls of the St. Nicholas in a drunken stupor, ringing a bell in an attempt to call for a maid. He awakened Colonel Charles Loring, who went out in the hallway to remonstrate. Enraged, Graham drew a sword from his cane, and without warning, plunged it into the Colonel, producing a fatal wound.

Go left on Spring Street and walk to the corner of Mercer.

17 This neighborhood, loosely the area bounded by the Bowery, Canal, West Broadway, and Houston Streets, was, during the 1850s, New York's first bona fide red-light district. Look over at 105 Mercer Street, the little Federal-style house on the west side of the street just above the corner. It is one of the very few surviving houses that saw employment as a brothel, and one of the oldest. It was built in 1831 and was being used as a bordello by the next year. At one time the area abounded in similar buildings put to similar uses; 105 Mercer is now the last reminder.

It was run by a Mrs. Smith during its boom years, but little else is known about the house. But we can get an idea of its character by glimpsing at a neighbor, as described in an 1859 underground guide to brothels entitled *Directory to the Seraglios of New York*:

> Mrs. Parker, No. 101 Mercer St.
> This is one of the most fashionable and quiet resorts in town, and within a few moments drive of the principal hotels, &c. Strangers visiting the city would do well to give this house a call, partake of its wines and agreeable lady boarders. The apartments are nicely furnished, and every thing is conducted in the best style. Mrs. Parker is very sociable, agreeable and witty, and strangers are always welcome by her and her pretty boarders.

The red-light district here was so notorious that it became an irresistible stop for adventurous tourists out for a dose of the sinful side of the big city. Numerous books and exposés detailed its charms, simultaneously warning and titillating readers, and there was a thriving trade in brothel guides and racy magazines. Establishments such as Harry Hill's Concert Saloon (see p. 33) were must-sees, and well-known brothel keepers such as Josephine Woods and Julia Brown were counted as forbidden yet thrilling celebrities.

The heart of the district was here, close to Broadway's hotels and theaters. Greene, Mercer, and Wooster were lined, practically wall-to-wall, with brothels; in fact, something like three-quarters of the city's disorderly houses were located in what is now called SoHo. At its height, during the 1850s, there were at least 30 brothels on Mercer Street, 14 on Greene, 14 on Wooster, and 12 on Howard Street.

Lloyd Morris describes Greene Street during its scarlet heyday:

> Along its whole length, on both sides, nearly every house was a brothel. Over the front doors, gas lamps blazed in bowls of tinted glass, usually red but of other colors also. On these lamps the names of the proprietor, or of the establishment, were etched in clear white: "Flora," "Lizzie," "The Gem," "The Forget-Me-Not," "Sinbad the Sailor," "The Black Crook." As you went northward along Greene Street, the quality of the brothels improved and their charges mounted. There were establishments catering to clerks and small tradesmen; up near Clinton Place [now West 8th Street] were the houses for more prosperous members of the middle class. All along Greene Street the shutters were tightly closed, but here or there you could see a light peeping through from a parlor or upper room. Every house had its pianist, who entertained in the parlor where liquor was sold, and the whole street echoed with the popular music of the day.

But brothels were hardly the end. In addition the neighborhood offered the pleasures of houses of assignation, which provided a room and a bed by the hour; concert saloons and dance halls, where one could buy a drink and a waitress; and, of course, a multitude of streetwalkers, or cruisers as they were called.

Broadway was the favorite cruising path for streetwalkers. Walt Whitman remarked in 1857 that "after dark any man passing along Broadway, between Houston and Fulton streets, finds the western sidewalk full of prostitutes, jaunting up and down there, by ones, two, or threes—on the look-out for customers." The *New York Tribune*, attesting to their density, reported in 1854 that "one is so accustomed to the sight of these gaudily dressed butterflies that the streets look very strange without them."

By the end of the Civil War, the bloom had faded. Though many second- and third-class brothels remained, the focus of commercialized sex moved uptown along with the rest of the city, settling in the Tenderloin, west of Madison Square Park. The decline is indicated succinctly by a brothel guide printed in 1870, ten years after the one cited above. "The house No. 101 is of the third class, and contains nothing worthy of attention." The dwellings in SoHo were replaced by the now characteristic cast iron warehouses of the dry goods business, one of the few trades more profitable than sex.

Continue west one more block on Spring Street and then take a right on Greene. Walk just a few feet and, on the west side of Greene, you'll see an alley, the very heart of the enduring mystery of Elma Sands.

18 In 1799, Aaron Burr, that great rapscallion of early American history, chartered the Manhattan Water Company, ostensibly to bring a reliable supply of safe water to the city. He laid several miles of wooden pipes, and had several wells dug, but water was not really on his brain. The Federalist Burr created the company to get around a monopoly on banking enjoyed by the Republican party, and, by invoking a little-noted clause in the by-laws of the company, used its excess capital to establish the Manhattan Bank (which is still doing business as Chase Manhattan). In carrying out his scheme Burr drilled a well that is still extant somewhere beneath the concrete in this alley. On January 2, 1800, the soggy body of Gulielma Sands was found in this well, instigating Manhattan's first notorious murder case and its most enduring murder mystery.

Young Gulielma Sands had left home, the boardinghouse of her aunt and uncle Catherine and Elias Ring, on the evening of December 22, 1799. Before departing, the young woman, called Elma, or sometimes Elmore, had whispered to her aunt that she was to be secretly married that very night to a fellow boarder, Levi Hinckley Weeks. Catherine Ring later testified that she thought she heard the two leaving together. When Elma was found in the well, suspicion naturally fell upon Weeks, and he was quickly arrested.

The defendant was the brother of Ezra Weeks, a prominent builder and architect in the city. Ezra had the means to hire a crack legal team for his brother, an all-star lineup perhaps unparalleled to this day: Livingston Brockholst (later a U.S. Supreme Court Justice), Aaron Burr, and Alexander Hamilton. Though the latter two would soon be dueling in Weehawken, in this case they worked together effectively, and successfully, to defend Levi Weeks.

Catherine Ring's testimony about hearing the couple leave together turned out to be just about all there was to the case against Weeks. There were several witnesses testifying to seeing a couple (or two men and a woman) in a one-horse sleigh, and a Susanna Broad claimed she saw the sleigh of Ezra Weeks, the defendant's brother, being taken out that evening. Others saw sleigh tracks around the well. But no one could positively identify Levi or Elma as the sleigh-riders, and Susanna Broad grew befuddled when she tried to remember the exact night, or even the exact month, when she saw Ezra's sleigh. No one saw the pair together that night, there was no physical evidence to link the pair, there was no established motive (an autopsy revealed that Elma was not pregnant).

In addition, Weeks had a solid alibi—his brother Ezra, and others (including, incidentally, John McComb Jr., one of the architects of City Hall) testified that the defendant was at Ezra's home, and though he did pop out for a few minutes around eight (for Catherine Ring saw him at her boardinghouse), he came right back. The judge, none other than the famous disappearing Justice Lansing (see p. 8), instructed the jury to return a not guilty verdict and, after retiring for but three minutes, they did so. The general feeling at the time was that Levi's connections had enabled him to elude justice, and most accounts of the case, up to the present day, have agreed. But given the very weak prosecution case, it is hard to see how any other verdict could have been returned.

There was one other attractive suspect, one Richard David Croucher. He was a fellow lodger in the Ring boardinghouse, and after the discovery of Elma's body, was, according to one suspicious witness, "extremely busy among the crowd to spread improper insinuation and prejudices against the prisoner [Levi Weeks]." Croucher, besides bearing a proper Dickensian name for a villain, displayed a suitably villainous character. Six months after the trial he was tried and convicted for rape, and then, after somehow wrangling a pardon, moved to Virginia where he got himself tried and convicted again, this time for fraud. He returned to England at some point and was executed there for what is described only as "a heinous crime." There is a legend that during the trial, Burr or Hamilton, in a moment of high courtroom drama, thrust a candelabra before Croucher's face, and, while the flames flickered eerily over his features, cried "Behold the murderer, gentlemen!" But, unfortunately, this did not really happen, and Croucher too had an alibi, having been a guest at a child's birthday party, of all things.

The verdict did not dispel the cloud that hung over Levi Weeks, and he was forced to leave the city. He eventually settled into a successful career as an architect in Natchez, Mississippi, where he died in 1817.

Return to Broadway via Spring Street and walk north. At 579 Broadway, just shy of the corner of Prince Street on the right side, Stanwix Hall once stood, site of a cause célèbre of the nineteenth century, the killing of Bill "the Butcher" Poole.

19 One of the uglier episodes in the history of organized politics in the United States was the rise, in the mid-nineteenth century, of the Native American Party (also known as the Know-Nothings): a xenophobic, racist, and patriotic political group opposed to immigration and given to mob tactics and violence. They were very popular in New York, and one of the best-known of the ilk was William Poole, a butcher by trade, who wielded a great deal of political power on the lower West Side.

Poole had an enemy in John Morrissey, a then-famous prizefighter, and his gang. Morrissey, a Democrat, was staunchly opposed to the nativist Know-Nothings, though his feud with Bill the Butcher seemed as personal as it was political.

The fall of a "true American." Lewis Baker shoots xenophobe Bill "the Butcher" Poole.

By early 1855, after several violent incidents between them, tension was at a breaking point. It broke on February 24, 1855 in the newly opened Stanwix Hall, an ornate saloon opposite the fashionable Metropolitan Hotel. Poole was in the barroom about an hour after midnight when several of Morrissey's gang—Lewis Baker, James Turner, Patrick McLaughlin (also called "Paudeen") and several others—filed in, armed and dangerous. Paudeen sidled up to Poole and muttered, "What are you looking at, you black-muzzled bastard?" He then spit three times into Poole's muzzle for emphasis. Poole, realizing he was in a bit of a jam, placed a stack of gold coins on the bar and offered a hundred dollar bet for a fair fight. But he couldn't resist adding that Paudeen was not included in the offer, as he wasn't worth it. This gratuitous remark turned out to be a major mistake. Turner yelled, "Sail in!" and leveled a Colt revolver at Poole. He was a bad aim, however, and fired his first shot through his own arm. He got off a second shot that hit Poole in the leg, and the Know-Nothing staggered toward Baker. Baker drew his own pistol and fired twice at Poole's chest at close range. He and his henchman then exited.

Poole lived for fourteen days with a bullet in his heart. His last words were: "I die a true American!" whereupon he dramatically expired. Baker hid out in Jersey City for a couple of weeks and then made a run for the Canary Islands. His brig was intercepted, however, and he was returned to New York City. Baker was tried three times for the murder, but in every case the jury failed to agree and he was released. Paudeen was killed three years later in a dance hall owned by Butt Allen in Howard Street. John Morrissey, who was not directly involved, retired from prize fighting in 1857, and became a successful gambling-house proprietor in the city and Saratoga and later a congressman and state senator (see p. 46).

Poole's murder became a rallying cause for the Native American Party, and his funeral was remarkable. More than five thousand mourners, and a half-dozen brass bands, followed the hearse down Broadway. George Templeton Strong recorded in his diary on March 13, 1855: "... two hundred thousand people, they say, were in Broadway; the street was crowded from Bleecker Street to the Ferry."

ALSO INFAMOUS

Harry Hill's Concert Hall, at 22–32 East Houston Street, was the nineteenth century's most popular and notorious dance hall and saloon. A "reputable vile house," as one contemporary put it, the middle class could here go slumming in relative safety, for though the place was full of thieves, and all the waitresses were prostitutes, Harry Hill insisted that no criminal activity take place on the premises—customers had to do their sinning elsewhere. This combination of security and salaciousness gave the dive a national reputation. Lloyd Morris claimed "No visitor to New York would have thought of returning home without having gone at least once to Harry Hill's place . . . ."

Walk two blocks up to Bleecker Street. Pause at the northeast corner.

20 This handsome building was once the headquarters of the Manhattan Savings Institution. Gaze up at the gable on the Broadway side and you can see the monogram, an intertwined M S I, still extant. This was the site (in the bank's first building, preceding this one) of the nineteenth century's most infamous and lucrative bank robbery, dashingly carried out on October 27, 1878 by the era's most famous yegg men (i.e. safe crackers or bank burglars).

The perpetrators were a loose confederacy of proud professionals grouped around the imposing figure of George Leonidas Leslie (see p. 34). They included Jimmy Hope and his son John Hope, Jim Brady, Abe Coakley, Red Leary, Shang Draper, Johnny Dobbs, "Worcester Sam" Perris, "Banjo Pete" Emerson, and Edward "Eddie Goodie" Gearing. Chief of Detectives Thomas Byrnes called them "one of the strongest bands of burglars and thieves that ever existed." Police Chief George Walling claimed, with more than a hint of awe, that "the operations of the Leslie gang . . . in nine years, in this city alone, amounted to a round half million dollars. Throughout the United States their plunderings cannot have been less than $7,000,000, comprising 80 percent of all the bank robberies perpetrated from 1860 to the date of Leslie's death."

The gang planned the Manhattan Savings Institution job for three years, and Leslie made two attempts to pick the vault before finally admitting that a less tidy assault was necessary. The poorly paid night watchman, Patrick Shevlin, was enlisted, as well as a crooked cop, John Nugent, who was enthusiastic enough to volunteer to carry out the bags of loot. At about six o'clock on the morning of October 27, 1878, four members of the gang—Jimmy Hope, William Kelly, Abe Coakley, and Pete Emerson—burst into the bank and tied up the janitor, his wife, and his mother-in-law. Leaving behind one man to guard the terrified family, the others went into the vault with hammers and chisels and in two and a half hours had cleaned out the place.

The gang made off with an enormous haul, especially by nineteenth-century standards: $2,747,700, of which $12,764 was in cash, and the remainder in bonds (compare this to the famous Brink's robbery of 1950, which netted $2,775,395).

After several months of detective work, consisting mainly of putting the screws to amateur Shevlin, the police arrested several of the thieves, but John Hope, William Kelly and Pete Emerson were the only ones ever convicted of the job. Policeman John Nugent apparently got off by bribing a juror, but he was later convicted in Hoboken of highway robbery. Johnny Dobbs died in the alcoholic ward of Bellevue Hospital in the mid 1890s. Chief of Detectives Byrnes' reference work *Professional Criminals of America* gives us the histories of other gang members, but only up to 1886: at that time Jimmy Hope was doing time in California's San Quentin prison; Jim Brady and Eddie Goodie were in Auburn prison; Sam Perris was a fugitive from justice, wanted for a murder committed during a bank robbery in Maine. Red Leary made a famous escape from the Ludlow Street jail in 1879, but was recaptured in February of 1881. The bonds were non-negotiable and unusable by the burglars, but the cash was never recovered.

MUG SHOTS

GEORGE LEONIDAS LESLIE
King of the Bank Robbers

George Leonidas Leslie, alias Western George, George L. Howard, George Herbert, George L. Lester, J. G. Allison, George K. Leslie, C. G. Green, and more, was New York's premier bank thief in the late nineteenth century, and its most famous before the advent of Willie Sutton. Known as "The King of the Bank Robbers" and "the ace burglar of American criminal history," Leslie was born in the 1830s of a prosperous family and attended college in Cincinnati. Cultured and courtly, he frequented the theater, art exhibits, and society soirees, always impeccably dressed. But, like a true-to-life Raffles, he led a double life, mingling with respectable folk by day, and mixing in the society of thieves, burglars, confidence men, fences, prostitutes, and rogues by night. In July 1870, he married Mary Henrietta Coath; at sixteen years old, she was half his age. He represented himself as a government revenue detective and his wife did not find out his occupation or even his real name for five years. "The revelation was of course a fearful, a staggering shock to her," related a biographer, "but her love survived it, and she apparently without hesitation, elected to continue at his side wherever he might go."

Leslie had a hand in most of the lucrative bank robberies of the day, including the Manhattan Savings Institution, the South Kensington National Bank in Philadelphia, the Third National Bank in Baltimore, the Saratoga County Bank in Waterford, New York, the First National Bank in Quincy, Illinois, and others.

He was an excellent safe-cracker, but preferred to play the role of tactician, planning burglaries for others to carry out. He was so adept at this that yegg men throughout the country called on him to plan their break-ins or look over their plans. Leslie was one of the first of that now ubiquitous breed, the consultant. Though criminally active for a good twenty years, he was never convicted and never served time. Leslie came to an ignominious end though, especially for such a dapper gent. His decomposed body was found on June 4, 1878 by Tramps' Rock, an outcropping near Yonkers. The murder caused quite a stir at the time, and much speculation over who carried out the deed, and why. The story goes that he was set up and killed by fellow thieves Shang Draper, Johnny Dobbs, and Sam Perris, with help from pals Johnny Irving and Billy Porter, either because he was paying too much attention to Irving's sister Babe (in an alternate version, Shang Draper's wife Jennie) or for squealing about a bank job.

Walk to Bond Street, take a right and proceed to 31 Bond Street. Though the brownstone that made this address notable is gone, if you glance about you'll see several similar surviving town houses on the street.

21 The prolific diarist George Templeton Strong, whose volumes of daybooks offer a fascinating glimpse of everyday life in nineteenth century New York, wrote on February 1, 1857:

An epidemic of crime this winter. 'Garotting' [mugging] stories abound, some true, some no doubt fictitious, devised to explain the absence of one's watch and pocketbook after a secret visit to some disreputable place, or to put a good face on some tipsy street fracas. But a tradesman was attacked the other afternoon in broad daylight at his own shop door in the Third Avenue near Thirteenth Street by a couple of men, one of whom was caught, and will probably get his deserts in the State Prison, for life—the doom of two of the fraternity already tried and sentenced. Most of my friends are investing in revolvers and carry them about at night, and if I expected to have to do a great deal of late street-walking off Broadway, I think I should make the like provision; though it's a very bad practice carrying concealed weapons. Moreover, there was an uncommonly shocking murder in Bond Street (No. 31) Friday night; one Burdell, a dentist, strangled and riddled with stabs in his own room by some person unknown who must have been concealed in the room. Motive unknown, evidently not plunder.

He continues four days later: "The excitement about the matter exceeds that produced by any crime of violence committed here in my time, even the Colt and Helen Jewett cases. Through all this miserable weather a crowd of several hundred people of all classes is in permanent position in front of the house."

In the summer of 1856, Harvey Burdell, a successful bachelor dentist living and working at 31 Bond Street, took up with Emma Cunningham, and installed her, with her family of three daughters and two sons, in his house. After a brief spell, however, they had a falling out: Burdell, a mild and tightfisted man, found Cunningham, a strident and determined widow, too much to handle. Very soon they were at each other's throats, and in a very public way, with arguments and accusations and suits being flung about in the streets and courts. She filed a breach of promise suit against the dentist, claiming he reneged on a promise of marriage. Burdell then accused his ex-lover of stealing an IOU from his safe; and so on. Burdell was desperate to get this rancorous woman out of his house. Cunningham was desperate to get a claim to his property, and when the breach of promise suit failed, she took an unusual step: she married the doctor without his knowledge.

On October 28, she took part in a marriage with a confederate named John J. Eckel, another boarder at 31 Bond Street, standing in for the dentist. She tucked the certificate away for future misuse—unworried, or unaware, that the groom's name was misspelled as "Berdell." Further proof that the marriage was false is contained in Burdell's letters, which contain curious language for a newly married man. In a letter to his cousin, written a day or two after the ceremony, he wrote: "All her designs were to get me to marry her; but

Nineteenth-century crime tour? Gawkers mill about the site of the Burdell murder.

the old hag has failed and damned her soul to hell. I would sooner marry an old toad than to marry such a thing as she is." In a later letter he referred to Cunningham as "the old she devil" and "this monstrous b——h of Hell."

And then, amidst the terrible epidemic of garrotting that winter, came the even more horrible visitation of murder. On the evening of January 30, 1857, two or three passersby later reported hearing a strangled, cut-off cry of "Murd——," in Bond Street, and in the morning Burdell was found dead in his office amidst streaks and puddles of blood, stabbed fifteen times. Bloody palm prints appeared on the stairway wall down to the basement, indicating the killer's path of escape, although the office door was closed and the key still in the lock, on the outside.

Not surprisingly, suspicion very quickly fell on Emma Cunningham, or Emma Burdell as she now insisted on calling herself, and John Eckel. District Attorney A. Oakey Hall, later an infamous member of the Boss Tweed Ring, prosecuted the case against Cunningham, but there was little hard or convincing evidence with which to convict. No eyewitnesses, no murder weapon, no bloodstains on the clothes or bodies of Cunningham or Eckel. After thirty-five minutes the jury returned a verdict of not guilty. Charges against Eckel, who was to be tried separately, were dropped.

Then came the amazing coda to this case, for indefatigable Emma was not through. A surrogate's court had decided that Cunningham's claim of marriage was not legally binding. She had only one other route to the Doctor's property and soon announced that she was pregnant by Burdell and would produce his heir. And as the months went by, during which time she still resided at 31 Bond, she grew noticeably rounder.

She was not, however, with child. Pillows were easy enough to stuff under a petticoat, but it was obvious that the successful completion of the scheme required a partner. Cunningham took the unavoidable step of letting her family doctor, David Uhl, in on her secret, and offered him a thousand dollars to help her out. "She told me then," he recounted, "very plainly, that she was not in the family way, and that we would have to get hold of a child in some way or other." Uhl, feigning compliance, ran right off to District Attorney Hall, who set up an elaborate plan, right out of a Victorian penny dreadful, to produce a baby and entrap Cunningham. They rented and furnished a room, tucked a man in bed to impersonate a friendless mother willing to give up her child, and "borrowed" a baby from Bellevue Hospital. At the last minute Hall realized he had forgotten something very important and dispatched a doctor to run up to Bellevue again and pick up a placenta.

On Monday, August 3, with everything in place, Uhl went over to Bond Street and told Cunningham, busy faking labor pains, that a baby was ready. That evening, Cunningham, swathed in black clothing and a veil, skulked out to pick up the youngster while another accomplice went out for a bucket of cow blood. Meanwhile, the entire drama was being watched by detectives stationed up and down Bond Street, and those leaving the house on their furtive errands were tailed.

Cunningham returned to Bond Street with her contraband and picked up where she had left off. At the appropriately dramatic moment, when Cunningham, with hair disheveled and brow brushed with sweat, produced her child, detectives burst in and grabbed the evidence.

Apparently, however, she had committed no crime—the police having swooped in before she made any formal and fraudulent bid for the Burdell estate—and was released. Her final public appearance was ten days later, when she was forcibly carried from 31 Bond Street on a mattress, characteristically refusing to the last to give up. She reportedly moved to California.

Eckel was later imprisoned in the Albany penitentiary for complicity in some whiskey frauds and died there. The borrowed baby and her mother, Matilda Anderson, appeared in a successful run at Barnum's Museum, advertised as the "Bogus Burdell Baby." District Attorney Hall wrote a satirical play on the case called *The Coroner's Inquest,* and then went on to become a mayor and Tweed accomplice.

Harvey Burdell was buried in a family plot in Greenwood Cemetery in Brooklyn. The obscure dentist enjoyed a huge funeral procession down Broadway. Reported the *New York Times,* "since the funeral of Poole, nothing has been in the way of a funeral cortege like that."

Return to Broadway and walk up to 673 Broadway, the building on the southwest corner of West Third Street and Broadway. This was the address of the Grand Central Hotel and the setting of one of the great crimes of New York City: the killing of "Jubilee" Jim Fisk.

22 Like his life, Jim Fisk's murder, on January 6, 1872, was grandiose: the frenzied finale to a steamy love triangle played out amidst the no-holds-barred world of high finance. The story absolutely enthralled New York.

Ostentatious, eccentric, portly Jim Fisk had worked his way up from Vermont circus barker to Wall Street financier. He made his fortune by taking over the Erie Railroad line with Jay Gould in an incredible and completely illegal series of shenanigans involving secret deals, watered stock, backstabbing, and outright theft. In an age of cutthroat capitalism and rapacious industrialists, Fisk was known as the "Napoleon of finance." He bought the Narragansett Steamship Line and dubbed himself an admiral. He purchased the penurious Ninth Regiment of the New York State National Guard and thereby became a Colonel. He was fond of his National Guard uniform and wore it at all public functions.

The Grand Central Opera House on 23rd Street and Eighth Avenue was another purchase and became his headquarters. He installed his mistress, Helen Josephine Mansfield, in a mansion nearby. Mansfield was held to be a great beauty at the time—judging from her portraits, standards were then more flexible.

Fisk's restless profit-searching brought to his attention Edward S. Stoke's Brooklyn Oil Refinery, and the fateful third point of the triangle made its appearance. Fisk bought a partnership in Stoke's successful business in 1869, and the two men became friends, often dining together in Fisk's mansion at 313 West 23rd Street in the company of his mistress. Mansfield and Stokes soon commenced an affair. Fisk and Stokes, suddenly rivals, began a furious legal battle. Fisk had Stokes arrested on a charge of embezzlement. Stokes had

Fisk arrested on a charge of false imprisonment. Mansfield threatened to sue Fisk over money that he owed her. Fisk accused Stokes and Mansfield of blackmail. Mansfield brought suit against Fisk for libel.

By January 6, 1872, Stokes had evidently tired of this ersatz battling and settled on stronger medicine. After an upsetting court appearance (and, interestingly, lunch at Delmonico's, in the very building where John Colt killed his publisher Samuel Adams thirty years previously), Stokes went to the Grand Central Hotel. At around four o'clock, Fisk arrived to pay a call on the widow of an old friend. He had taken exactly two steps up the staircase when he looked and saw Stokes at the top, descending. Stokes pulled out a four-barrelled pistol and fired several times, hitting his nemesis in the abdomen and arm and sending him tumbling to the floor. Fisk was variously reported as crying out "For God's sake will nobody protect me?" or, less sensationally, "Oh!" Big Jim was hauled upstairs and identified Stokes as his assailant. He died the next day. Stokes quietly surrendered.

The shootist said he encountered Fisk purely by accident and without malice aforethought. He gave this account during his third trial:

> I went down on the right-hand side of the private staircase. When I had gone down several steps, I saw Fisk coming. He came in with a rush—sprang through the doors on to the private staircase. I at the time was on the right side going down. We were then in a line. I jumped from the left to the right, and cried out, "Don't shoot!" and immediately pulled my pistol and fired two shots as quick as that. I saw his pistol. He pulled his pistol up in this way in both hands.

The stature of both principals, and their very public and very scandalous quarrel, guaranteed keen interest in Stokes's three trials. The first began on June 19, 1872, six months after the shooting, and resulted in a hung jury after forty hours of deliberation. A second trial, with the defense counsel assisted by rising young lawyer John R. Dos Passos (father of the novelist), ended with a verdict of murder in the first degree. Stokes was sentenced to be hanged on February 28, 1873; however, a writ of error and a new trial were granted, and Stokes went once more before the bar in the dark shadow of the gallows. This go-round was the charmer, and Stokes was awarded a verdict of manslaughter in the third degree and sentenced to four years in Sing Sing.

There may have been something more than luck—or justice—at work here. A story that surfaced a half-century later has it that there was an eyewitness—never heard in court—who saw the entire inci-

A clash of financial titans. Stokes claimed self-defense against a gun-toting Fisk.

dent on the staircase. Before the law could reach him, the legal firm of Howe & Hummel (see p. 83) paid him a huge amount of money to clear out of the country and never come back. He lived out his days in Yokohama, Japan.

Stokes emerged from prison as something of a celebrity and bought an interest in the Hoffman House, a popular saloon next to the Fifth Avenue Hotel opposite Madison Square Park. He died in 1901. Helen Josephine Mansfield married Robert L. Reade, the brother of the Viscountess Falkland, in 1891, but divorced him eight years later. She died in poverty in Paris in 1931. The scene of the crime, The Grand Central Hotel, collapsed on August 3, 1973.

Continue three blocks to Waverly Place, and back, briefly, to the twentieth century, for the Carl Andre case, an unsettling incident of recent vintage.

23 Early Sunday morning, September 8, 1985, a call was placed to a 911 operator: "What happened was we had . . . my wife is an artist and I am an artist and we had a quarrel about the fact that I was more, eh, exposed to the public than she was and she went to the bedroom and I went after her and she went out of the window." The voice was that of the renowned sculptor Carl Andre, one of the seminal figures of the Minimalist school and an artist whose work appears in the Whitney and Guggenheim Museums and many major collections in Europe. His wife was Ana Mendieta, also a sculptor, and just beginning to receive recognition for her work. She lay now thirty-two floors beneath her apartment, on the roof of the Delion Delicatessen at the northwest corner of Broadway and Waverly Place—but did she stumble, or jump, or was she pushed?

Andre told police that he and his wife had been watching television when she left to go to sleep. He remained watching until 3:30 AM, when he walked into the bedroom and found she was not there. But inconsistencies in his story, as well as the different version he gave 911, led to his arrest for murder. The state claimed that after a quarrel Andre pushed Mendieta out the window.

Evidence that had appeared convincing before trial began to break down in court. A witness who testified to hearing a woman's scream turned out to have a history of auditory hallucinations. The bedroom from which Mendietta plunged was disheveled, but its previous condition could not be determined. There was a scratch on Andre's nose, but the time or date of its appearance was unknown. The unusual characteristics of the windowsill, which was 20 inches wide and came up to Mendieta's chest (she was 4 foot 8 inches), seemed to make an accident unlikely, but did nothing to resolve the question of homicide. The state of the relationship between the two artists (some said Mendieta intended to ask for a divorce that night) was never nailed down. There were plenty of questions and conjectures, but few solid conclusions.

The case split the clubby downtown art world into two antagonistic camps: Mendieta's supporters said Andre was jealous of his wife's increasing success and had a history of violence against women. The

Andre partisans said Mendieta was a temperamental woman obsessed by death. Their battle was waged in newspaper articles, on leaflets, and even in artworks. The battle sundered the staid art world, but had no effect on the trial. On February 11, 1988, at the end of an unusual trial in which Andre waived his right to a jury, he was acquitted of second-degree murder.

Just to your right is Astor Place; walk half a block to face the District 65 Building on the north side of the street. This building occupies the site of the Astor Place Opera House, the focus of the Astor Place Riot, which raged here May 10, 1849.

(24) The Astor Place Riot, one of the bloodiest days in New York's history, had its roots in a banal squabble between two arrogant actors.

Actor William Macready, Englishman, and actor Edwin Forrest, Native Son, had once been friends. Macready had helped Forrest get his start in London, and Forrest had married an English woman he met through the older actor. But over the years, professional competition and personal egotism had created friction and then outright antipathy. Their rivalry was exacerbated, and then exploited, by a growing nativist movement, then organized as the Order of United Americans, forerunner of the Know-Nothings and a group with much strength in the organized gangs of the Bowery and other working class areas. The slights supposedly delivered by an effete, aristocratic Macready to a bold, democratic Forrest—billed everywhere as "The *American* Tragedian"—were transformed into insults piercing the very soul of the American character. When the English actor arrived in the United States for an 1849 tour, nativists were incensed.

An attempt by Macready to play Macbeth at the Astor Place Opera House on May 7, 1849 proved unsuccessful, as he was driven from the stage by an unruly crowd throwing, as he later cataloged, "eggs of doubtful purity, potatoes, a bottle of pungent and nauseating asafoetida, old shoes, and a copper coin."

Convinced by city elders, including Washington Irving and Herman Melville, to try again, he announced a return to the Opera House stage for May 10. This proved to be, to put it mildly, a miscalculation. Nativist elements, fired up by the temerity of this fop and organized by local ward leaders, regrouped. One of the principal instigators of the protest was Edward Z. C. Judson, a popular author who used the pen name "Ned Buntline" and who was the man that dubbed William C. Cody "Buffalo Bill." He later served a year in prison for his role in the riot.

Astor Place, from Broadway to Third Avenue, began to fill up early on the evening of the 10th. By curtain time there were thousands of unruly citizens—estimates ran up to 20,000—in the street, and a packed house inside. It was clear that the situation was uncontrollable.

When Macready hit the boards, the audience erupted: rowdies hurled insults, invectives, and soon chairs at the actor; by the second act, paving stones from outside were raining down on the audience and stage, but the indomitable Englishman pressed on. "The audience has paid for so much, and law compels me to give it; they would have cause for riot, if all were not properly done," he primly said.

Outside, the mob, stretching from Broadway to Third Avenue and wrapping around the Opera House on both Astor Place and Eighth Street, grew increasingly aggressive, stoning both the building and the police cordon around it. Reported the *New York Tribune*: "As one window after another cracked, the pieces of bricks and paving-stones rattled in on the terraces and lobbies, the confusion increased, till the Opera House resembled a fortress besieged by an invading army rather than a place meant for the peaceful amusement of a civilized community."

The police force, obviously insufficient, became trapped with their backs up against the building, and the National Guard from the Seventh Regiment, already mobilized and prepared, was called in. They marched up Broadway to Astor Place, wheeled right and, though coming under fierce bombardment, managed to force through the crowd to a position in the rear of the Opera House on Eighth Street. They succeeded in clearing this thoroughfare, but were less successful on the south side of the building. They marched back down on Broadway and turned again into Astor Place, but the crowd was so thick and belligerent that they were forced to proceed in single file, squeezing themselves between the building and the mob.

Here they found themselves in much the same situation the police had suffered only a few hours before: thoroughly outnumbered, pelted by rocks, and in danger of being overwhelmed. A fateful order was given for the Guard to fire point blank into the crowd. A first volley was aimed above the heads of the demonstrators, but, as this proved unconvincing, two more volleys followed, both directed squarely at the crowd (though many guardsmen refused to fire or aimed their weapons in the air).

The crowd scattered, leaving in its wake dozens of dead and wounded on the street. Sporadic fighting continued until midnight, at which time nervous soldiers fired another volley at the stragglers still in the area, felling a few more. That put an end to the battle.

The eventual death toll stood at thirty-one civilians dead, some thirty or forty wounded from gunfire, and more than one hundred

Pugilist and politician, John Morrissey.

soldiers, police, and civilians injured by paving stones, clubs, or other weapons. Eighty-six rioters were arrested, including the aforementioned E. Z. C. Judson. A coroner's jury exonerated the guardsmen, though it criticized the police for not being prepared.

Macready had been smuggled out of the theater in disguise and left the city the next morning. He never returned to the United States and died in England on April 27, 1873. Forrest, though tainted by association with the riot and by a later scandalous divorce from his wife, continued with a successful theatrical career. He died on December 12, 1872.

ALSO INFAMOUS

The large apartment building at 70 E. 10th Street, between Broadway and Fourth Avenue, was the home of Leon Klinghoffer, the sole victim in the hijacking of the Mediterranean cruise ship *Achille Lauro*. Klinghoffer was shot in the head and thrown overboard on October 8, 1985, by members of the Palestine Liberation Front (a breakaway group from the Palestine Liberation Organization).

Half a block beyond 10th Street, on the east side, we reencounter John Morrissey, whom you recall was mixing it up with Bill "the Butcher" Poole last we checked.

25 A good decade or so after that trouble, Morrissey had ascended into the ownership of a casino, known by its address, 818 Broadway.

A contemporary describes it:

> Until early in the nineties there still existed in New York what was probably the best known gambling house in the country, old "818" Broadway. This was in its heyday the headquarters of John Morrissey, pugilist, adventurer, gambler, and finally Member of Congress. In the nineties it was run by Lucius Appleby, of bookmaking fame, and by Gus Abel. It was the resort to which country people, curious to see a grand gambling establishment, were generally taken. At 12 o'clock every night a sumptuous supper was served, including wines, to all present, without charge.

Another chronicler writes that "[Morrissey's] house in New York was the most elegantly furnished of any of the kind in the state. It was always conducted on principles of the highest honor, as gamblers understand that term. His table, attendants, cooking, and company were exceeded by nothing this side of the Atlantic."

Though gambling was prohibited under the strict Green Law of 1851 (named after reformer Jonathan F. Green), little effort was made at enforcement: casinos were too lucrative for the cop on the beat, the ward politician, and their bosses. In fact, New York was a wide-open town for gambling. A writer in 1872 asserted that the city hosted 200 gambling houses, and 350 to 400 lottery offices, policy shops, and other "gambling hells" as they were called. Two decades earlier a visitor estimated that some 30,000 people in New York earned a living from gambling and similar activities.

Morrissey, born in Ireland in 1834, came to New York as a child and while still in his early twenties became a gang leader and political player in the lower West Side. After a brief career as a prize fighter, he opened a series of gambling joints, using his political connections to keep the heat off, and by 1867 he had established the Saratoga Racetrack and Club House in Saratoga Springs, the plushest casino on the East Coast. He became sufficiently renowned, and sufficiently respectable, to win public office, and served two terms as a United States Congressman and two more as a State Senator. He maintained, as both politician and gambling house proprietor, a reputation for scrupulous honesty. Morrissey died, after losing most of his fortune gambling in the stock market, in 1878.

Continue up to Union Square and pause for a moment. Have a seat in the park if you wish.

ALSO INFAMOUS

On the day after Christmas, 1920, gang leader Monk Eastman (see p. 201), was found dead in front of the Bluebird Cafe at 62 East 14th Street, just west of the southwest corner of Fourth Avenue. The once-powerful Eastman, by that time reduced to peddling narcotics, was shot five times by Prohibition Enforcement Agent Jerry Bohan, who drew a two-year rap for manslaughter.

26 Union Square was notorious in the early years of the twentieth century as a magnet for radical and socialist rallies, and one in particular earns a place in this book. The Unemployed Conference of New York City called a mass meeting for March 28, 1908. Their application for a permit was denied and those arriving in the Square that day found it filled with hundreds of police. Most of the would-be protestors left, and by 3:30 P.M. only a thousand or so were milling desultorily about. Suddenly, the unmistakable thunder of a bomb burst forth, a blast so great that people a block away were thrown to their knees. Protestors, police, and passersby scattered in panic, not knowing where the bomb had exploded, who was hurt, or whether there were to be more.

"In a moment," reported the *New York Times*, "all was pandemonium. The police closed in on the crowd, using their clubs right and left, while the mounted men, under Inspector Schmittberger, formed in phalanxes and charged at the mob of unemployed that skirted the park . . . . The fleeing throng started in to sing the 'Marseillaise' and jeer at the police."

The bomb had exploded just to the south of where the flagpole now rises. And it did little damage except to its makers—Selig Silverstein and Ignatz Hildebrand, two anarchists intent on dispatching a few of the assembled policemen. Instead, the bomb went off prematurely as Silverstein began his lob into the ranks, blowing off his hand, blowing out his eyes, and delivering a fatal wound. Hildebrand was killed instantly.

In a dying statement, Silverstein, 22, declared: "Yes I made the bomb, and I came to the Park to kill the police with it. The police are no good. They drove us out of the park, and I hate them. I am very sorry that I did not make good. As for my life, why that is nothing. It was the police that I wanted."

Now stroll over to the west side of the park at 15th Street for another incident with a radical tinge. This occurred down the block at the corner of Fifth Avenue and 15th Street.

27 Anarchist-cum-socialist-cum-labor unionist Carlo Tresca was assassinated at the northwest corner of Fifth Avenue and 15th Street on January 11, 1943. Such was the unceasing political involvement of Tresca, and such were his entanglements, that equally reasonable cases can be made that he was killed by fascists, communists, or gangsters. In fact, the puzzle has never been definitively solved.

Tresca came from Italy in 1904, and his energy, intelligence, and charisma quickly made him an important player in the lively left-wing labor movement of the day and a leader of the small but vocal Italian anarchist community. He was active in the famous Lawrence and Patterson strikes in Massachusetts, in the defense of Sacco and Vanzetti (in fact, he spoke to a huge rally here in Union Square on the eve of the anarchists' execution), and in support of the Loyalists in Spain. He was an implacable foe of Mussolini's fascism and Stalin's communism.

On the evening of January 11, 1943, Tresca and his friend Giuseppe Calabi left the office of Tresca's newspaper, *Il Martello*, at the southwest corner of Fifth Avenue and 15th Street, and headed for some food and beer at a nearby bar. As they paused at the northwest corner, a man appeared out of the darkness and fired four shots, one hitting Tresca in the lung, another in the head. The assassin quickly recrossed 15th Street, jumped into a waiting sedan, and disappeared into the night. The fiery agitator was pronounced dead on arrival at St. Vincent's Hospital.

Who shot Carlo Tresca? The immediate answer is simple: Carmine Galante. Galante later rose to become a leader in the Bonanno Mafia family (and was killed in Brooklyn in 1979), but at this time he was a small-time gangster and gun-for-hire. Although an informant and circumstantial evidence implicated Galante, he was never charged; there is little doubt, however, that he was the triggerman.

But the ultimate answer, the name of Galante's employer, is unknown. The background and issues involved were at times so labyrinthine and arcane that they can be merely hinted at here. Plausible cases can be made for at least three suspects:

1). Mafia boss Vito Genovese (then living in Italy and evidently on good terms with high Fascist officials), had him killed, either at the behest of Mussolini, or because Tresca threatened to expose Genovese's criminal background to the Italian government. Genovese had access to Galante, of course, since they were fellow Mafioso.

2). Vittorio Vidali, a member of the Soviet secret police implicated in Trotsky's assassination, had him shot for his anti-Communist activities, particularly his attempts to squeeze Communists out of a role in plans for post-war Italy. Vidali could have made contact with Galante through mob connections in the Communist-controlled National Maritime Union.

3). Newspaper owner and ex-Mussolini supporter Generoso Pope had him killed for his continued opposition to Pope's bid for power in the emerging post-Mussolini antifascist Italian and Italian-American political scene. Pope's right-hand man was Frank Garofalo, a one-time associate of Lucky Luciano who knew Galante quite well. Garofalo had once physically threatened Tresca.

The likeliest answer is number three, but the debate continues.

Walk up to 33 Union Square West.

28 In 1968, artist, filmmaker, and celebrity Andy Warhol was at the height of his hipness. Working with a coterie of artists and hustlers drawn from the darker corners of the urban underground, he had just set up a workshop and studio—The Factory—on the fifth floor of this building and was producing avant-garde movies, hanging out in trendy bars, and getting lots of unfavorable media coverage (which he cherished).

One of the players in his informal Factory gang was Valerie Solanas, a particularly unstable member of the motley group. She had acted in one of Warhol's early films and then continued to dog him, becoming increasingly belligerent. When Warhol arrived at the Factory on June 3, 1968, Solanas was waiting for him, and they rode up in the elevator together. Warhol noticed that Solanas looked a little nervous.

Upstairs, Warhol sat behind his desk and took a phone call. As he spoke, gazing distractedly at his reflection in the glass desktop, Solanas walked up in front of him and pulled out a .32-caliber pistol from a brown paper bag and fired point-blank three times. Only one bullet managed to find Warhol, slamming into his right side, exiting through his left, and piercing a collection of organs in between. He slumped under the desk, bleeding, while Solanas stalked through the office looking for other victims. She managed to wound visiting critic Mario Amaya with a bullet in the side and was set to shoot assistant John Hughes through the head when her pistol jammed. She pulled out a spare .22 but suddenly reconsidered and left the office. Four hours later she surrendered to a policeman in Times Square and explained that she had shot Warhol because "he had too much control over my life."

Warhol, so seriously injured that he was pronounced dead soon after entering the emergency room, pulled through, emerging in two months without a spleen but otherwise intact.

For motive, Solanas offered a self-written manifesto from a self-formed group (with one member) called SCUM—Society for Cutting Up Men, which called for a revolution to "eliminate the male sex and begin to create a swinging, groovy out-of-sight female world." She was remanded for psychiatric testing, and later drew a three-year sentence for the shooting. She died of emphysema in 1988.

Walk around now to the top of the Square and 33 Union Square North, the Century Building.

29 The assassination of Hovannes Tavshanjian on July 22, 1907, just a few feet east of the front entrance, could well be the first instance of foreign terrorism in the United States. However, the story, full of political intrigue and passion, is now forgotten.

The *New York Times* contained the following report on its front page:

> H.S. Tavshanjian, a wealthy importer of Oriental rugs, was shot and almost instantly killed as he was about to enter the Century Building, 33 Union Square North, yesterday afternoon, to go to his place of business on the third floor. His murderer is Bedros Hanparzoumian [sic], an Armenian of 24, who, in the new precinct station house in West 20th Street a little later said that he had "saved his country" by his act.

Though the Armenian community in New York City around the turn of the century was small, about 2,500 in 1908, and scattered, it was a community crackling with political intensity. The Turkish subjugation of the homeland, and the massacres beginning in 1894–96, had galvanized the expatriates and led to fierce activity by several nationalist groups vying for the loyalty—and money—of Armenian Americans.

One of these was the Social Democratic Hnchagian (Clarion) Party, organized in Geneva in 1887 around a vague platform of nationalism and socialism. By 1907, they had splintered several times. One particularly radical wing was the Reformed Hnchags, or, as they modestly called themselves, the Constantinople Armenian Revolutionary Terrorists' Organization. Their charming symbol showed three hands driving daggers into a red heart. Nothing spared for the cause, their tactics included blackmail, extortion, and murder.

The Reformed Hnchags had passed a death sentence upon Hovannes Tavshanjian simply because he had failed to "donate" $25,000, an omission they considered a betrayal of the mother country. His executioner, Bedros Hampartzumian, was apparently imported from Constantinople for the job.

The day after the assassination, six other wealthy Armenian businessmen received threats. A typical one read: "We have just killed Tavshanjian, who would not agree to our demands and who advised you not to. You see what has happened to him. So take warning and be prepared to give us the money we ask. If you do not pay you will live only two weeks."

The murder and blatant extortion appalled the Armenian community no less than the rest of the city, and cooperation by previously reticent members led to a fairly speedy wrap-up. The assassin Hampartzumian was convicted and electrocuted at Sing Sing on December 6, 1909. The leader of the Reformed Hnchags in the United States, Hevont Martoogesian, a pastor of the Armenian Apostolic Church at Seventh Avenue and 39th Street, was indicted on four counts of blackmail for sending extortion letters and served a two-year sentence.

The last leg of our tour will take us off Broadway and into Gramercy Square, the bucolic little park built by developer Samuel Ruggles in 1831 in imitation of the private squares of London. Despite its pastoral pretensions, this little green place in the city has experienced two or three exciting crimes of note. Walk up Park Avenue South, take a right at 20th Street and stop at 9 & 10 Gramercy Park.

30 In the middle of the nineteenth century these two brownstones were the site of Miss Haines's Academy for Girls. The residents of Gramercy Park would watch, with some amusement, as the school's French teacher, Miss Henrietta Desportes, took her young charges for their constitutional each day.

At the same time, however, the prim residents were scandalized at the presence of the school teacher, for she had a scarlet past: the demure Henrietta Desportes had been intimately involved in one of the most sensational murder cases of the century.

On August 18, 1847, three thousand miles away in Paris, Fanny Sebastiani, the Duchesse de Choiseul-Praslin, was found brutally murdered in her bedroom. While standing trial for the foul deed, her husband, the Duc de Choiseul-Praslin, committed suicide by swallowing arsenic (he spent six days in agony before expiring). His guilt was not in question. The case scandalized the continent and made headlines even on this side of the Atlantic. It's said that by exposing the depravity and decadence of the aristocracy, the murder, trial, and suicide served as a significant factor in the downfall of French King Louis-Philippe and the outbreak of the Revolution of 1848.

Henrietta Desportes had been the governess for the Duc and Duchesse de Choiseul-Praslin. Though she had left their employ previous to the murder, she was rumored to be the mistress and perhaps accomplice of the Duc. Legally exonerated, but living under a cloud of suspicion, she removed herself from France and came to Gramercy

Park. She eventually married Henry Field, brother of Cyrus Field, the promoter of the transatlantic cable, and the couple moved off to a country home in New England. She died in Stockbridge, Massachusetts on March 6, 1875. As long as she and her husband lived in New York, however, Mrs. Cyrus Field barred the young French woman from her door, and persisted in calling her "that murderess."

Saunter over two doors, to 12 Gramercy Park.

31 You recall that we left dapper crook Gerald Chapman (see p. 21), perpetrator of the Leonard Street mail robbery, counting his loot in Long Island, with the police hot on his trail. In the midst of this nationwide manhunt, where did Chapman choose to hide? Not one to skulk, he settled on a flamboyant residence smack in the middle of the city, right here at 12 Gramercy Park.

Posing as G. Vincent Colwell, a young society man just over from England, the robber leased this house as a very public kind of hideout, entertaining lavishly with dinner parties and evening musicales, usually with his good friend George "Dutch" Anderson. He strolled around the park in his tailored suits, spats, black homburg, and, perched aristocratically on his nose, pince-nez glasses. He was known in the neighborhood as "The Count of Gramercy Park." This aristocratic interlude, however, was shortlived.

On July 3, 1922, a little over six months after the Leonard Street Robbery, the cops finally figured out that Colwell was Chapman (evidently on a tip from driver Charlie Loerber) and nabbed him here in his rented mansion. Chapman and Anderson were sentenced to twenty-five years in the federal penitentiary in Atlanta.

But his story does not end there. Chapman escaped from Atlanta, was wounded and captured in Athens, Georgia, and then broke free again from a hospital ward. These wily exploits earned him a national reputation. Later Anderson, having escaped from the Atlanta Pen through a sixty-foot tunnel, joined him. Back on the East Coast, the two worked on an elaborate counterfeiting scheme, but Chapman, a creature of habit, couldn't resist cracking a safe or two, and while cleaning out a department store in New Britain, Connecticut on October 11, 1924, he killed a policeman. He was captured shortly afterwards.

An interesting little legal point cropped up here. Chapman had been returned to federal custody to serve out his twenty-five-year sentence in Atlanta. Connecticut wanted him for murder, but the law at the time stated that a person in federal custody could not be tried by a state court until the federal government had released him. The feds were willing to pardon their prisoner, but Chapman refused the honor! A dusty old decision by the Supreme Court stated that a pardon is like a gift, and not valid until accepted. Chapman was quite willing to cool his heels in the penitentiary for a few decades, considering the alternative that awaited him in Connecticut. President Calvin Coolidge solved the problem by drawing up an executive order that commuted—not pardoned—Chapman's sentence. Gerald Chapman was shipped unwillingly from his federal cell to a courtroom in Connecticut, where he was convicted of murder. He was hanged on April 5, 1926.

ALSO INFAMOUS

Actor Edwin Booth, brother of presidential assassin John Wilkes Booth, founded a theatrical club, The Players, at 16 Gramercy Park South, in 1888. Architect Stanford White, victim of another assassin (see p. 163), did the exterior and interior design work.

Walk up on Gramercy Park West and proceed right to the northwest corner of Lexington Avenue and the site of the shooting of David Graham Phillips.

32 Phillips, neglected today, was a prominent turn-of-the-century newspaperman, muckraker, and novelist, considered by contemporaries "the most distinguished American novelist of his time," and noted in the *Literary History of the United States* as "perhaps the ablest novelist associated with the muckrakers." He was a prolific writer whose work eventually filled seven volumes, but only two of his novels are even dimly remembered today: his first, *The Great God Success,* and his last, published posthumously, *Susan Lenox, Her Fall and Rise* (and known now as a movie with Greta Garbo and Clark Gable). It was one of his articles, "The Treason of the Senate," that provoked Teddy Roosevelt's "Muck-rake" speech and that now venerable neologism.

In the summer of 1910, at the height of his success, he began receiving anonymous letters full of vehement rants on his supposed cynical treatment of American womanhood. Phillips, as a muckraker, was used to receiving abusive letters, and didn't seem concerned. He carried on his business as usual, unaware that not only was his noisome critic writing letters, but also watching his apartment and tracing his every move. The letter writer and snoop was Fitzhugh Coyle Goldsborough, a member of an old and well-known Washington family and a violinist with the Pittsburgh Orchestra. Goldsborough was insane, and was convinced that all of Phillips's novels were thinly disguised attacks on his family, and that, in particular, the female protagonist of his latest novel, *The Fashionable Adventures of Joshua Craig*, was a libel on his beloved sister. Goldsborough had taken an apartment around the corner so he could spy on Phillips's flat in the National Arts Club, 15 Gramercy Park South.

About one-thirty in the afternoon of January 23, 1911, Phillips, following his usual routine, left the Club (the building with all the wild wrought iron directly across the park), and walked along the west side, the way you just passed, to pick up his mail at the Princeton Club, located in a brownstone here on the corner. He was within a few doors of the club when Goldsborough, popped up and, shouting, "I've been waiting six months to get you!" or, according to another version, "Now I've got you!" or perhaps something equally dramatic and misquotable, fired six shots point-blank at the writer. The disturbed man then pointed the gun at his temple and killed himself. Phillips died the next night at Bellevue Hospital.

The killing, which outraged the city, led to the passage of the Sullivan Law, the country's first modern gun control law.

Nearest subway: 14th Street–Union Square L N R 4 5 6; 23rd Street 6
Nearest bus lines: M 1; M 2; M 3; M 23; M 101; M 102

Lower Manhattan: The Financial Center and Civic Center

A Criminal Sketch of Lower Manhattan

Even in Dutch days the east side of Manhattan, where this tour begins, was a little disreputable. New Amsterdam's fort and church were constructed on the high ground by Broadway in the west; the east side became a tight neighborhood of tradesmen and artisans and rough and tumble docksides. Low taverns and their tough customers abounded. The City Tavern, which was later converted into the Dutch Stadt Huys, or City Hall, was built at Pearl Street and Coenties Alley in 1642. Philip Gerritsen, the first proprietor of the City Tavern, was stabbed three months after he opened the place, an illustration of the nature of the establishment. The popular Blue Dove was also on Pearl Street, between Whitehall and State Streets. It was a favorite of the rattle watch, New Amsterdam's earliest police force, and thus is the city's first example of that well-known institution, the cop bar.

The bad behavior engendered by these taverns extended beyond their thresholds. After too many drinks on a May night in 1663, Jasper Abrahamsen and Hendrick Jansen went careening up Pearl Street beating up passersby and storming into homes demanding

The Financial Center and the Civic Center

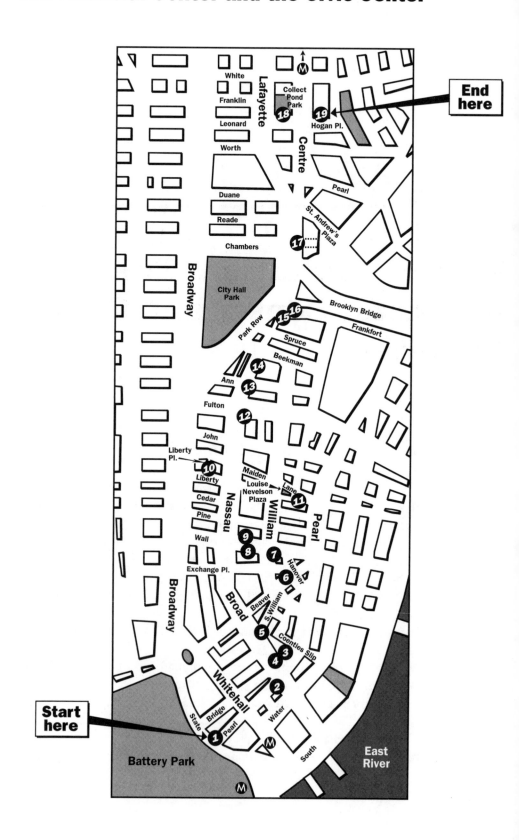

food and drink. They were sentenced to be " . . . bound to a stake and severely flogged, and the Hangman shall make a gash in [the] left cheek or jaw so that the blood flows . . . ." In addition the pair were banished from the city. To add insult to injury, they had to pay the costs of their punishments.

Throughout the Dutch and British periods crime remained slight by our standards, but this was the area of the city hardest hit. The small stores and workshops that were concentrated here were subject to burglary, the Battery became a favorite promenade for prostitutes, and rowdy sailors congregated close to the East River wharves.

In August of 1786 Isaac Willetts advertised a reward "for the detection of the robbers who broke into his house, No. 2 Pearl Street, close to the Battery, and took cash to the amount of £575:16:8 in gold and silver." A substantial loss, but Willetts' troubles were not over. Watching out for the culprits a few days later, he spied "a number of men looking about the house, who he suspected to be part of a gang at present infesting the city. He fired among them, but did not happen to hurt any; on which they seized him and beat him in a shocking manner, and then made off."

The *New York Post* reported on November 29, 1802, that: "It is necessary to caution the public against a gang of villains it appears is infesting the city. A man's great coat and hat were reported stolen from the hall of a dwelling on Pearl Street, and the office of Boyd and Dey on Pine Street was broken open and robbed of a considerable amount of money."

The burst of trade following the War of 1812 and the opening of the Erie Canal in 1825 turned New York into a great commercial center but also produced New York's first crime wave. Between 1814 and 1834 the city's population increased by about 65 percent each decade, while the number of criminal complaints in the same twenty years rose more than four times. In the ten months from May 1839 to February 1840, 23 murders were recorded. The most notorious of New York's slums, the unredeemable Five Points (see p. 87), came to life in the late 1830s.

In 1853 the chief of police stated that more crime took place on the piers and slips east of South Street and west of West Street than in the rest of the city put together. Dockside gangs such as the Daybreak Boys, Buckoos, Hookers, Swamp Angels, Slaughter Housers, Short Tails, Patsy Conroys, and the Border Gang pilfered from the piers, burgled outlying ships, and caroused through the streets. A vivid sense of the docks and their denizens comes from an anonymous observer of 1874, who reported:

> The neighborhood of Water Street is about the most notorious in the metropolis for deeds of violence, flagrant vice, and scenes of

debauchery. It abounds in lodging-houses for sailors, liquor-stores of the lowest class without number, dance-houses and concert saloons (at the very thought of which poor Decency hides her eyes in agony), and various other low places of amusement. Brothels of the worst description swarm in all directions . . . . The use of deadly weapons, too, is so common that murder provokes no sentiment of horror among the denizens of Water Street, but only excites in them a morbid curiosity . . . .

Crowded onto Water Street were, at 340, Mother McBride's dance house; at 316, John Allen's, the most notorious of all Water Street dives, whose proprietor was known as "The Wickedest Man in New York"; at 319, the Saranac; and at 337 1/2, The Pipe, "kept by Butch Haley, famous dive for thieves and cut-throats." Most are long gone, of course, but Kit Burn's Sportsmen's Hall, with its famous rat-baiting pit, where bets were placed on fights to the death between small dogs and large water rats, remains at 273 Water Street. It is Manhattan's third oldest structure, but now lies neglected and unnoted. At 279, Tom Norton's, "a bagnio filled up with river pirates and Water St. hags," is still open for business, now as the Bridge Cafe.

This wide-open district began to fade at the end of the nineteenth century, a result of the disruption caused by the Brooklyn Bridge, the rise of the Hudson River docks, and reform. Criminal activity shifted to the west side docks, where it was rationalized and controlled by Joe Ryan's corrupt International Longshoremen's Association. The remaining locus of waterfront crime on the east side was the Fulton Fish Market, which was the base of Joseph "Socks" Lanza, who organized the United Seafood Workers' Union in 1922 and built an empire based on payoffs and extortion. According to federal officials, the Fulton Fish Market is now in the hands of the Genovese Mafia family.

Stalking Lower Manhattan _____

Nearest subway: Whitehall St. R line; South Ferry 1 & 9 lines
Nearest bus line: M 6; M 15

Our tour begins at the northeast corner of State Street and Pearl Street.

1 Battery Park, built mostly from landfill, lies behind you. In colonial days the shoreline of the island was hard by this spot, and the Bat-

A nineteenth-century pickpocket caught in the act on the Battery.

tery only a narrow walk (literally, at that time, a battery of guns) along what is now State Street. Enough room, however, for vice. Scottish physician Alexander Hamilton visited the city in 1744 and reported in his diary that "Mr. J[effery]s told me that to walk out after dusk upon this platform [the Battery] was a good way for a stranger to fit himself with a courtezan, for that place was the generall rendezvous of the fair sex of that profession after sun set. He told me there was a good choice of pritty lasses among them, both Dutch and English." The situation in the Battery was changed and yet not much different a century and a half later. "The grass has disappeared," griped a city guidebook in 1879, "the iron fence is broken, the wall promenade near the sea gone to decay, freshly-arrived foreigners, ragged, tattered, and drunken men and women sit under the old trees, and the Battery is now as unsafe a place at night as can be found in the city."

Walk up Pearl Street past Whitehall and pause at the southeast corner
of Pearl and Broad Streets.

2 In 1776 the area between Whitehall, Broad Street, and the shoreline (then at Water Street), was completely burned out in a fire set by departing Revolutionaries before the occupation by the British.

The temporary structures put up afterward gave the neighborhood the nicknames "Canvas Town" or "Topsail Town," after the material used for roofs. Close to soldier's barracks and sailor's ships, this was a popular red-light district throughout the 1780s and '90s. In 1784, in an early stab at urban renewal, the sheriff demolished several disreputable houses. As with modern attempts, the disrepute remained.

Continue up Pearl Street to the plaza on the west side of the street.

3 In Dutch days the Stadt Huys, or city hall, the birthplace of law and order in New Amsterdam, stood here. You'll see a large freestanding plaque in the plaza that delivers some history of the building; its location is outlined in yellow brick.

Built in 1642 as a tavern, it was converted 11 years later to a municipal complex, complete with council chambers, courthouse, jail, and debtors' prison. To round off this full-service center, a pillory, cage, and ducking stool were placed prominently on the other side of Coenties Slip in 1692.

The administration of justice in the Dutch period was quite simple: all judicial, legislative, and executive power was concentrated in the Director, aided by the Council. The Director was assisted by the *schout-fiscal*, an appointee of the Director, who acted as public prosecutor, public defender, and sheriff. It was his job as well to patrol the streets for miscreants and sinners. Although Roman-Dutch law theoretically prevailed, the Director pretty much did what he wanted, prosecuting some crimes and ignoring others. Keep in mind that New Amsterdam was owned by the Dutch West India Company, and was more a private concern than a municipality.

The crimes dealt with were, for the most part, tranquil affairs by our standards. A good example is that of the very first court proceeding here in the Stadt Huys, on February 10, 1653, a case of slander brought by Joost Goderis against several citizens who taunted him as a cuckold. The outcome is unrecorded.

Capital punishment was rare. One notable exception was the case of Jan Quisthout van der Linde, a soldier from Brussels, convicted of "a crime condemned of God as an abomination"—sodomy. On June 17, 1660, he was tied in a sack and thrown into the bay.

Go back to Broad Street and look left toward the intersection of Broad and Water streets.

No waiting. Stocks and whipping post were located conveniently close to the Stadt Huys.

4 In British colonial days the shore ran along Water Street and a pier extended from Broad Street into the East River. Nearby stood the little shop of John Peter Zenger, printer of religious tracts, handbills, and a newspaper, and an early American hero of the free press.

Zenger immigrated to New York from Germany as a young boy and was apprenticed to the city's only printer, William Bradford. In 1725 Bradford, with Zenger at his elbow, began publication of New York's first newspaper, the *New York Weekly Gazette*, a mouthpiece for Governor William Cosby. The next year the young printer struck out on his own.

Through the 1720s and '30s the New York political scene was dominated by two loose groupings: a clique supporting wealthy merchants, large landowners, and the Anglican church, and backed by Governor Cosby; and a faction led by politicians Robert Hunter and Lewis Morris drawing for support on artisans, shopkeepers, and farmers. The rivalry between the two groups flared when Governor Cosby, in a jurisdictional dispute, fired the uncompliant chief justice, Morris. Undaunted, Morris quickly got himself elected to the state assembly, and, looking for an instrument with which to fight Cosby, turned to Zenger. The young printer turned out the first issue of the anti-administration *New York Weekly Journal* on November 1, 1733.

The Cosby administration did not take kindly to the slings and arrows of the *Journal* (most of which were written by financial backer

James Alexander, not Zenger). In early November, 1734, the sheriff burned a number of offending newssheets, but when this inflammatory treatment failed to deter the attacks, Attorney General Richard Bradley charged Zenger with seditious libel and arrested the printer.

Zenger spent almost a year languishing in jail (then located on Wall Street where Federal Hall National Memorial now stands) while awaiting trial, but his backers were busy. When the printer's original lawyers were disbarred by a Cosby judge, they secretly arranged to substitute Andrew Hamilton from Philadelphia. Hamilton was at the time one of the most famous lawyers in the colonies. His surprise appearance in the courtroom on the first day of trial was a public relations coup for the Morris camp.

The trial began on August 4, 1735. The prosecution's case was based simply on the fact that Zenger published the offending papers; the truth or falseness of the attacks on the governor were irrelevant. But, in a bold and brilliant move, Hamilton made that question the crux of his defense. He freely agreed that Zenger produced the newspapers, thereby both admitting to and frustrating the prosecution case. He maintained though, that the crime of libel involved the production of false statements—the indictment charged Zenger with material "false, scandalous, and seditious"—and stated that unless the prosecution could prove Zenger's attacks to be untrue, the printer had committed no crime. "I cannot think it proper for me . . . to Deny Publication of a Complaint, which I think is the Right of every free-born Subject to Make, when the matters so published can be supported with Truth."

This was not at all the accepted interpretation of the libel law. Legal precedent backed the Attorney General, who declared that "supposing [the libels] were True, the Law says they are not the less Libellous for that . . . the Law says, their being True is an Aggravation of the Crime." A fierce courtroom battle ensued, with both sides insisting on contradictory definitions of libel, and the common law and the judge clearly on the side of the prosecution.

Finally, Hamilton gave a stirring summation to the jury:

> . . . the question before the Court and you gentlemen of the jury is not of small or private concern, it is not the cause of a poor printer, nor of New York alone, which you are now trying: No! It may in its consequence affect every freeman that lives under a British government on the main of America. It is the best cause. It is the cause of liberty; and I make no doubt but your upright conduct this day will not only entitle you to the love and esteem of your fellow citizens; but every man who prefers freedom to a life of slavery will bless and honor you as men who have baffled the attempt of tyranny; and by an impartial and uncorrupt verdict, have laid a noble foundation for securing to ourselves, our posterity, and our neighbors that to which nature and

the laws of our country have given us a right—the liberty—both of exposing and opposing arbitrary power (in these parts of the world, at least) by speaking and writing truth.

The jury was moved more by Hamilton's words than the letter of the law, and brought in a verdict of not guilty, thereby establishing a vital precedent for freedom of the press. Jubilant New Yorkers sent Hamilton back home with a lavish testimonial dinner and ball attended by the mayor. Zenger, however, had to spend the celebratory night alone in jail, waiting for money to be raised to pay the costs of his long imprisonment.

Walk a block up Broad Street to South William Street.

5 In 1741 Robert and Rebecca Hogg owned a little general merchandise store at the northeast corner of South William (which at the time was called Jew's Alley) and Broad Streets. On the night of February 28, the shop was relieved of a sack of money, silver candlesticks, and cloth. This modest burglary was the spark of the "New York Conspiracy" or "Great Negro Plot," whose course throughout the year would terrorize the city and result in the deaths of thirty-four people at the hands of local justice.

On the other side of town, just above Trinity Church, John Hughson, barkeeper and part-time fence, operated a low tavern. Mary Burton was an indentured servant at the tavern, and, under hints that a loose tongue could gain her freedom, she revealed to the Hoggs that the culprits in the burglary were Caesar (a slave owned by John Vaarck) and Prince (the slave of merchant John Auboyneau) and that the loot was hidden at Hughson's. At this point it looked like a fairly standard affair. The two burglars were thrown in prison, there most likely to face whipping or banishment, and Hughson was questioned. But events occurred that made the burglary a fatal one.

Several weeks after the burglary, a long run of fires unsettled the city. In many cases, arson was obvious, and people began to sniff around for clues and culprits. Cuff Philipse, a black slave, was seen running from one fire; another slave, Quaco, was overheard saying to a friend "Fire, Fire, Scorch, Scorch, A LITTLE, damn it, BY-AND-BY."

Amidst mounting panic, a special session of the court was convened to investigate the suspicious fires. The first witness was Mary Burton, the indentured servant at Hughson's. She spun a shocking tale:

> Caesar, Prince, and Mr. Philipse's negro man, Cuffee, used to meet frequently at my master's house, and I've heard them talk frequently of

burning the fort and [say] that they'd go down to the Fly and burn the whole town. My master and mistress said they'd aid and assist them as much as they could. In their common conversation they used to say that when all this was done, Caesar'd be governor and Hughson, my master, should be king.

This news broke like a storm upon the city. An eyewitness had given substance to the rumors of a conspiracy. Enthusiastically, the magistrates pressed her to reveal more, and she eagerly did so. Then the magistrates arrested Margaret Kerry Sorubeiro, usually called Peggy, a prostitute who lived at Hughson's. She began to name names. The questioning, sweetened by promises of immunity or mercy, was continued with others, with similar results, until the conspiracy had grown to huge proportions.

On May 30, seventeen slaves were arrested. On June 12, another nine were picked up. The pace quickened when an offer of pardon was declared in the middle of June. Those brought before the court had a choice: confess to a plot and receive immunity, or admit nothing and become a suspect: the decision, for most, was clear. By July 4, nearly two hundred blacks languished in prison. The conspiracy grew not only in size but also in lurid detail: meetings at Hughson's tavern were said to include strange rituals of witchcraft and, just as bad in the magistrates' eyes, Roman Catholic trappings.

The general outlines of the conspiracy, as pieced together by the judges, was that John Hughson, along with an itinerant school-teacher named John Ury (who was accused of being a Catholic priest) had organized upwards of two hundred slaves into a cabal. They were to burn the city, kill the whites, and put themselves in power. The details were no clearer than this.

Between May 11 and August 29, 1741, the "New York Conspiracy" claimed thirty-four victims. Vaarck and Auboyneau were hanged for the robbery at the Hoggs's on May 11. Philipse was burned at the stake on May 30. John Hughson, his wife Sarah, and Sorubeiro were executed on June 12 for conspiracy. Quaco Walter was hanged on July 18. In sum, thirteen blacks were burned at the stake, and seventeen blacks and four whites were hanged.

Accounts of the "New York Conspiracy" usually treat it as an example of mass hysteria, a city gone mad, and claim that the plot had no basis in fact. It's certain that many confessions were coerced and fabricated, and that Ury, among others, was an innocent victim. But a more recent argument by historian T. J. Davis makes the case that there was indeed a modest plot among some slaves to torch buildings and attempt revolt. Arson was definitely the cause of several of the blazes, and some of the early confessions ring true. Another impressive argument for this interpretation is the common-sense notion that the slave community was likely to have often been active in defiance and resistance.

Continue one block up Broad Street. Take a right on Beaver Street and walk up to Hanover Street.

6 Before achieving immortality as the world's most famous pirate, Captain William Kidd lived respectably and prosperously in New York City in the late seventeenth century. He owned several trading vessels and considerable property. Between 1691 and 1695 he lived in a stately mansion in fashionable Hanover Square, around the southwest corner of the intersection of Hanover and Beaver Streets.

Born about 1645 in the small Scottish fishing village of Greenock, Kidd came to New York in the late '80s, already an accomplished seaman and privateer. He was in London on business in 1695 when he was approached by Robert Livingston, another New Yorker, with an interesting business proposition. The East India Company was having a great deal of trouble with piracy in the Indian Ocean and proposed to send a private vessel to combat the menace. Livingston had formed a corporation with several other prominent people to finance an expedition in return for a share of the spoils. Livingston offered the captaincy to Kidd, and in April of 1696 Kidd sailed out of England in the *Adventure Galley*, putting in first at New York, and then proceeding to the Indian Ocean.

At some point while bobbing about on the waves, Kidd went bad. The *Adventure Galley* hoisted up, at least metaphorically, the Jolly Roger, and, over the next two years, roamed about looting, burning, and killing.

Kidd did quite well as a buccaneer. Sailing a captured vessel, the *Quedagh Merchant*, and loaded up with ill-gotten gain, he headed back toward the New World, reaching Anguilla in the West Indies in April 1699. There he learned that tales of his exploits had preceded him and that he was a wanted man.

Kidd returned to Boston and launched what proved to be an unsuccessful defense. He was removed to England, where he was convicted of one count of murder and five counts of piracy and executed on May 23, 1701, at Execution Dock just outside of London.

Turn left on Hanover Street and proceed to Wall Street. Turn left again and pause at William Street.

7 Dollar for dollar and pound for pound, Wall Street must be the most criminal slice of the city. The fruits of all the flamboyant robberies and rip-offs of desperate folk elsewhere are bagatelle compared with the hauls of the well-tailored men of Wall Street. The outright swindles and larcenies could fill a volume, but in addition, there are numberless daily deals and transactions and practices that bounce and skip around the line of ethical demarcation like a loose football. "The very style of business done in the street," explains a guidebook of 1879, "blunts the moral sense." This criminal review of Wall Street, therefore, is severely abridged.

The first New York City bank robbery (technically a bank burglary), took place at the City Bank, which stood close to the northeast corner of Wall and William Streets, then 52 Wall Street, on March 20, 1831. Edward Smith broke into the bank and took off with $200,000 in bills and Spanish doubloons. He was captured a week later and soon sentenced to five years of hard labor. $175,738 was recovered.

Continue to 23 Wall Street, the Morgan Guaranty Trust Company and pause opposite the entrance to 30 Wall Street. Here you can still see, in the white granite wall, the pits and scars of the famous, fatal, and still unsolved bombing of September 16, 1920.

8 Around noon on that day, a tired old wagon, drawn by a tired old horse, came to rest outside 30 Wall Street, then the Assay Office, across the street. A few minutes later, wagon and horse burst apart with terrific force and shattering sound. The blast was huge: windows for blocks around were blown out, nearby awnings caught fire, bars on the windows of the Assay Office were bent. Thirty people were killed immediately; ten more died later. Hundreds were injured. There was pandemonium in the street as dazed people wandered about in the dust and smoke, and crowds first stampeded out of the immediate area and then, to help or to gawk, rushed back in. Within five minutes a crowd of ten thousand had assembled; by the evening over forty thousand stood by. First aid and clean-up, performed by literally thousands of policemen, volunteers, and federal troops called in from Governors Island, lasted long into the night. All that remained of the vehicle were fragments of the axles and two hooves of the departed horse. The driver had either made good his escape or been blown to pieces.

It was immediately assumed that the explosion was an anarchist plot, for these dangerous radicals were much in the American news at the time. In April of the previous year, bombs had been mailed to J. P. Morgan, John D. Rockefeller, Attorney General A. Mitchell Palmer and others; a few days later, bombs went off in New York, Cleveland, Philadelphia, a few other cities, and at Palmer's house in

Washington. That fall the attorney general launched his infamous Palmer Raids, rounding up thousands of suspected radicals throughout the country. The bombing of Wall Street, it was assumed, must be the opening salvo of radical retaliation.

Two alternative theories, neither given much credence, have been voiced. One is that the explosion was part of a robbery attempt, for on that day $900 million in gold was being moved under armed guard from the Sub-Treasury Building to the Assay Office. Workers were carrying boxes of gold bars over a wooden ramp slung across an alleyway between the two buildings, and the wagon was parked opposite this ramp. The workers, however, had knocked off for lunch right at noon and closed up the two side entrances of the buildings, thereby saving their lives, and, possibly, the gold. The other theory holds that the explosion was an accident, carelessness from someone working on one of the numerous construction projects going on in the neighborhood. But evidence indicated that five hundred pounds of cut-up lead sash weights were placed in the dynamite, making that explanation hard to maintain.

One of the greatest manhunts in the city's history followed. Hundreds of police were mobilized; the state rounded up dozens of suspects and followed up scores of insignificant clues, elusive sightings, and contradictory stories. Arthur Carey, then head of the Homicide Squad, recounted later that the horseshoes were traced to an Italian blacksmith, who claimed to have made them for a pair of fellow countrymen the morning of the explosion. He agreed to go through the Italian section of town with detectives to try and spot his customers, but only if given anonymity. Unfortunately, says Carey, his role as a witness was revealed in the press and the terrified blacksmith refused to cooperate further. But there were several blacksmiths who claimed to have made the shoes (not surprising, really, since over the years the police stopped in at over 4,000 stables all over the East Coast). And anyway, would the men involved have been traipsing about their old neighborhood when every cop in the five boroughs was in a frothy rage to find them?

The investigation continued for years, but the search for justice was an entirely frustrated one. The Wall Street bombing remains a complete mystery.

Step up to the Federal Hall National Memorial at 26 Wall Street.

9 In 1699 a new city hall was built on this site to replace the dilapidated Stadt Huys, the site of which we traipsed by at Pearl and Broad Streets at the beginning of this tour. A courtroom was set up on the first floor and jail cells installed in the rear. The attic was used

FAMOUS WALL STREET FINANCIAL MALFEASANCES

William Duer, 1792—Trading on insider information, and using fronts and secret agreements, Duer, Assistant Secretary of the Treasury in George Washington's second term, sunk hundreds of thousands into the newly sprung markets for bank and debt securities. His activities in the market were so great that a general panic resulted when he crashed in March 1792. Some placed the losses in New York as high as $5 million. He was thrown into debtors' prison, where he died on May 7, 1799.

    Robert Schuyler, 1854—Schuyler, president of both the New Haven and Harlem railroads and one of the city's elite, counterfeited 20,000 shares of New Haven stock and pocketed $2 million from their sale. New Yorkers were stunned to find out that Schuyler had lived a double life for years, keeping another family under the name of Spicer. Schuyler/Spicer fled to Canada and was never brought to justice.

    Cornelius Vanderbilt, Daniel Drew, Jay Gould, Jim Fisk, 1868—In one of the most infamous episodes in Wall Street history, these robber barons conducted a titanic battle for control of the Erie Railroad. Vanderbilt attempted to dominate the line by buying as much stock as possible, while Drew, Gould, and Fisk fended him off by printing an ever greater supply of bogus shares. Vanderbilt tried to have the three arrested for fraud; they fled to safety in New Jersey, then tried to bribe the legislature to legalize, *ex post facto*, their counterfeiting. Eventually they signed a peace treaty that made them all as happy and rich as before.

    Richard Whitney, 1938—Whitney served as the President of the New York Stock Exchange from 1929 to 1931 and was a pillar of the financial community. But when he fell into debt he began to steal bonds—eventually a million dollars' worth—from clients of his brokerage firm and pledge them as his own as collateral for bank loans. On March 10, 1938, Whitney was indicted for embezzlement and the *New York Daily News* gasped, "Not in our time, in our fathers' time nor in our grandfathers' time has there been such a social debacle. . . ." Whitney plead guilty and got five to ten in Sing Sing, though he was released on good behavior in August 1941.

    Equity Funding, 1973—The officers of this financial services institution created 64,000 fictitious life insurance policies, forged death certificates, and counterfeited bonds in order to create $100 million in fake assets. Twenty-two men were indicted.

    Michael Milken, Ivan Boesky, et al., 1987–90—An informal network of traders and lawyers, including junk-bond king Milken and top arbitrageur Boesky built immense fortunes on insider trading and securities frauds. The public marveled at the genius and pluck of these men, only to learn that the game was rigged. Boesky was fined $100 million and served two years in prison. Milken was fined $600 million and served twenty-two months; he later agreed to pay an additional $500 million to settle civil lawsuits, which still left him with a fortune of at least $125 million.

as a debtors' prison. The instruments of justice, including a pillory and a gallows, were located across the street where the New York Stock Exchange now stands. In 1789 the building served as the nation's capitol, but was demolished in 1812 when the present city hall, New York's third, was built. The building here now was built in 1842. There is a museum inside with an exhibit on the Zenger trial (see p. 61).

Turn right on Nassau Street and walk the three blocks to Liberty Street. To your left, at the site now occupied by the Chamber of Commerce building at 59 Liberty Street, the northwest corner of Liberty Street and Liberty Place, is an unexpected New York connection to a celebrated crime.

10 The assassin of President James Garfield, Charles Guiteau, was a New York resident in the early 1870s, plying his trade as a lawyer in an office here at 59 Liberty Street. His practice in New York consisted primarily of bill collecting (not unusual for low-echelon lawyers of the time) and selling insurance. He was spectacularly unsuccessful, and often resorted to fraud and cheating in order to get by. The lawyer from whom he sublet his office, D. McLane Shaw, evicted him for his questionable business practices.

Beside being a petty criminal and failure, Guiteau was also insane, and his condition worsened over the years. In 1881 he moved to Washington in the delusion that he was about to be appointed a consul, and, in May of that year, decided that he must assassinate the President. On July 2, 1881, Guiteau followed President Garfield to the Baltimore and Potomac Station and shot the unguarded President in the back.

Garfield died two and a half months later, on September 19. At his trial for murder, Guiteau claimed, basically, that God told him to kill the President. He was convicted despite his providential dispensation, and on June 30, 1882, he was hanged.

Two other presidential assassins had connections to New York. John Wilkes Booth, besides being a megalomaniac and murderer, was an actor. He performed often in New York, the last time on November 25, 1864 in a gala presentation with his two brothers Edwin and Junius at the Winter Garden, Broadway at Bond Street, later the Grand Central Hotel and the site of the killing of "Jubilee" Jim Fisk (see p. 39). The young Lee Harvey Oswald lived during part of the summer of 1952 in the apartment of his older brother at 325 East 92nd Street. His mother thought New York was a bad influence on little Oswald, already a problem child at the age of thirteen, and took him south. He returned to the city years later with his Soviet wife Marina and spent a night in a seedy Times Square hotel.

Turn right and walk east on Liberty Street to Louise Nevelson Plaza. Just below the easternmost point of the plaza, is 78-88 Maiden Lane, the site of another unexpected New York connection to a well-known crime.

11 In 1910, Hawley Harvey Crippen poisoned his wife Cora, stashed her under the floorboards of his London bungalow, and ran off with his mistress Ethel Le Neve. With his young lover disguised as a boy, the pair attempted an escape to the United States on a steamship, but, in the first use of radio-telegraphy in the name of the law, were discovered mid-Atlantic and hauled back. Crippen was hanged; Le Neve, in a separate trial, was acquitted. Crippen's case is one of Britain's most famous: According to writer Martin Fido, "for fifty years after his arrest he was *the* classic murderer in most English eyes." Interestingly, Crippen was an American, and lived in New York for a time. Circa 1891, he practiced homeopathic medicine at 78 Maiden Lane.

Return to Nassau Street, take a right and walk three blocks to Fulton Street.

12 In the 1630s, when this area was far outside of the city limits of New Amsterdam, there was a little farm here that belonged to Anthony Jansen or van Vaes, also called Anthony the Turk. This intersection stands in what was the northwest corner of the estate, which extended more or less from Ann Street on the north to Maiden Lane on the south, Broadway on the west and Pearl Street on the east. Jansen was a colorful character, but more interesting was his wife, Grietse Reyniers, for she was the city's very first prostitute.

She arrived in New Amsterdam in 1633, complete with a scarlet past. Testifying years later in a court case, one settler remembered Reyniers from an Amsterdam tavern, where he observed her entertaining Dutch soldiers in a back room. The landlady, he reported, peeked through a hole in the door to discover Reyniers servicing the soldiers in her petticoat.

Reyniers was a constant headache for the fusty city fathers. Her spirit is evident in a number of surviving anecdotes, but is best illustrated by a story that surfaced soon after her arrival. She seems to have plied her trade even on the ship that brought her to the New World, for as the *Southberg* departed, some of the sailors called out to her as she stood on the strand, "Whore, whore, two pounds butter whore!" Whereupon Reyniers hoisted her skirt, mooned the crew, and yelled, "Blaes my daer achterin!"

Reyniers and husband Jansen were later banished to Long Island.

Walk up to Ann Street. This small unassuming block was, in the middle of the eighteenth century, one of the centers of the city's considerable gambling industry.

13 Gambling has always contributed a fair share to New York's economy, whether suppressed, or, as now, actively promoted by the government. In early days gambling was informal, generally conducted in taverns or coffee houses. Sometimes a private room in the back or the attic would be outfitted with gaming devices, and these eventually developed into separate gambling dens. These ranged from the low joints of the slums, invariably crooked, to luxurious uptown casinos that catered to the dapper elite. Popular betting devices before the Civil War included racing (whether by horse, foot, or ship); lotteries (both private and state-sponsored); policy (numbers); fistfighting and wrestling; cockfights and dog baiting; and, increasingly as mid-century drew near, gaming such as cards, dice, and roulette. A class of professional gamblers began to emerge for the first time in the 1780s.

The first successful, well-known professional gambler in New York—and hence the nation—was Reuben Parsons. From inauspicious beginnings as a losing player, he pulled hard on his bootstraps and by the 1830s had become "The Great American Faro Banker." (Faro was a popular card game of the time.) He launched a number of profitable houses and bankrolled quite a few more. His touch failed only when he faced the accomplished gamblers of Wall Street and lost his considerable fortune in the stock market. He died penniless in 1875.

Gambling dens, or gambling "hells" as they were called in the nineteenth century, were spread liberally throughout the city, but there was an especially thick agglomeration here on Ann Street and nearby. This was due to the many "day houses" which popped up here just after mid-century. Prior to that time, most gambling houses had been uptown, run like private clubs with lavish dinners and a full bar, and open only at night. Day houses opened their doors in the afternoon and early evenings, and catered to businessmen during their working day. They were easily accessible, eliminated the expense of providing meals, and removed the need for alibis to abandoned wives and families. The first was opened in the 1850s by

Reuben Parsons and Sherlock Hillman on Liberty Street and was hugely successful and soon imitated. James D. McCabe Jr., in his 1882 guidebook *New York by Sunlight and Gaslight* explained:

> The "Day Houses" are down-town institutions. Ann street, in the rear of the *Herald* office, and several streets adjacent or convenient to Wall street, are the principal neighborhoods infested with them. Not long since a single block in Ann street contained five of these houses, and the majority, though several times raided by the police, still continue to flourish. The "Day Houses" occupy the upper floors of buildings, the street floors of which are devoted to legitimate business, and claim to be "Club Houses." They are managed by the lowest class of gamblers, skin games only are played in them, and the players have no possible chance of success. Yet they manage to do a profitable business. Their visitors are Wall street brokers, clerks, salesmen, and men in regular business, who too often risk here money that is not their own.

It was in one such day house, at 12 Ann Street, that Cornelius Vanderbilt Jr., profligate son of the Commodore, spent his last night. On April 2, 1882, after a debauched time drinking and gambling here, Vanderbilt returned to his room in the Glenham Hotel at Fifth Avenue and 22nd Street (still extant) and shot himself to death.

Continue half a block on Nassau Street. In 1841, the boardinghouse of Mrs. Phoebe Rogers stood at 126 Nassau, between Beekman and Ann Streets. Here is the spot where the mystery of Mary Cecilia Rogers, one of New York's most famous and venerable murder cases, began.

14 On Wednesday, July 28, 1841, readers of the *New York Sun* spotted this advertisement on the third page of their penny paper: "Left her home on Sunday morning, July 25, a young lady; had on a white dress, black shawl, blue scarf, Leghorn hat, light colored shoes, and parasol light-colored; it is supposed some accident has befallen her. Whoever will give information respecting her at 126 Nassau Shall be rewarded for their trouble."

Mary Rogers, the young lady in question, turned up the same day, and what befell her was more than an accident. She was found floating in the Hudson near Hoboken, quite obviously murdered. Roger's shocking and mysterious death immediately consumed the city. A lasting place was ensured several years later when Edgar Allen Poe published "The Mystery of Marie Roget," a Frenchified version of the murder, considered by many critics to be the second detective story ever written (Poe's "The Murders in the Rue Morgue" is considered the first).

Mary Rogers was born in New York City in 1820. In 1836 she was hired by John Anderson to work the counter in his tobacco store on Broadway. The novelty of a striking young girl in this male preserve attracted plenty of customers and loiterers, including (at least according to legend) Washington Irving, James Fenimore Cooper, General Winfield Scott, James Gordon Bennet, and Edgar Allen Poe. She was known around town as "the Beautiful Seegar Girl."

A curious incident occurred while she was in Anderson's employ, something that foreshadowed her later fate. In October of 1838, Rogers disappeared, leaving, it was said, a suicide note. Her notoriety was such that her disappearance made the papers. She was back hawking cigars in a week or two, claiming that she was vacationing with relatives in Brooklyn and didn't know what the fuss was about. There were whispers of an elopement, or, in even more hushed tones, an abortion.

Mary Rogers retired from the "seegar" business at the age of 19 to help her mother run a boardinghouse here at 126 Nassau Street. On the Sunday previously noted, July 25, 1841, she walked out of the boardinghouse, telling her fiancé, a dissolute cork cutter named Daniel Payne, that she was off to visit a cousin in Jane Street and would return that evening. But, it later turned out, Cousin Downing had no appointment with Rogers, and did not see her that evening.

Mary Rogers did not return that night, and as her absence grew longer, her mother and her friends fretted. Payne searched in likely spots without success, and on Tuesday evening placed the ad in the paper. At three-thirty the next day, as readers were scanning the plea in the paper and pondering this strange happenstance, Roger's body was spotted in the shallow water just off Elysian Fields, a popular picnic spot in what was then a rural and bucolic Hoboken, New Jersey. (An Elysian Park still exists in more or less the same spot, across the Hudson from 14th Street.)

A strip of lace was found tight around her neck: death was due to strangulation. Another strip, probably a gag, hung loose about her neck. A piece of material from her dress (she was found fully clothed) had been torn off and wrapped around her waist, apparently as a handle to drag her body to the river. Bruises were found on her throat, and abrasions on her back.

The shocking murder of the "beautiful seegar girl" became the lead story in every city paper. An outraged city cried for a solution, but the police (existing then only in a rather primitive form) were of little help. They scurried about frantically, but their investigatory skills were next to nil. They failed even to establish the time or place of death. Several of Mary's old boyfriends were arrested, only to be quickly released. A few men were arrested after being accused in anonymous letters, but soon let go. The strip around Roger's neck was tied in a sailor's knot, so several seamen were arrested and, again, almost immediately released. Four weeks after the discovery of the body, the police had only embarrassment to show for their efforts.

On August 25 came a startling development. In Weehawken, not far from Elysian Fields, and close by a tavern called the Nick Moore House, articles of Mary's clothing—gloves, a petticoat, a handkerchief bearing the initials "M. R."—were discovered inside a hollow thicket of briar bushes. The owner of the Nick Moore House, Fredericka Loss (whose sons discovered the clothes) suddenly remembered seeing Mary in her tavern on that Sunday a month earlier, accompanied by a "swarthy man," the young girl drinking a proper glass of lemonade.

This discovery created only new mysteries, for the placement and condition of the articles indicated that they were almost certainly planted long after the discovery of the body. And here the important evidence ran out, and the mystery of Mary Rogers comes to its inconclusive and unsatisfying impasse. No circumstantial evidence, smoking gun, or deathbed confession follows (though an interesting coda, described below, capped things off).

Detectives in armchairs have the following suspects and proposed solutions to mull over:

There was Rogers' fiancé, Daniel Payne, who was the last to acknowledge seeing her alive on Sunday morning. But he was able to produce affidavits swearing to his whereabouts (mostly in various bars) for all of that day.

There was a former suitor, Alfred Crommelin, who joined the search for her and identified her body in Hoboken. In the first hysterical days of the investigation he was arrested, but a case has never been made against him, and no one has considered him a heavyweight contender.

Various seamen were suspected, and several arrested, but a case could be made against none.

There was the "swarthy man" who was supposedly seen with Mary in Hoboken, but his very existence is doubtful, due only to some hazy recollections by two witnesses a month after the murder.

There were gangs of ruffians—Victorian juvenile delinquents—who frequented the area around Elysian Fields, but none were ever connected with the case.

Poe's culprit was ". . . a young naval officer, much noted for his debaucheries." Poe believed that Rogers' 1838 disappearance was a brief elopement with this sailor, and that a second attempt ended in Rogers' murder in the thicket. But Poe's retelling of the events is inaccurate and his solution not very likely.

The most popular theory has been that Rogers underwent an unsuccessful abortion at the Nick Moore House, and that her body was deposited in the river under cover of night. Local authorities evidently suspected the Nick Moore House of being an abortion site; Rogers was known to have tried to sell an IOU for $52 just prior to her disappearance, that being just about the going rate for the operation; and her earlier weeklong vanishing act makes sense as a previous abortion. According to this version, the clothes found in the thicket were planted by Loss's sons to get rid of incriminating evidence and draw attention away from the tavern.

But other evidence militates against the abortion theory. If Rogers died during or just after an operation, why was she found fully clothed? What of her death by strangulation? The bruises on her throat and abrasions on her back seem inconsistent with an abortion.

A variation of this theory asserts that Rogers underwent a *successful* abortion on Sunday at the Nick Moore House, but was later, probably on Tuesday, beaten to death by Daniel Payne, whose sworn affidavits covering his activities that Sunday become meaningless. This theory may help explain the incredible closing scene of the drama.

In a page torn from the grandest of Grand Guignol, Daniel Payne, on October 7, 1841, crossed the river into Hoboken to commit suicide. He got drunk, downed a vial of laudanum, and staggered to the infamous thicket, where he penned a note: "To the World—Here I am on the very spot. May God forgive me for my misspent life." He then made his way down to the shoreline, and close by the little cove where Mary's body was brought ashore, expired, a victim of either alcohol poisoning or, more likely, exposure.

For over 150 years the case of Mary Rogers has endured as one of the most prominent and provocative of mysteries in New York's long and full criminal history.

Go another block past Spruce Street to Pace College Plaza, the site of the *New York Tribune* office in the second half of the nineteenth century, when this area teemed with newspapers and newsmen and was known as Printing House Square.

15 In 1869, the *Tribune* found itself not just reporting the news, but smack in the middle of the day's most scandalous murder and love triangle, the Richardson-Sage-McFarland tragedy.

Albert Deane Richardson was a well-known author and a journalist for the *Tribune*. During the Civil War he had been sent by his paper to report from behind enemy lines, been captured, and then escaped from a Confederate prison camp. His exploits became a best-seller after the war.

Daniel McFarland invokes the "unwritten law" at the point of a gun.

Daniel McFarland was an Irish immigrant who had gone to Dartmouth, been admitted to the Massachusetts bar, but had never practiced as a lawyer. He married nineteen-year-old Abby Sage of Massachusetts in 1857. Sage later wrote that "when I married him, he represented himself to be a member of the bar in Madison, Wisconsin, with a flourishing law practice, brilliant political prospects, and possessed of property to the amount of $20,000 to $30,000. He also professed to be a man of temperate habits, [and] of the purest morals . . . ." None of these representations turned out to be true. He was an alcoholic and given to binges and bouts of violent fury. What little money he had was quickly lost dabbling in Wisconsin real estate. Just before the Civil War, he took his wife to New York City in an unsuccessful search for work and money, and for several years the impecunious couple shuttled almost monthly from boardinghouse to boardinghouse, avoiding bill collectors, pawning jewelry, and selling furniture.

In order to make ends meet, Sage took up public speaking and acting, and eventually landed a part with Edwin Booth at the Winter Garden playing Nerissa in *The Merchant of Venice*. Unseemly employment, of course, for a proper New England woman, but there were bills to be paid. She soon fell in with an arty, bohemian crowd of actresses and literati, and through these friends she met, sometime in 1866, Albert D. Richardson. A love affair quickly flamed.

At the end of February 1867, Sage moved out of the boarding-house she shared with her husband at 72 Amity Street (now West Third), and in the company of her father and several close friends, told her husband she was leaving him. McFarland took the separation badly. Three weeks later, he intercepted Richardson on the street and, unveiling a pistol, wounded the journalist in the hip. Richardson did not press charges.

Evidently frustrated by his lack of marksmanship, McFarland then turned to the law. He sued Richardson for alienation of affection and took his wife to court for custody of their children. Sage settled the case out of court by giving up her eldest son Percy, and then moved to Indiana, at that time the state with the most permissive divorce laws in the country, to establish residence and put asunder her legal entanglement with McFarland.

In 1869 she returned to New York City divorced, in the eyes of Indiana law. But the proceeding, conducted without the presence, or even the knowledge, of McFarland, was not recognized by the state of New York. Abby Sage considered herself a single woman again; Daniel McFarland assumed she was his wife.

On November 25, 1869, McFarland entered the offices of the *Tribune* and sat down at a desk in the counting room. A little after five-thirty in the evening, Richardson entered to get his mail. Mc-Farland immediately sprang up and delivered a shot to the journalist's midsection. Richardson fell wounded and the assassin sauntered out for a bowl of beef stew at a restaurant. He was arrested later that night in a hotel.

Richardson lingered for a week and died on December 2, 1869. Two days before expiring, lying on his deathbed, he and Abby Sage were married by the country's most famous clergyman, Henry Ward Beecher.

Entwined in a love triangle, involving some of New York's most famous citizens, wrapped up with volatile subjects such as feminism, the sanctity of marriage, and free love, the Richardson-Sage-McFarland trial was a smash hit. As contemporary Charles Sutton wrote,

> . . . all of society watched the affair eagerly, for all of society knew that there was more than the life of a man at stake; that the murder and trial were not accidental events that were likely to have occurred at any time, but that they were outgrowing incidents of this progressive modern age. Men, with handsome wives who had a taste for literature and literary society not shared by their husbands, thought and said that McFarland did right. The wives of these men, remembering their own

unhappy condition, and with their heart [*sic*] yearning for an affinity, hoped he would be hanged. . . . Every tea-table was a battle ground.

Lines were drawn between conservatives lauding McFarland as a virtuous husband defending his marriage from a libertine, and progressives and feminists upholding Sage as a suffering wife rightfully escaping from an abusive relationship.

The trial opened April 4, 1870. Defense lawyer John Graham based much of his case around the notion of "natural justice" or the "unwritten law"—basically, a husband's inalienable right to kill his wife's seducer. This "right" was invoked successfully in a number of prominent nineteenth-century cases, the most famous being the Washington D.C. trial of Congressman Daniel Sickles for killing his wife's lover Philip Barton Key (see p. 120). Graham had been on the defense team for that trial. Though a powerful emotional cudgel, the unwritten law was rather tenuous legally, so Graham also argued that McFarland was temporarily insane.

In addition, the defense opined vigorously on the characters of those involved: McFarland was a virtuous husband, Richardson was a libertine, Sage was an ungrateful spouse driven by passion and ambition.

Under the onslaught of Graham's emotional attack, the prosecution's straightforward case that McFarland shot Richardson with malice aforethought was ignored, and in less than two hours the jury brought back a verdict of not guilty.

At the close of the trial, public opinion favored McFarland, applauding the verdict as a vindication of marriage and a repudiation of radical, feminist notions. But shortly thereafter, Sage published a long article detailing her version of events. Its sordid details and sober tone won her much sympathy. She was further vindicated when, not six months after the trial, McFarland was arrested and jailed for public drunkenness. Having sealed his historical reputation, Daniel McFarland disappears and is heard of no more.

Abby Sage went on to a long career as a lecturer and writer, especially successful at adapting prose works for the theater. She died in Rome in 1900.

ALSO INFAMOUS

The southeast corner of Frankfort and Nassau Streets (now Pace Plaza) is the site of the first home of Tammany Hall, the political machine founded by William Mooney in 1789. Mooney got things off to a proper Tammany start: In 1809 he was removed as superintendent of the city's almshouse for stealing $5,000 in money and supplies.

Stay where you are for another incident at this spot.

16 England's Glorious Revolution of 1688, which replaced Catholic King James II with the Protestants William and Mary, was a dramatic and traumatic event for New Yorkers. Long-standing tensions—between Protestant and Catholic, Dutch and English, rich and poor—were brought to the breaking point. Long-unresolved political grievances, such as the recent and unpopular consolidation of the colony with New England, came to the fore.

With the sudden change of monarchs in the mother country, the city found itself with a chief executive that it did not trust. Not only had Lt. Governor Francis Nicholson loyally served the disliked Catholic James II, but he now stalled in recognizing William and Mary, adding to suspicions.

In this unsettled atmosphere, talk grew dark and foreboding. A rumor erupted of a Catholic assault upon the city. Nicholson, it was whispered, was among the plotters (despite the inconvenient fact that he was Protestant). Soon it was said that Nicholson planned to burn the city. Then came another rumor that a thousand French and Indians were about to attack Albany. On May 31, 1689, with the tension at a breaking point, the city militia, under the command of Jacob Leisler, took control of Fort James, ousted Nicholson, and pulled off something of their own little revolution.

Leisler was a wealthy merchant of German Calvinist background, prominent in the city but without prior political experience. He had immigrated to New Amsterdam in 1660 as a twenty-year-old soldier, and through a judicious marriage to a rich widow, came into money and status. For two years, this contentious and quick-tempered man almost single-handedly controlled New York Colony.

Although he was rabidly anti-Catholic, he did a credible job initially. He took steps to protect the colony from French and Indian attack, and was instrumental in convening the first inter-Colonial congress. But he soon became despotic and erratic, and the colony turned against him, firing off several petitions of complaint to England.

After much dawdling, William and Mary, in late 1690, dispatched a new governor, Colonel Henry Sloughter, to put New York back in order. Although Leisler had ostensibly taken control of the city to establish the rule of William and Mary, he now delayed handing power over to their agent. Partisans on both sides skirmished in the streets of New York for several weeks before Leisler's militiamen, weary and besieged in Fort James, surrendered. Leisler and his aides were charged with treason. Found guilty, Leisler and his lieutenant and son-in-law Jacob Milborne were executed on May 16, 1691, at about the spot where the statue of Ben Franklin now stands. The execution order stated that Leisler and Milborne be hanged "by the Neck and being Alive their bodys be Cutt downe to the Earth and Their Bowells be taken out and they being Alive, burnt before their faces; that their heads shall be struck off and their Bodys Cutt in four parts."

Turn to your left, cross Park Row and walk past City Hall. Cross Chambers Street and then turn right and cross Centre Street. Through the arch of the Municipal Building, you will see Police Headquarters. Since 1972 this building has served as the base of operations for New York's Finest.

17 For over 150 years Manhattan used various inadequate citizen's patrols, military squads, and "rattle watches" to protect the city. Soldiers provided the earliest security force. From 1697 to 1731 the city relied upon four "bellmen" for policing, clearly inadequate for a city of nearly ten thousand. Later schemes proved even worse, such as the citizen's watch established in 1742. Those with money or better things to do could pay for substitutes, and the caliber of the watch left much to be desired. The *New York Gazette* of February 21, 1757 complained that they were a "Parcle of idle, drinking, vigilant Snorers, who never quell'd any nocturnal Tumult in their Lives; (Nor as we can learn, were ever the discoverers of a Fire breaking out,) but would, perhaps, be as ready to join in a Burglary as any Thief in Christendom."

In 1845, following the example of London, a professional police department was finally established, but this, too, proved inadequate in a number of ways. Policemen (who wore no uniforms) were political appointees, and served only one year. There were no physical or mental requirements or tests, and the force was made up of only eight hundred men. It was not until 1853 that the department was uniformed and not until 1884 that a civil-service system was instituted for the police department. George Matsell, the first chief of police, must have had great expectations when he coined the phrase "the finest police force in the world."

Reformers and civic leaders were, until the 1930s, quite critical of the police department and vocal about police brutality, corruption, and favoritism. Dr. Charles Parkhurst, head of the Society for the Prevention of Crime, once said in the 1890s, "Our motto was 'Down With the Police.' " Certainly there was a good deal of class prejudice behind these criticisms, since most reformers were upper-class and many cops working-class and recent immigrants, but their views that the force was an obstacle to good government and law and order does provide a dramatic contrast to today's unceasing calls for greater police power and budgets.

Today the NYPD numbers approximately 28,000. But this is certainly not the limit of police power in New York City. There is, in addition to the New York City Police Department, a New York City Transit Police, a New York City Housing Authority Police, a Port Authority Police Department, a Department of Sanitation Police, and a New York City Uniformed Court Police, among others.

The first woman, Mary Hamilton, was admitted to the Police Department in 1888. Samuel Battle, the first black policeman, joined the force in 1911.

POLICE INVESTIGATIONS AND SCANDALS

The Lexow Committee, 1894—The Reverend Charles Parkhurst's revelations of big city vice and police complicity sparked this investigation, named for committee chairman Senator Charles Lexow. They looked into city elections fraud (at the time elections were a police responsibility), prostitution payoffs, and police brutality. One of its achievements was getting Theodore Roosevelt named as Police Commissioner.

The Mazet Committee, 1899—A state legislature version of the Lexow Committee, they focused on William Devery, a colorful but thoroughly corrupt police chief. At the conclusion of the hearings, he was fired.

The Curran Committee, 1912—In the fallout from the Becker-Rosenthal Case (see pp. 190), lawyer Henry H. Curran was appointed by the Board of Alderman to investigate police corruption. Curran recommended that Police Commissioner Rhinelander Waldo be fired, but the Board refused.

The Seabury Investigation, 1931—Upright, avuncular Samuel Seabury looked into corruption among the police, the courts, and the city government. The investigation forced the resignation of Mayor Jimmy Walker for accepting pay-offs.

The Harry Gross Trial, 1951—The trial of one of the city's biggest bookmakers revealed extensive police protection of his operations. Over 100 cops left the force, voluntarily or otherwise.

The Knapp Commission, 1972—The accusations of Frank Serpico spawned this investigation, which found corruption to be widespread. An extensive reorganization of the department followed.

The Mollen Commission, 1992—Like clockwork, the twenty-year cycle of corruption scandels and inquiries continues. This panel found that the department tolerated corruption and called for an independent oversight agency.

Further north is the heart of man-made justice in New York City. On the east side of Centre Street is the Surrogate's Court. Another block up is the United States Court House. Above that is the Supreme Court of the State of New York. Keep walking up another block to the corner of Hogan Place and Centre Street. Look over at the small park, Collect Pond Park, on the east side of Centre Street. If you're tired, cross the street and take a seat.

18 This park was once Collect Pond, an early Manhattan landmark; a small spit that reached into the pond was a favorite execution spot in colonial New York. Over two hundred years later, the pond, now landfill, is still used for judgment and punishment. On the east side of Centre Street is the Criminal Courts Building and Men's House of Detention, directly to the north is the Civil Court Building, and on the west side, across Lafayette Street, the Family Court building. On the spot now occupied by the park stood the first and second of New York's infamous Tombs prisons.

In 1833, the city discovered that the Bridewell, the prison in City Hall Park, was falling apart and commissioned a new prison here on the present site of the Park. Completed in 1838, The Tombs has endured through four buildings and two locations, lent its name to countless other lesser jails, and achieved nationwide fame.

The design was cribbed from an illustration of an Egyptian mausoleum—hence the prison's nickname—that appeared in a popular travel book of the day. It consisted of a four-story structure built around a central yard in which another building, housing the men's prison, stood. The honor of the first night's stay belongs to two otherwise undistinguished thieves, "Snuffy" Joe Bernard and Andrew Morrison. The first execution there, carried out January 12, 1839, dispatched Edward Coleman, a leader of an early Five Points gang dubbed the Forty Thieves. On July 28, 1838, he encountered his wife on Broadway, at Walker Street, pulled out a razor, and cut her neck open. The *Sun* reported: "It appears that the horrible deed resulted from Coleman's belief in her infidelity and if the statements of their acquaintances are correct his belief was not without cause." The last execution in the Tombs took place on December 5, 1889, when Harry Carlton was hanged for killing policeman James Brennan on 59th Street.

The Tombs was built to hold two hundred prisoners, but was often overloaded. At one point in 1870 there were five hundred prisoners confined there. Built on ground reclaimed from Collect Pond, the place was often damp and musty, and it was not uncommon for water to come up through the drain pipes and flood the cells. In 1874 a journalist had himself committed to the prison for ten days and reported on his uncomfortable stay:

You enter a wide, arched, gloomy hall, on one side of which are three large cells, about fifteen feet square, with open barred grates the whole front of them, and open grates as partitions between them; there are eight bunks in each cell—the yard workmen, the tier men and other prisoners doing work occupy these bunks, the other prisoners accommodate themselves as best they can upon the floor. . . . For hours it is a miniature hell—there is no such thing as sleep—vermin of every kind crawl over you and *eat* you. You are on fire, you tear your flesh with your nails; huge rats rush between your legs or over your body; vulgarity, obscenity, profanity of every description reigns supreme.

A bridge connected the men's prison inside the courtyard to the building surrounding it: the Bridge of Sighs, so dubbed because it formed the path from cell to scaffold for condemned prisoners. In 1894 the Centre Street Criminal Court was built just to the north, and a bridge connecting the two, arching over Franklin Street, then took over the somber moniker.

The original Tombs was demolished in 1896 and construction began on a replacement in the same spot the next year. The second Tombs exchanged the Egyptian motif for a Norman castle style, with round, turreted corners topped by cones.

The third Tombs, the New York City Criminal Courts Building and Men's House of Detention, a slick, steely Art Deco edifice built in 1939, is still standing across the street. A fourth version of the House of Detention, officially the White Street Correctional Facility, was built in 1989, and a new Bridge of Sighs was thoughtfully erected.

MUG SHOTS

WILLIAM HOWE AND ABRAHAM HUMMEL
Crooked Lawyers

In the last quarter or so of the nineteenth century, William "the Weeper" Howe and Abraham "Little Abie," or more poetically, "the Light of the Tenderloin" Hummel were the most notorious, scurrilous, audacious—and popular—lawyers of their day. Even in the debased coinage of the Gilded Age, Howe and Hummel had national reputations as shameless but brilliant scoundrels. Between their incorporation in 1869 and their ignominious demise in 1907, their skill in satisfying clients, whether by embracing or abandoning justice, was a source of admiration and incredulity.

Howe was the eldest, a robust and flamboyant man, given to a highly personal wardrobe of dark purple or green waistcoats, checkered pants, and unsubtle jewelry. "When engaged in the trial of a celebrated case," related his *New York Times* obituary, "he would

often change his clothing for every session of the court . . . .
Diamonds in clusters, horseshoes, sunbursts and other forms adhered
to the person of Mr. Howe wherever it was possible to place them."

Howe's success did not lay in book-learning, but in his bombastic,
high-Victorian courtroom delivery. "He was the most accomplished
weeper of his day," said contemporary Samuel Hopkins Adams. "He
could and would cry over any case, no matter how commonplace.
His voice would quaver, his jowls would quiver, his great shoulders
would shake, and presently authentic tears would well up in his
bulbous eyes and dribble over. It was a sickening spectacle, but it
often carried a jury to extraordinary conclusions." Howe would strut,
kneel, grimace, or beg, as the occasion demanded. He once delivered
a three-hour-long summation entirely on his knees.

Howe found the perfect partner in Abe Hummel, his opposite in
every way—except greed. "Little Abie" was short and slouched, with
bird-like limbs and a huge head. His contribution to the firm was a
steel-trap legal mind that could always find just the right technical
loophole or legal cranny. In contrast to the motley Howe, Hummel
dressed almost always in black. "He looks like an abortion," said
client Stanford White.

Howe and Hummel served as the unofficial bar of the New York
underworld, and the most notorious of New York's criminal element
were satisfied clients of the firm: the infamous fence "Mother"
Mandlebaum, bank robber George Leonidas Leslie (see p. 34), the
Whyos Gang, all the major madams, all the major policy-shop owners
and bookmakers, and a large number of the city's amateur and
professional desperados. When 74 brothel owners were rounded up
during a reform drive in 1884, every one turned out to be a Howe
and Hummel client. In January of 1873, of the 25 prisoners awaiting
trial in the Tombs prison for murder or manslaughter, 23 were Howe
and Hummel clients.

Many of the country's well-known celebrities rubbed shoulders
with the riff-raff in the Howe and Hummel waiting room. The firm
represented the boxer John L. Sullivan, actors Edwin Booth and John
Barrymore, actresses Lillian Russell and Lillian Langtry, P. T.
Barnum, Stanford White, and other quite respectable folk interested
in getting results.

The firm reached its peak at the end of the nineteenth century, but
barely survived into the twentieth. Howe died in 1902. Hummel was
only 53 at the time of his partner's death, but his career was drawing
to a close. In 1907, after a four-year struggle with the reform-minded
District Attorney William Travers Jerome, Hummel was convicted of
suborning perjury and sentenced to a year in prison, there, no doubt,
to rub elbows with many former clients. Immediately after his release,
Hummel retired to Europe, and died, forgotten, in London in 1926.

For the last stop on this tour, take a right on Hogan Place, named after Frank Hogan, the legendary district attorney of New York from 1941 to 1973, and enter the Criminal Courts structure.

19 Inside there is a permanent exhibit, (open Monday–Friday, 9 A.M. to 6 P.M.), on the sixth, eighth, and ninth floors, covering some of the famous cases that have passed through the district attorney's office here. There you will find some fascinating material on gangsters such as "Lucky" Luciano and Albert Anastasia, the crooked "$64,000 Question" contestant Charles Van Doren, John Lennon's assassin Mark Chapman, and other immoral, if not immortal, names of New York history.

Nearest subway: Canal Street 6, J, M, N, R, Z
Nearest bus line: M 15

3

The Five Points, Chinatown, and Little Italy

A Criminal Sketch of the Five Points

New York is a city known for its eminent slums, and the Five Points—the name derives from the intersection of three streets at what is now the southwest corner of Columbus Park—was the first and perhaps the most disreputable of them all. The Five Points slum was so removed from the long arm of the law, so decrepit and noisome and evil that it became a national symbol of urban decay and depravity. The *Police Gazette* lamented: "Here is vice at its lowest ebb, a crawling and fetid vice, a vice of rags and filth. The place was the terror of every officer, for it was all but worth one's life to go into the houses singlehanded." The *Daily Tribune* called it "the great center ulcer of wretchedness—the very rotting skeleton of civilization." Charles Dickens, after a celebrated (and well-guarded) tour, wrote of the " . . . hideous tenements which take their name from robbery and murder; all that is loathsome, drooping, and decayed is here."

The results of a survey done around 1850 bear out the purple prose in stark figures. In one Five Points block,

> . . . of 614 children only 1 in 66 attended any school. Out of 916 adults, 605 could neither read nor write. In the same block there were 33 underground lodging-houses, ten feet below the sidewalk, and 20 of the vilest grog-shops in the city. During five hours on the Sabbath, two of these grog-shops were visited by 1054 persons,—450 men and 445 women, 91 boys and 68 girls.

Drinking on a Sunday is no longer considered the worst of crimes, but the Five Points was guilty of other sins as well.

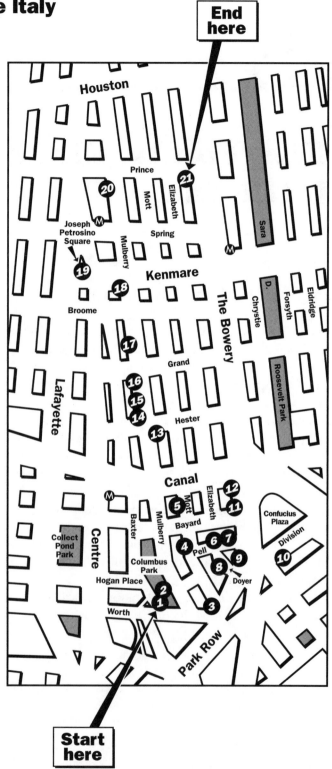

**The Five Points,
Chinatown,
and Little Italy**

End
here

Houston

Prince

20

Mott

Elizabeth

Sara

Joseph
Petrosino
Square

Spring

M

Mulberry

19

Kenmare

18

The Bowery

D.

Chrystie

Forsyth

Eldridge

Broome

Roosevelt Park

17

Grand

Lafayette

16

15

14

Hester

13

Canal

12

M

Baxter

Mulberry

5

Mott

Elizabeth

11

Confucius
Plaza

Bayard

Collect
Pond
Park

Centre

4

6 7

Division

Pell

9

Columbus
Park

8

10

Hogan Place

Doyer

2

1

3

Worth

Park Row

Start
here

The area teemed with prostitutes, and the ironically named Paradise Square, a tiny park located just to the west of what is now the corner of Baxter and Worth, was a notorious area for streetwalkers. There were scores of brothels and dance-halls (more or less the same thing) around the Square and in adjoining streets; these were considered a long step down from the establishments in SoHo (see p. 28).

The first organized gangs in the city came from the Five Points— the Kerryonians, the Chichesters, the Roach Guards, and the most famous of them all, the Dead Rabbits. These were predominantly Irish gangs, but the neighborhood was quite mixed, and one observer noted in 1869 that "some of the most brutal and desperate men of the locality are English."

While we know exactly how many people were drinking on Sundays, the rate of homicide in the district is harder to come by. It is said that Murderer's Alley, a small street located by the infamous Old Brewery tenement, alone averaged two murders a year around the 1850s. Twenty years later, the *Police Gazette* mentioned a Baxter Street den that had been the scene of seven murders.

Attempts to clean up the Five Points mess began early. In 1830 Jacob Hays, leading a squad of officers, raided the neighborhood, to no lasting effect. Frustrated city officials proposed razing the district (thereby saving the neighborhood by destroying it) several times in the early 1830s, but property owners—i.e. slumlords—blocked the moves. In 1850 Police Captain John J. McManus swept through and arrested most of the saloon and brothel keepers, but again to no avail.

Old time religion was more successful. In midcentury two (competing) Protestant missions, which offered food, shelter, vocational training, and rigorous praying, set up shop in the Five Points. Though it's easy to scoff at the narrow Victorian attitudes of the reformers of the Five Points Mission and the Five Points House of Industry, these institutions do seem to have had an effect. "[The Five Points] is bad enough now," a city guide noted in 1869, "— bad as it can be, one who saw it for the first time would think; but, compared to what it was fifteen years ago, it is as a white-sanded floor to the Augean Stable."

The nucleus of poverty and crime shifted in succeeding decades from Park Street to Baxter Street to Mulberry Street, by which time the character and ethnicities of the district had changed so much that the appellation Five Points faded, to be replaced by Mulberry Bend and Little Italy and Chinatown. In their time, each were characterized as dark quarters of "vice at its lowest ebb." The rich criminal histories of those neighborhoods will be described at their thresholds.

Stalking the Five Points, Chinatown, and Little Italy _____

> Nearest subway: Canal Street 6, J, M, N, R, Z
> Nearest bus line: M15

This tour picks up just about where the last ended (ambitious walkers can combine them). Start at the southwest corner of Columbus Park.

1 Look southwest at the octagonal New York County Courthouse. It occupies the site of the "Old Brewery," the single most famous tenement in the city's history. On this rookery the *Police Gazette* waxed rhapsodic:

> The wickedest house on the wickedest street that ever existed in New York, yes, and in all the country and possibly all the world, was the building known as the Old Brewery on the street known as 'Cutthroat Lane' [now Park Street, which once continued west of Baxter]. . . . For a full score of the sixty years that this structure stood, the debasements within its confines were so utterly repugnant as to make any unvarnished relation of its putridity seem nothing less than the play of an unsound and exaggerated imagination. . . . When the building was razed in December, 1852, to make way for the mission house sponsored by the Conference of the Methodist Episcopal Church, the wreckers carried out human bones by the sacks-full.

It was indeed once a brewery, built by a man named Coulter, but converted sometime around 1800 into a residence; its three stories turned to five and its floors divided into a confusing maze of tiny warrens, hallways, and garrets. There were close to a hundred rooms; only a few boasted windows. There were over a thousand tenants.

Turn around now to face Columbus Park, once called Mulberry Bend Park and prior to that plain old Mulberry Bend, a crooked street of tenements.

2 Seventy-five years after the heyday of the Five Points, the neighborhood was still poor. Charles Gardner was a private detective who accompanied the crusading Dr. Charles Parkhurst on his famous peregrinations (see p. 170) and took the Reverend Doctor to Mulberry Bend in 1892. According to Gardner, it vied with the Five Points:

"The wickedest house on the wickedest street." The Old Brewery.

> As we passed along the street our progress was very difficult. There
> was absolutely no place, no spot, no inch that was not occupied by a
> man, woman or child. Leaden-eyed, pale-faced men, wildly talking and
> gesticulating in the patois of all Italy, made a part of the mass.
> Haggard, dirty and uncomely women paced the narrow way. Babies,
> mere bundles of rags and dirt, lay on the filthy pavement, sprawled out
> in infant helplessness. Half-clad girls in the bitter March air shivered
> with cold. The crowd moved and swirled, like a human cataract, hither
> and thither, with a babel of sound bewildering to the ear. The
> pavements were slippery with garbage and filth.

In his classic study of New York slum life, *How the Other Half
Lives*, Jacob Riis called the Bend the " . . . foul core of New York's
slums."

Walk along the southern end of the park until reaching Mott Street. Turn
left into Mott Street and you are in Chinatown.

❸ The identity of the first permanent Chinese resident in New York is
a matter of historical controversy, and dates for his arrival range from
1844 to 1862. It is certain, however, that by the 1870s there were
somewhere around seventy-five males and that by the 1890s there
were at least 4,000 Chinese residents living in the three or four small
blocks around Mott, Pell, and Doyers Streets. (Today there are ap-

proximately 150,000 Chinese living in a Chinatown that has greatly overflowed its traditional boundaries.)

For the rest of the population in New York, the customs and culture of Chinatown were a mystery and the residents not just unknown but vaguely threatening. Prejudice and stereotyping played a large role in early perceptions of Chinatown as a dark quarter of Oriental subterfuge and heathen ruthlessness. Many nineteenth-century books touching on the subject solemnly state that all the Chinese in New York were opium users and chronic gamblers. Visitors in the 1920s and '30s walked the streets in mortal fear of receiving a Tong hatchet in the back. (The other side of this fear is the violent bigotry directed at the Chinese, as illustrated by the murder of Lee Teep, related on p. 109.)

But—these sometimes vicious, sometimes ridiculous characterizations aside—Chinatown did and does, like any other part of the city, have its share of crime. Let's take a look.

Walk over to 17 Mott Street and pause for a brief history of Chinatown's famous Tongs.

4 The struggles of the Tongs makes a story every bit as thrilling as the well-worn history of the Mafia, and the rise and fall and deaths of *caporegimas* and hitmen are easily matched in excitement by the struggles and stories of *dai lows* and *boo how doys*. The Tongs, which merely means "association" in Chinese, are an American invention. They developed in the Chinese community in San Francisco after the Civil War to counter the dominant power of the traditional family guilds, based on bloodlines, that had been imported from China. Tongs were open to anyone regardless of kinship, and their membership was often secret, two advantages they held over the numerically stronger family guilds. Though formed to defend the legitimate interests of the smaller families, a function they have always and still serve, they quickly got involved in lucrative gambling interests, drug trafficking, protection rackets, extortion, and similar unseemly activities.

The first successful Tong established in New York was the Hip Sing ("United in Victory") Tong, imported from Portland, Oregon by Laing Yue in the early 1890s. Its first headquarters was 10 Pell Street. It quickly dominated the burgeoning vice of the enclave. One head count in 1898 gave them 450 members—this is out of a total Chinatown population of about 4,000.

In response to the stranglehold of the Hip Sings, the On Leong ("Peaceful and Virtuous") Tong was organized in the late 1890s by Moy Dong Yue. The On Leongs quickly established their turf on

Mott Street, while the Hip Sings claimed Doyers and Pell, these three streets comprising the whole of Chinatown at the time. This territorial division still holds. A third Tong, the Tung On, emerged recently and controls territory along Division Street that 15 or 20 years ago was outside of the traditional boundaries of Chinatown.

Skirmishing between the Hip Sings and the On Leongs was constant, but the first war did not erupt until 1909, and it was not between the two Tongs, but between the On Leongs and the Four Brothers, one of the old-style family guilds. It started under rather unusual circumstances.

In San Francisco, a member of the Four Brothers, Low Hee Tong, purchased a concubine, the sixteen-year-old Bow Kum. After four years she was removed by a Christian mission, and shortly thereafter met and married a farmer named Tchin Len, who brought her east to New York's Chinatown. But Low, with backing from the Four Brothers in New York, demanded the return of the woman or payment of her purchase price: $3,000. Tchin refused, but decided it was a good time to join the On Leongs. (Another version of the story, however, states that Tchin's marriage to Bow was a device to remove her from the Christian mission, and that Tchin intended to force her into prostitution.)

On August 15, 1909, a *boo how doy* (hitman) entered Tchin's home at 17 Mott Street, the very building before you, and stabbed Bow to death, thus unleashing a great battle between the two groups. The usually quoted figure of 50 deaths sounds inflated, but a good many died nevertheless, including a prominent Chinese comedian, Dop Doy Hong (see pg. 97). A truce was not arranged until over a year later. Three soldiers (to use Mafia parlance) of the Four Brothers—Low Fong, Low Tching, and Chu Wah—were charged with the murder of Bow, but all were eventually released.

During this conflict the Hip Sings officially remained neutral, but actually supported and provided material help to the On Leongs. But as soon as the truce was signed, the two rival tongs went back to squabbling, and low-intensity skirmishes and occasional hit and run missions were the norm over the course of many years.

Walk up the block to 53 Mott Street.

5 The store at 53 Mott Street was, until a few years ago, Tai Pei Liquors, the business of Fok Leung Woo, also known as Peter Woo. Woo came to the United States in the 1930s and was, at various times, a shrimp and lobster wholesaler, a landlord, a restaurateur, and a liquor store owner. But law enforcement officials say Woo ran another, more profitable business on the side: heroin smuggling. He was arrested in February 1989 for his role in the White Mare case, a drug deal that, when uncovered by the police, became the largest single seizure ever of heroin in the U.S., weighing in at 800 pounds. (The French Connection payload, by contrast, was only 246 pounds.) The drug, from Thailand, was 90 percent pure and worth $1 billion.

Woo was the U.S. point man between wholesaler Chan Hok Pang, a confidant of Kuhn Sa, overlord of the "Golden Triangle" poppy growing region in Southeast Asia, and a Chicago dealer named Simon Auyeung. Both Auyeung and Woo were members of the On Leong Tong, whose headquarters are just up the street at 83 Mott Street at the corner of Canal Street. Auyeung was, in addition, an FBI informer. When the deal was done, the Feds swooped down on three locations in Queens and nabbed the heroin, $3 million in cash, and nineteen people, Peter Woo among them.

The White Mare case is illustrative of the changing dynamics of the heroin trade in New York, the world's largest retail market for the drug. From early in this century, heroin processing and distribution were controlled to a great extent by Europeans and the Mafia. But as the Mafia has deteriorated in the last decade or two, Asian smugglers have taken over, bringing the drug in through Southeast Asian routes. Law enforcement estimates now put the Chinese and Tong share of the heroin market at 70–80 percent.

Turn back to Pell Street and stop in front of number 10.

6 In the 1890s, there was an opium den here, one of about twenty in Chinatown at the time.

The mystery, fear, and romance of opium was for a long time entwined with the popular idea of Chinatown. Late nineteenth century guidebooks delighted in discussing Chinatown's opium dens, often going into great detail on the process and equipment used, and they soon became a tourist staple. At the turn of the century Chuck Connors, a well-known Chinatown roustabout, fitted up a room or two in appropriate decor and hired actors to simulate stupefaction. He then hired himself out as guide to slumming visitors.

Though there were certainly real opium dens here, and opium addicts, use of the drug was an activity that went on mostly outside of this neighborhood, principally in the Tenderloin or in private houses. An estimate in the 1880s puts the number of opium users at that time (when there were about 100,000 Chinese in the United States and approximately 4,000 in New York's Chinatown) at over 500,000. Opium was, at the time, the most popular drug in America.

The Tongs' control of the drug trade diminished in the twentieth century but, as mentioned above, they are now bouncing back. Opium dens, however (at least as anything more than a broken couch in a tenement apartment), are a thing of the past.

Walk over to 16 Pell, where there is a plaque marking the present headquarters of the Hip Sing Tong. Here we pick up the story of the Tongs again.

7 In 1924, major fighting broke out between the Hip Sings and the On Leongs, resulting in the biggest and bloodiest Tong War in New York history.

In the spring of that year a new faction of the On Leongs emerged that succeeded in ousting the old guard, including Moy Dong Yue, the founder of the New York branch, from national leadership positions. The expelled leaders did something unheard of: they switched their allegiance to the Hip Sings. It was a tremendous slap in the face. All Chinatown knew conflict was imminent.

In the early evening of October 7, 1924, the first shots were fired by On Leongs attempting to storm Hip Sing headquarters on Pell Street. A few hours later a Hip Sing member, Lem Hing, became the first fatality when On Leong bullets felled him in a restaurant on Delancey Street. Within a week five Hip Sings had been killed. By the time the dust settled and peace was officially declared, on March 26, 1925, it is said 70 men were killed. Even so, the Tongs continued to fight sporadically into the early '30s, when the violence finally petered out.

ALSO INFAMOUS

Twelve Pell Street is often pointed out as the site of Mike Salter's "The Pelham," saloon, where singing waiter Irving Berlin got his start. Less well-known is the fact that the two stories above were, at the same time, an opium den.

Stroll down Doyer Street until it turns sharply east.

8 More murders occurred here, it is said, than at any other spot in the world. A slight exaggeration, no doubt, but "Bloody Angle," as this little crook in Doyers Street is dubbed, has seen its share of sanguinary mayhem during the various Tong Wars that raged throughout Chinatown during the first three decades of this century.

Gang activity waned from the 1930s to the '50s, but the explosive growth of Asian immigration since the '60s, which breathed new life into Chinatown, also fueled a rebirth of the gangs. New agglomerations arose, such as the White Eagles, the Black Eagles, the Flying Dragons, and the Ghost Shadows. The '80s saw the emergence of new gangs such as the Tun-an, the Golden Star, the Chung-i, the White Tigers, the Fu-ching, and the Hung-ching. Today, gangs such as Born to Kill, comprised of Vietnamese, are said to be particularly fierce and remain especially feared. (Born to Kill was dealt a heavy blow, however, on October 23, 1992, when its founder and leader David Thai was sentenced to life in prison.)

Although the On Leong and Hip Sing Tongs have attempted to reform their image—they are now known officially as the On Leong Merchants' Association and the Hip Sing Public Association—it is generally agreed both within the community and among the law enforcement establishment that they are still behind some of the gangs. It is said the Ghost Shadows, which controls Mott and Bayard Streets, is affiliated with the On Leong Tong, the Flying Dragons of Pell and Doyer Streets is in with the Hip Sing Tong, and that the Tung On Boys, with turf on East Broadway and Division Street, is associated with the Tung On Tong.

Following the successful prosecutions against the Mafia in the 1980s, city and federal law enforcement agencies focused their attentions on the Tongs. By early 1995, the reputed leaders of all three major Manhattan gangs were under indictment. This hardly means an end to gang activity—only a shake-up and new struggles for control.

MUG SHOTS

SING DOCK
Tong Hitman

Overshadowed by the better-known exploits of Mafiosi, the dubious achievements of the early Tong members remain sadly obscure. Undeservedly neglected is Sing Dock, the chief *boo how doy*, or hitman, of the Hip Sing Tong in the late nineteenth and early twentieth centuries. A methodical man who always carefully mapped out his assassinations and escape plans, he became known as "The Scientific Killer," and, in Tong circles, his exploits were well known and well regarded.

Sing was born in San Francisco around 1873, the son of Gout Sum Choy and Wu Shee, who owned a small general store in that city. He was brought back to China as a child by his parents and schooled there, but at fourteen he returned to San Francisco with his father. He eventually joined the Hip Ying Tong, where he soon became a valued *boo how doy*. Eventually his main allegiance shifted to the Hip Sing Tong, one of the two groups active in New York. He rose to be the mainstay of the coterie of killers, the "inner council of seven" of the Hip Sings, a sort of Tong version of the better-known Murder, Inc. of Albert Anastasia. They took care of the hits and rubouts that were from time to time necessary in the course of Tong business. The "Scientific Killer" carefully worked out battle plans and methodically trained and drilled his loyal killers.

He came to New York and settled at 13 Pell Street around 1905. Here he planned one especially vicious hit on behalf of the Hip Sings. On August 6 of that year a performance was to be held in the Chinese Theatre at 5–7 Doyers Street. Because the actor was sympathetic to the On Leongs, Sing knew that many members of that rival Tong would be in attendance. He realized that patrons would be searched that evening upon entering the hall, and so in the afternoon before the performance he smuggled in some pistols and hid them in accessible spots around the theater. Shortly after 10:00 PM, with the theater packed with four hundred people, a Hip Sing ignited a bunch of firecrackers and, in the same moment, fellow Tong members reclaimed their pistols and began blazing away. Total havoc followed as the audience screamed and fled in panic and On Leong members produced their own guns to return fire or their own knives to meet the enemy hand-to-hand. Reported the *New York Times* the following morning, "The seats, curtains, and scenery were riddled with lead. The floor was littered with pigtails, pistols, hats, coats, and debris which had been shot from the ceiling and walls." Four lay dead or fatally injured: Lee Yuck, Lee Yee Sing, Yu Yuck, and Wu Sing. Sing called this massacre "The New York Theater Party," which indicates that he was either incredibly ruthless or scathingly arch.

On March 12, 1911, at Hip Sing headquarters at 16 Bowery, Sing was shot in the stomach by fellow Hip Sing and former protege Yee Toy, and died the next day at Hudson Street Hospital. Some reports say that Yee shot in self defense, another that the two had argued over gambling debts, another that the spat was purely personal. Yee Toy went down a year later outside of his home at 12 Pell Street, across the way from his mentor's last address.

Walk out of Doyers Street, turn left and proceed to 12 Bowery.

9 One of the more notable fatalities of the 1909–10 Tong War between the On Leongs and the Four Brothers occurred here at 12 Bowery. Dop Doy Hong ("Comedian" Hong, known in the white press as Ah Hoon), a prominent player at the Chinese Theatre on Doyers, was killed here on December 30, 1909.

The legendary version of this murder, reported in the newspapers at the time and repeated in Herbert Asbury's *Gangs of New York*, is that Dop, who supported the On Leongs and ridiculed the Four Brothers in his stage act, knew that he was in mortal danger and was closely guarded both on stage and in his room, sleeping with armed guards outside his door. His killer supposedly foiled these elaborate precautions by lowering himself down an airshaft one night in a boatswain's chair and shooting the sleeping Dop through the window.

The truth is more prosaic. Dop did not know he was in any danger, and had no reason to: civilians unconnected with the Tongs were rarely harmed. He was not guarded. When he finished his performance, he walked through a rear passageway that connected the theater with sleeping quarters here at 12 Bowery, which backed the theater building. Two *boo how doy* entered the theater—they had easy access, as the building was owned by the Four Brothers—and hid in the hallway outside his room. After Dop Doy Hong entered, the pair simply knocked on the door, and when Hong answered, shot him and quickly exited. The motive for the killing of the comedian is unknown, but at the very least, his assassins seemed to lack a sense of humor.

Look over to the other side of the Bowery, just below the huge Confucius Plaza apartment blocks, to Division Street. Near the corner the headquarters for counterfeiter William Brockway once stood, then 3½ Division Street.

10 In the nineteenth century, counterfeiting in the United States was something of an art form, and during this time some of its most skilled and dedicated practitioners were at work. The greatest of them is generally conceded to be William Brockway, who did much of his work in New York and at one time conducted an operation out of an office at 3½ Division Street.

Brockway was born in New Haven, Connecticut, in 1822 and began his career there. He seems to have gone about preparing for his illicit calling quite diligently. At a young age he got a job with an engraver-printer named Ezra Becker, who printed notes for several New Haven banks. In his spare time he sat in on electrochemistry and law classes at Yale. His first productions, which appeared in 1849, startled authorities with their quality. In the 1850s and '60s he worked in Philadelphia, successfully counterfeiting for almost 20 years and producing everything from $1,000 government bonds to 50 cent fractional bills. He used the best engravers, often hiring them away from legitimate banknote companies. His bonds were so

Dour counterfeiter William E. Brockway.

good the Treasury Department was convinced someone had stolen the original plates, and offered a $20,000 reward for their return.

Brockway moved to Brooklyn in 1875 and set to work on U.S. Treasury bonds, producing fake notes worth at least $204,000. When nabbed in 1880, he was given thirty years, but his sentence was suspended on condition that he surrender his plates and his trade secrets (and promise to never again practice his craft). He led some Secret Service agents to a hidden cache in Richmond Hill, Queens, where twenty-three steel and copper plates for banknotes and bonds and a jar full of $50,000 worth of counterfeit $100 bills were hidden. The agents were stunned by the quantity and quality of the material.

But Brockway couldn't give up the life. Just three years later he set up a factory here at 3½ Division Street, putting a couple of engravers to work forging railroad bonds. They were all set to put $54,000 of worthless paper into circulation when they were nabbed. This time William Brockway wasn't able to make a deal, and was sentenced to five years in Sing Sing. He was released in 1887, but, at the age of sixty-five, wasn't done yet. He got together with an old cellmate, Orlando E. Bradford (a descendent of Plymouth Colony's William Bradford), and produced over half a million dollars worth of U.S. and Canadian banknotes. But the engraver they hired turned out to be an informer, and Brockway went back to prison. He was released in 1904 and apparently kept straight for the remainder of his life. He died in 1920.

ALSO INFAMOUS

The Edward Mooney residence, at 18 Bowery (the southwest corner of Pell Street and the Bowery), is noted in every guide book as Manhattan's oldest extant row house, built in 1785–89. Less often mentioned is that in the 1830s and '40s it was a brothel.

Continue up the Bowery past Bayard Street and pause in front of 42 Bowery, which was, over a century and a half ago, the headquarters of the Bowery B'hoys gang.

11 The gangs of the nineteenth century were not only criminal enterprises, but political power bases as well. They served as enforcers, vote getters, and ballot-box stuffers for ward and district politicians, who curried their favor and turned a blind eye to their predations.

Early gangs included the Forty Thieves, which arose around 1825 and is said to be the very first organized gang in the city; the Kerryonians, all natives of County Kerry, Ireland; the Chichesters; the Roach Guards; the Plug Uglies, named for the plug hats they adopted as an emblem; the Shirt Tails; the Atlantic Guards; and the Bowery B'hoys. Perhaps paramount in its day was the Dead Rabbits gang. "Rabbit" was contemporary slang for a rowdy, and a "dead rabbit" was a very rowdy, athletic fellow. Originally members of the Roach Guards gang, they broke away some time in the 1830s.

Arrayed against these Five Points gangs were the Bowery B'hoys and its allies and offshoots, such as the Atlantic Guards, the O'Connell Guards, and the True Blue Americans. Besides carping over territory, the gangs had political differences. The Bowery B'hoys were supporters of the Native American Party and the Know-Nothings—xenophobic, anti-immigrant political movements. The Dead Rabbits, made up in good measure of Irish immigrants, were ruffled by the nativism of the boys from the Bowery.

The two gangs squared off in the Dead Rabbits' Riot, which began here outside the Bowery B'hoys headquarters at 42 Bowery on July 3, 1857, and over the next two days engulfed the Bowery and Chatham Square in the worst violence in the city since the Astor Place riot of 1849 (see p. 43).

It had been a tough summer for the city. In the middle of June the Police Riot (see p. 147), which featured rival city-controlled and state-controlled police forces fighting for supremacy, had stunned New York. The city was left without effective law enforcement, and lawless elements, including the gangs of the Five Points and the Bowery, made the most of a bad situation.

On the morning of July 3, a contingent of Dead Rabbits stormed the headquarters of the Bowery B'hoys, but were quickly turned away. The next day they returned, again to be repulsed, and fell back to Centre Street where they rallied. When the police entered the fray, however, the rival gangs immediately made common cause and turned on them (this was, by the way, the state-controlled Metropolitan Police; the city-controlled Municipal Police were later accused of abetting the rioters). Though the police drove the rioters from the street, the gangs attained the roofs of nearby buildings, and, raining clubs and stones upon the cops below, forced them to retreat.

When the gangs regrouped an hour later, they were armed and ready, and the scene of fighting shifted to the Five Points. The *New York Times* reported: "Brick-bats, stones and clubs were flying thickly around, and from the windows in all directions, and men ran wildly about brandishing firearms. Wounded men lay on the sidewalks and were trampled upon. Now the Rabbits would make a combined rush and force their antagonists up Bayard street to the Bowery. Then the fugitives, being reinforced, would turn on their pursuers and compel a retreat to Mulberry, Elizabeth and Baxter streets."

At the height of the conflict, upwards of 1,000 gang members were involved, massed behind barricades, and the riot took on the aspect of a regular battle. Rumors spread through the city that the Dead Rabbits intended to pillage the Bowery and that the nativist Bowery B'hoys were set on sacking (Old) St. Patrick's Cathedral on Mulberry Street.

By the early evening the hapless police were forced to call on the state militia to save them. At around 9:00 two columns of the Seventy-first and the Eighth regiments swaggered into the fray with clubs swinging and were finally able to quell the riot.

Over a hundred men were injured and eight died. The incident convinced the state government that a radical reorganization of police practice was needed, and they instituted, among other changes, the modern system of precincts.

Lest anyone think the affair wasn't serious, a trip up to the New York National Guard's Camp Smith, across the Hudson from West Point, will reveal, still proudly displayed on the grounds, a three-foot long cannon captured from the Dead Rabbits.

Continue north on the Bowery and pause at the corner of Canal Street.

12 The Bowery, enshrined in the folklore of New York, is the most famous street of last resort in the world. In the nineteenth century it was an entertainment district for the working class, full of cheap theaters, huge beer gardens, and crowded dance halls. Shooting galleries, lottery shops, clothing stores, and street musicians vied for the attention and money of the weekend crowds. Although famous for its bright lights and exuberant spirit, the thoroughfare was always considered a little disreputable. An 1872 guidebook warned that, "respectable people avoid the Bowery as far as possible at night. Every species of crime and vice is abroad at this time watching for its victims."

The Bowery began its long decline during the 1870s. The theaters moved uptown and the bustling beer halls were reduced to dank saloons. Fake auction houses and dime museums appeared next to beer dives and pawnshops. By 1901, Jacob Riis could complain of the cheap flop houses—"nurseries of crime"—lining the street. When the Great Depression hit, the street became the preserve of the luckless drifter and the solitary drinking man. The Bowery remains desolate and forlorn, although the expansion of Chinatown has breathed some bustle into its lower end. Of the dozens of gin-joints and dives that once inhabited the street and contributed to its sordid national reputation, none remain—Al's Bar at 108 Bowery, where pints of Wild Irish Rose could be had, closed in 1994.

Continue walking up the Bowery and turn left on Hester Street. Proceed to Mulberry Street and Little Italy.

13 Here, on the streets of Little Italy, the makers of the modern Mafia lived and worked. In the late nineteenth and early twentieth centuries, among the waves of Italian immigrants who worked hard and honestly, were criminals who built powerful and widespread illicit enterprises. Their organizations have been known variously as the Black Hand, the Cammorra, the Mala Vita, the Unione Siciliane, La Cosa Nostra, and the Mafia.

The beginnings of the Mafia in the United States are unknown. Secret Service Agent William J. Flynn claimed that the Mafia was active in counterfeiting in New York as early as 1884, and the earliest recorded Mafia hit appears to the assassination of Antonio Flaccomio in 1888 (see p. 213). But the first Mafiosi that can be connected to now-familiar family trees are the group of counterfeiters and Black Hand extortionists headed by Guiseppe Morello and Ignazio Saietta (usually called Ignazio Lupo or, redundantly, "Lupo the Wolf," and a stepbrother to the more famous gangster Ciro "the Artichoke King" Terranova), which was active in the first decade of this century (see p. 110).

The term "Black Hand" claims a rather elastic definition. It has often been used to refer to crimes involving Italians or occurring in Italian neighborhoods. From the turn of the century to the 1950s, it was the preferred term for organized crime in general ("Mafia" was used briefly in the nineteenth century and was only revived in the 1950s during the Kefauver hearings on organized crime). But most accurately, it refers to a specific type of crime, usually extortion or kidnapping, accompanied by threats or a note invoking the name or symbols of the Black Hand.

The Black Hand was never an organized criminal conspiracy. It was a criminal methodology inspired by the media. In 1903, a reporter from the *New York Herald* used the term Black Hand in a story on an extortion case involving Italians. Other reporters picked up on this arresting image and began using it to describe crimes occurring in the various Italian districts in New York. If the newspapers were going to scare the hell out of readers with panicked stories of an organized and bloodthirsty gang, certainly extortionists were not going to disabuse anyone of the notion. A fanciful drawing of a black fist with a dagger, a few obscure and meaningless symbols and initials scattered about, and the term *Mano Nera* at the bottom almost always assured compliance.

That the crimes were serious and numerous is beyond dispute. A *New York Times* article of 1911, headlined "Black Hand Crimes Doubled in Year Just Ended" lists seventy bombings, six kidnappings, and sixteen murders attributed to Black Hand activities for that year alone. That was the high-water mark, but during the heyday of the menace (between 1903 and 1915), there must have been thousands of crimes and a palpable sense of fear in these streets.

By the late teens, criminal activities such as extortion and racketeering were becoming more sophisticated and organized, and the decentralized Black Hand began to die out. Prohibition marked the real end though, since bootlegging and related activities were so much more profitable. In catering to the country's thirst, criminals from this neighborhood—Charles "Lucky" Luciano, Vito Genovese, Salvatore Maranzano, and others—were transformed from local thugs to national figures. The aggressive and hierarchical structures that they put in place during Prohibition facilitated their success in other fields as well, including drug dealing, loan-sharking, labor racketeering, gambling, hijacking, fencing, and extortion.

By the early 1930s the Mafia in New York had coalesced into five groups or families: the Gambino Family, the Genovese Family, the Lucchese Family, the Colombo Family, and the Bonanno Family. They work separate territories and to some extent specialize in distinct criminal activities.

The Mafia has fallen on hard times recently. Heat from government prosecutions has sapped their strength, and the Gambino and Genovese Families (with about 450 members each), appear to be the only families of any vitality at the moment.

A casual walk up Mulberry Street reveals some characteristic crimes. Immediately on the left, at 129 Mulberry, is Umberto's Clam House, site of one of the city's most famous mob hits, that of flamboyant Joey Gallo, assassinated here in the early morning of April 7, 1972.

14 "Crazy Joe" Gallo and his two brothers Larry and Albert "Kid Blast" Gallo headed up a maverick Mafia crew of the Colombo family. Working out of the Red Hook section of south Brooklyn, the Gallo siblings were involved in extortion, union racketeering, and other favorite organized crime money makers. But in the early '60s, claiming that the Don was stingy and disrespectful, the Gallos rebelled, starting a shooting war intended to wring concessions from boss Joseph Profaci and his successors Joseph Magliocco and Joseph Colombo. Instead Joey Gallo brought a contract upon his head.

The huge success of Mario Puzo's novel *The Godfather* in 1970 had produced a wave of Mafia chic, and Joey Gallo, who had an impeccable Mob pedigree and was young and engaging, became an unlikely celebrity. He hung out with a group of writers, actors, and trendsetters and went to parties and expensive restaurants on the Upper East Side. He was said to be a thrilling conversationalist who could easily mix bits of Camus (whom he had read in prison) with tales of his own criminal escapades. He styled himself on Richard Widmark's suave gangster in *Kiss of Death*.

On April 6, 1972, Gallo was celebrating his forty-third birthday with, among others, his bride of three weeks, Sina Gallo, and her daughter Lisa. After a night at the Copacabana, they ended up at Umberto's for an early morning snack. By accident they were spotted entering the restaurant by a rival mobster who, within minutes, rounded up some gunmen friends. Sometime around 5:00 A.M., three men burst in the side door and unloaded their pistols at the diners. Joey, hit three times and mortally wounded, upended the table to protect his family (who were, miraculously, unharmed), staggered outside, and collapsed in the middle of Hester Street.

Another gustatory landmark is the Cafe Biondo, just up the street at 141 Mulberry Street.

15 The owner was once Joseph "Joe Butch" Corrao, called by the *New York Times* a capo in the Gambino family. He was involved in two extraordinary cases that make him out as a sort of spymaster in a Mafia counterintelligence effort. Corrao was the conduit for two moles the Mob managed to place in the law enforcement network. One was Mildred Russo, an elderly woman who, as a deputy clerk in the United States District Court, handled sealed indictments. She would tip off Corrao whenever a secret indictment of Mob members came into her hands. In 1984, she was caught, sentenced to one year's house arrest, and sequestered in her apartment down the way at 20 Mulberry Street.

The second case is more startling: a Mafia mole under deep cover in the NYPD. William Peist was a New York City Police Detective and a member of an elite intelligence unit whose specific task was keeping tabs on organized crime. But, according to a Federal indictment handed down in December 1991, Peist secretly worked for the bad guys, passing information to Corrao on police investigations, telephone taps, and electronic bugs. He proved so valuable that John Gotti, head of the Gambino family, put him on retainer. In his most chilling betrayal, the Feds say, Peist, assigned to guard jurors during Gotti's 1990 trial, divulged to Corrao the names and addresses of several of the citizens he was sworn to protect. In 1993, he pleaded guilty to selling police information to Gotti and other organized crime figures and was sentenced to seven years and three months in prison.

Continue up to Grand Street.

16 Joe "the Boss" Masseria was the first recognized Mafia boss of real strength. His dominance, however, was not achieved without a struggle, and one of the earliest Mafia power plays pitted Masseria and his gang against the minions of Umberto Valenti. A famous episode in that conflict occurred right around the corner in front of 190 Grand Street, when Masseria, accompanied by two henchmen, tried to put an end—quite literally—to the competition. On May 8, 1922, they waited in the doorway of 194 Grand Street, watching Valenti and Silva Tagliagamba saunter toward them. Impatiently, Masseria gave the order to fire when the pair were still two doors away, and in the blaze of bullets, four bystanders, in addition to Tagliagamba, were wounded. Valenti was unharmed. Masseria ran to Mulberry, turned right, and was just crossing Broome when he was arrested. Tagliagamba, after lingering for a month, died. Masseria was never tried for this murder, witnesses being scarce. Further fights, and the outcome of the feud, are described in the East Village tour (see p. 206).

Walk up to 163 Mulberry, Benito's II Restaurant.

17 In the 1950s and '60s Salvatore "Sally Bugs" Briguglio was a business agent for the corrupt and criminal Teamsters Local 560 of

Union City, New Jersey. Run by Anthony Provenzano, the local was involved in loan sharking, numbers, bookmaking, and the systematic pilferage of shipped goods. Briguglio was a suspect in the murder of Anthony Castellito, who was set to challenge the presidency of Provenzano when he disappeared in 1961. But more famously, he was also a suspect in the 1975 disappearance of Teamster chief Jimmy Hoffa. On March 21, 1978, Briguglio was shot and killed in front of 163 Mulberry Street, where Benito's II Restaurant now does business.

This address enjoys another gangland distinction: when young Lucky Luciano was arrested for the first time, on a narcotics charge in 1923, the future don turned informer and told police they could find a large quantity of morphine and heroin here. His ratting kept him out of prison and contributed to his rise.

Walk two blocks up to the corner of Mulberry and Kenmare Streets.

18 From 1920 to 1922, the famous "curb exchange" stood here, an open-air market where bootleggers and gangsters would gather to trade and barter their wares. The type or brand of liquor a bootlegger was able to make or obtain was not always the kind his customers wanted, so the curb exchange enabled him to informally exchange what he had for what he needed. It was Joe Masseria's early domination of these curbs that enabled him to rise to leadership.

TOP TEN MOB HITS IN MANHATTAN

Nathan "Kid Dropper" Kaplan—outside the Essex Market Courthouse, August 28, 1923. Kaplan had just been discharged on a weapons charge under the promise that he leave town forever, when, amidst an escort of eighty policemen, he was shot by teenager Louis Cohen on orders from rival "Little Augie" Orgen (see p. 168).

Jacob "Little Augie" Orgen—at the corner of Norfolk and Delancey Streets, October 15, 1927. Labor racketeers Louis "Lepke" Buchalter and Jacob "Gurrah" Shapiro killed Orgen and wounded Jack "Legs Diamond" Noland in a drive-by shooting (see p. 168).

Arnold Rothstein—in the Park Central Hotel (now the New York Sheraton), Seventh Avenue and 55th Street, November 4, 1928. Gambler and organized crime kingpin Rothstein, known as the man who fixed the 1919 World Series (he denied it), was shot in Room 349 and died two days later. Assassin unknown (see p. 252).

Salvatore Maranzano—in his office in the New York Central (now the Helmsley) Building, Park Avenue and 46th Street, September 10, 1931. Maranzano, early "boss of bosses," was killed in a take-over plot engineered by Lucky Luciano and Vito Genovese.

The hit men gained entry to his office by disguising themselves as federal agents (see p. 247).

Vincent "Mad Dog" Coll—in the London Drug Store, 314 West 23rd Street, February 8, 1932. Fighting a bitter war for a piece of Dutch Schultz's turf, Coll was killed in a phone booth by the Dutchman's employees.

Albert Anastasia—in the barbershop of the Park Sheraton Hotel (now the New York Sheraton), Seventh Avenue and 55th Street, October 25, 1957. Anastasia is often called "head executioner" of Murder, Inc. Assassins said to be the Gallo brothers.

Joseph Colombo Sr.—in Columbus Circle, June 28, 1971. Leader of the Profaci family, Colombo had organized the Italian-American Civil Rights League and was leading their Unity Day rally when he was shot by ne'er-do-well Jerome Johnson. Colombo died after a seven-year coma; Johnson was killed on the scene by an unknown gunmen. Johnson's motive is unknown, but there is speculation that he was hired by the Gallo brothers.

Joey Gallo—in Umberto's Clam House, 129 Mulberry Street, April 7, 1972 (see p. 104).

Neapolitan Noodle Hit—in the Neapolitan Noodle Restaurant, 320 East 79th Street, August 11, 1972. Four businessmen—Sheldon Epstein, Max Tekelch, Leon Schneider, and Jack Forein—were shot by a hired killer who mistook them for Colombo family members. Two of the innocent men, Epstein and Tekelch, died.

Paul Castellano—in front of Sparks Steak House, 210 East 46th Street, December 6, 1985. Castellano, godfather of the Gambino family, was killed in a power struggle for the top spot in the family. Assassins were part of John Gotti's crew (see p. 251).

Turn left on Kenmare and walk over two blocks to Lafayette Street and the small triangular park on the north, Joseph Petrosino Square.

19 The assassination of New York Police Lt. Giuseppe Petrosino on March 12, 1909, in Palermo, Italy—four thousand miles from this square named in his honor—was a seminal event in Mafia history. The chilling realization that the criminal organization could whack New York's preeminent detective while he was on a secret mission in a foreign country, and get away with it, led, more than any other single factor, to the myth of Mafia omnipotence.

Giuseppe Petrosino was born in Padula, Italy on August 30, 1860, and came to New York at the age of thirteen. In 1883 he joined the police department and became one of the very few Italian-speaking members of the force. This rare ability led to an early promotion, in 1890, to an investigative force assigned to keep tabs on the mysterious and growing Italian underworld of New York. This beat would keep him busy for the remainder of his life.

As Italian involvement in crime grew, Petrosino became the police department's resident expert. He was appointed head of the force's Italian Squad, a unit solely dedicated to eradicating the burgeoning crime of the city's Italian slums. Because the Black Hand was the object of so much media attention, Petrosino's deeds and pronouncements were often in the news, and he became a well-known figure. His fame was further bolstered by his work in the barrel murder case (see pp. 110).

In 1909 Petrosino went to Sicily to look into local police and court records, hoping to find evidence that would enable American authorities to deport undesirables back to Italy. He reached Palermo on February 28, 1909 and checked into Room 16 of the Hotel de France under the name of Simone Valenti di Giudea. Although his presence was intended to be a secret, it was, in fact, common knowledge by the time he reached Palermo. The day after his departure from New York the whole story was leaked to the press, and it was related in the Italian paper *Il Pungolo* after the detective was ashore. Petrosino was well known in Italy too, often called "the Italian Sherlock Holmes." The idea that his assassins knew of his plans through a sophisticated network of intelligence or powerful conspirators is unfounded.

Petrosino spent several days rummaging through records and meeting secretly with informers. Although he was wary of the Italian police, his research seemed to be going reasonably well. On March 6, Petrosino turned down the offer of a bodyguard. On March 12, while returning after dinner to his hotel through Palermo's Piazza Marina, he was hit by three bullets that killed him instantly.

The brazen, distant killing of this New York hero cop produced a sensation in the city. Newspapers were full of alarm, condemnations, and theories, and when Petrosino's body returned to New York, 200,000 followed his bier through the streets. Flags flew at half mast throughout the city.

The murder of Petrosino was never officially solved, but speculation has centered on Don Vito Cascio, a leading Mafioso of western Palermo and Sicily, and two of his henchmen, recently returned from America, Carlo Costantino and Antonino Passananti. The latter two were members of the Lupo-Morello gang and involved in the notorious barrel murder (see p. 110). However, none was brought to trial.

When Mussolini broke the Mafia and Vito Cascio was an aged man lingering in prison, he confessed, at least obliquely, to the Petrosino killing, reportedly claiming, "In my entire life I have killed only one person, and that I did *disinterestedly*. Petrosino was a courageous enemy; he did not deserve a dirty death at the hands of just any hired killer." Most students of the Mafia take him at his word. In 1987 this small park, once known as Kenmare Square Park, was renamed Petrosino Square in his honor.

Another fatality associated with this square has received much less attention. In a particularly nasty instance of the powerful and prevalent racism against early Chinese residents, Lee Teep was fatally wounded at this intersection on April 24, 1881. Though Lee may not have been the first Chinese murdered in New York, his case was the first in which a white New Yorker was charged with the murder of an Asian.

Around nine o'clock that evening Lee and two friends, Kwong Tong and Ah Sin, encountered four young white men at this intersection coming the opposite way. As they passed, one knocked Lee's hat off his head. As he bent over to pick it up, this same stranger, without provocation, stabbed Lee twice in the back. He died in St. Vincent's Hospital a week and a half later. John J. Corcoran was tried for first degree murder, but, amid indications of perjured testimony, he was acquitted.

Turn back and continue up Mulberry to 247, the Ravenite Social Club.

20 The Ravenite Social Club was a hangout of famous and flamboyant Gambino Family boss John Gotti in the 1980s, but the place has long been a Mafia favorite. It was founded in 1926 as the Alto Knights Social Club and frequented by Lucky Luciano. Carlo Gambino also took a shine to the place, and in 1957, upon his ascent to bosshood, renamed it the Ravenite Social Club, ostensibly for his favorite Edgar Allen Poe poem. Later on, Aniello Dellacroce, an underboss in the Gambino family and a Little Italy native, took over the club. Gotti began doing business here as a protégé of Dellacroce.

John Gotti, though he enjoyed only a brief reign, was one of the most popular and well-known Mafia bosses New York has ever produced. After an apprenticeship as a neighborhood tough and hijacker in Queens, he engineered a meteoric rise to the top of the Gambino family by planning the assassination of boss Paul Castellano at Sparks Steak House, 210 East 46th Street, in 1985 (see p. 251).

A charismatic and animated figure, the handsome and always impeccably dressed Gotti was a folk hero, considered by many to be this generation's version of Clyde Barrow or Al Capone. He was one of the few Mafia bosses who relished—in fact, invited—media attention, and the press treated him as a celebrity. The *New York Daily News* called him "the Dapper Don" for his sartorial habits. The *New York Times* dubbed him "a Mafia Caesar." He was also known as "the Teflon Don" because charges against him wouldn't stick. He was acquitted in three prominent cases over six years (before his conviction in a fourth), and each court victory fueled his status.

The Ravenite Club was subject to intense FBI surveillance in the late 1980s as the government made strident efforts to put Gotti behind bars. They found a vacant apartment across the street and set up a sophisticated video system to spy on the club. Gotti had the storefront bricked up. The Feds placed bugs in the club. Gotti went outside, or to an apartment above the club, to chat. Finally, the FBI was able to get into the upstairs apartment, where their bugs recorded sufficient dirt to charge Gotti.

On December 12, 1990, Gotti was arrested here at the club on Federal racketeering and murder charges. In a trial that received intense media attention and featured the surprise testimony of top fellow family member Sammy "the Bull" Gravano against his former boss, Gotti was convicted on April 2, 1992 and sentenced to life in prison.

Law enforcement officials charge that Gotti continues to direct his crew from prison and that their hangout has moved over to 140 Mulberry St., the Hawaiian Moonlighter's Club.

For the tour's last stop, take a right on Prince Street, go past Elizabeth and stop in front of 8 Prince Street, on the south side of the street. This unprepossessing building is a landmark in Mafia history.

21 A restaurant and saloon here at 8 Prince Street served as the headquarters of early Black Handers Ignazio Saietta and Guiseppe Morello, and a case could be made that this building is the birthplace of the what we now know as the Mafia in the United States. In 1911, the *New York Times* reported that:

> The saloon and spaghetti kitchen at 8 Prince Street is now run by Vito Vasile. It was the favorite rendezvous of the Lupo and Morello counterfeiting gang, and was the centre, in the early nineties, of another counterfeiting gang that was broken up by the United States Secret Service men. The men believed by the police to be responsible for the 'barrel murder' made No. 8 their headquarters, and always, when the detectives have wanted to get wind of an Italian criminal, they began their search at that number.

The "barrel murder" was a gruesome mob hit that made New Yorkers shudder. On April 14, 1903, on the northwest corner of East 11th Street and Avenue D (a corner which, because of urban renewal, no longer exists), a sugar barrel was found with a body stuffed inside. The victim had been roughly treated: he displayed close to fifteen stab wounds, and his neck had been cleanly cut from ear to ear. After some swift detective work by none other than Joseph Petrosino, the victim was identified as Beneditto Mondania. Accounts differ on the character of victim Mondania and the reason for his murder. Some say he was a member of the Lupo-Morello gang who wanted out of his lifetime membership, while others say he was the closest relative of a gang member suspected of turning informer.

The sugar barrel was traced to a cafe owned by a fellow gang member at 226 Elizabeth Street. The police rounded up Morello, Lupo, and eight other compatriots, but none were tried and no one was ever convicted of the murder. Secret Service man William J. Flynn and the NYPD were certain that the knife wielder was gang member Tomasso Petto, also called "The Ox." When Petto was murdered in 1905 in Brownton, Pennsylvania, many asserted that justice, though extralegal, had finally caught up with him.

Morello and Lupo used their Black Hand earnings to set up several legitimate businesses, including a real estate venture. Around 1908 their buildings went bust, and in order to pay off creditors, they decided to print their own money in a Catskills factory. But the gang was well-known and well-watched, and Flynn soon shut them down. In February 1910, Morello was sent to Atlanta Penitentiary for 25 years and Lupo for 30 years.

Nearest subway: Spring Street 6; Bowery J M
Nearest bus line: M 21; M 101; M 102

Greenwich Village

A Criminal Sketch of Greenwich Village _____

In the popular imagination, Greenwich Village is the haven of artists and anarchists, free-lovers and folk singers, homosexuals and hangers-on, destitute writers and unrecognized geniuses. Criminals do not immediately come to mind. But this quaint neighborhood actually has a surprisingly abundant history of lawlessness.

Rogues and robbers were among the Village's earliest inhabitants. The very first European to establish a farm here was the dissolute and corrupt New Amsterdam Director General Wouter van Twiller. Among the tens of thousands of acres of property that he stole were those that now make up Greenwich Village. The first British settler of note in the area, Admiral Sir Peter Warren, arrived in 1731, and amassed his large fortune by cheating on British naval regulations that forbade private trading while on voyages. And from 1794 to 1804 Aaron Burr, rogue and conniver, lived in a mansion at what is now Charlton and Hudson Streets. It was from this house, Richmond Hill, that he started off to Weehawken, New Jersey on July 11, 1804, to duel and kill Alexander Hamilton.

Because it was far away from New York in its early years, the Village was deemed a good spot to house and hang miscreants. In 1796 a large state prison was built in the block bounded by West 11th, Washington, Christopher, and West Streets (at the time the prison stood on the shore, West Street being built on later landfill). The phrase "to be sent up the river" is supposed to come from the practice of shipping prisoners from the Battery to this prison via the Hudson River. Like the prisons of today, this one was often over-crowded, at times holding more than twice its capacity of four hundred prisoners. And like today, the results were often violent: An uprising in 1803 resulted in the deaths of three convicts. The facility

Greenwich Village

was replaced in 1826 by the more spacious Sing Sing prison in upstate New York.

Criminals sentenced to death were also often sent to this neighborhood. In 1816 two hangings were carried out on a gallows at the
intersection of Bleecker and Mercer Streets; Ishmael Frazer was executed for arson and Diana Silleck for murder. In 1820 Rose Butler
was hanged in Potter's Field, near Washington Square, the last person executed in New York for arson. However, the oft repeated story
that the visit to New York of Revolutionary War hero Marquis de
Lafayette was feted with the simultaneous hanging of 20 highway-
men in Washington Square Park is untrue.

Misfortune gave the small village a boost when a yellow fever epidemic downtown in 1822 sparked a mass migration to the healthful
surroundings of the rural settlement. By 1830 the area was urban-
ized—and presumably dangerous—enough to be included on the
police night-watch.

As early as 1853 a reformer complained of the rampant crime on
the docks of the Hudson River, a phenomenon that would continue for the next hundred years. Just after the Civil War, the
Charlton Street gang worked the west side docks and pirated in the
Hudson River. In the early 1890s, when the Hudson piers were
busy enough to support more larceny, groups such as the Potashes
and the Boodle Gang made their bases here. The most famous and
successful of the Greenwich Village gangs were the Hudson
Dusters, who made their appearance in the late 1890s. From their
headquarters at 633 Hudson Street they controlled the territory
south of 13th Street and west of Broadway, but directed most of
their attention to thieving from the piers. The police succeeded in
destroying the Dusters in 1916.

Dockside thievery continued, however. In fact, the bulk of the
crime committed in Greenwich Village in the first few decades of
the twentieth century clustered about the piers that jutted into the
Hudson and that constituted at one time the world's greatest
port. Behind the walls of the loading docks, an enormous amount
of pilferage, racketeering, hijacking, theft, and extortion took place.
Occasionally this criminality spilled out into the neighborhood (see
p. 136).

Toward the close of the nineteenth century a red light district developed around West Third Street and Bleecker, which, though by
no means the largest in the city, was one of the most dissolute.
Brothels lined West Third from Broadway to Sixth Avenue, while
several well-known "concert saloons"—cheap dives that featured
lewd theatrical performances and scantily clad waitresses who doubled as prostitutes—took over Bleecker Street. These included The
Burnt Rag at 50 Bleecker Street, Theodore "The" Allen's Bal

A shocking glimpse of stocking (and the dire consequences) at the Bal Mabille.

Mabille at 59 Bleecker Street, and the Black and Tan in the basement of 153 Bleecker Street, which was notorious for its (then-shocking) interracial clientele. These saloons were closed in a reform drive of 1887 but that by no means dimmed the red glow of the neighborhood.

Policeman Cornelius Willemse, who was assigned to the neighborhood in 1906, described his beat:

> There was none of the glamor and bright lights that helped to gloss over the wide-open doings of the Tenderloin. Prostitution was at its most vicious form, a mere side-line for thievery. Dark, squalid houses stood side by side. Men could shoot from doorways, or spring out with a stiletto, razor or sandbag before a passer-by knew what was up. The saloons were dark, evil-looking places, the rendezvous for thieves and the lowest type of thugs.

At the same time, the south Village, a primarily Italian enclave, was subject to the predations of the Mafia. One of its most ruthless members, Vito Genovese, lived and worked in the south Village (see p. 152) and it remains home for the alleged inheritor of his family, Vincent "the Chin" Gigante (see p. 151).

Today, the Village's most prominent evildoing has moved to two other spots. The meat market by Ninth and Tenth Avenues below

14th Street is one of the city's hubs of prostitution. When the meat wholesalers close up in the evening, streetwalkers, many of them transvestites, line the eerie and deserted streets to wait for their customers to furtively drive up. Another vice center is Washington Square Park, which has served for the last twenty years as an open-air drug market. Popular among New York University students and out-of-towners, it is infamous for the inferior, and often fake, drugs dispensed.

Stalking Greenwich Village _____

Nearest subway: Eighth Street R; Astor Place 6
Nearest bus lines: M 2; M 3; M 5; M 6; M 13

Start on the northwest corner of Washington Place and Greene Street.
The building on this corner is still remembered for the tragic Triangle
Shirtwaist Factory fire that took place here in 1911.

① A shirtwaist is a woman's tailored blouse with a collar and cuffs similar to a man's shirt, but tapered to a fitted waistline and hooked or buttoned in the back to a skirt. It was a popular style for women around the turn of the century, and the look is known to us in Charles Dana Gibson's famous "Gibson Girls," who were often dressed in shirtwaists.

Isaac Harris and Max Blanck, the owners of the Triangle Shirtwaist Company, were the largest manufacturers of these articles in the country, and were known in the trade as the "shirtwaist kings." On the eighth, ninth, and tenth floors of this building (then called the Asch, and now the Brown, Building) they employed some five hundred people, mostly young immigrant Jewish women, in manufacturing these garments.

On Saturday, March 25, 1911, at about 5:45 P.M., quitting time, fire broke out on the eighth floor in a bin full of cloth scraps. Despite attempts by workers to douse the blaze, it moved quickly to hanging garments and wooden tables, then to the floors, partitions, and ceiling. In the crowded loft, panic spread even faster than the flames. Workers rushed toward the elevators and stairway on the Greene Street side of the building; others made for the exits in the opposite corner on the Washington Place side. There were pileups in both areas: the elevators could hold only a handful of people; the doors to the stairway, which swung inward, were difficult to open in the press of the crowd (and some stairway doors may have been locked, though this was never conclusively proved).

The flames and confusion soon spread to the other floors, where workers faced the same obstacles to escape. Some managed to make it to the roof and clamber onto neighboring buildings. Some got out safely down the stairs or elevators. Several used the fire escape in the rear of the building, but in opening the large iron fire shutters to get out, blocked the path for those above. The rickety fire escape filled with people and then collapsed. Soon, flames in the stairways and elevator shafts shut off those routes. There remained only one means of escape from the scorching flames.

A reporter for the *New York World* described the ghastly scene as it unfolded:

> No sign of life in the building had been observed by the spectators on the street when suddenly something that looked like a bale of dark dress goods was hurled from the eighth floor window.
>
> "Somebody's in there all right," exclaimed a spectator. "He's trying to save the best cloth."
>
> Another seeming bundle of cloth came hurtling through the same window, but this time a breeze tossed open the cloth and from the crowd of 500 persons there came a cry of horror.
>
> The breeze had disclosed the form of a girl shooting down to instant death on the stone pavement beneath.
>
> A united murmur of dread went up from the watching multitude, rising to a loud note of despair as three other girls at the same moment threw themselves from various windows and other girls could be seen clinging to the window frames, struggling for breath and trying to decide between the death within the factory room and the death on the stone pavement and sidewalk below.

One hundred and forty-six workers died, most of them young immigrants.

The building was put up without adequate emergency exits, without a usable fire escape, without sprinklers. There were never any fire drills, and indications existed that the stairway exits were kept locked. Yet the building passed all inspections and was perfectly legal. The owners of the Triangle Shirtwaist Factory, when brought before the courts on charges of manslaughter, were acquitted.

Outrage over the tragedy fueled changes in the garment industry, in union tactics and strength, and in the building codes. And though the fire gutted the top three floors, the building itself survives to this day. Plaques at the corner of the building commemorate those who died in the fire.

ALSO INFAMOUS

The most famous outlaw of the Wild West—Billy the Kid—is not normally associated with New York City, but we can proudly claim him as one of our own. He was born here in 1859 as Henry McCarty, and though there is some disagreement regarding his birthplace, at least one reliable source puts it at 210 Greene Street, just three blocks to the south on a site now obscured by the huge apartment blocks of Washington Square Village. He left the city with his family as a young boy, bound for New Mexico and a place in history.

Walk west on Washington Place towards Washington Square Park. Turn right on Washington Square East and then left on Washington Square North, skirting around the park. Take a right on Fifth Avenue and go past Eighth Street to the Brevoort Apartments, 11 Fifth Avenue, where Carmine DeSapio once had an apartment.

2 Carmine DeSapio was the end of the line for Tammany Hall, the last boss of New York's most venerated—and vilified—political institution. The Tammany Society and Columbian Order, as it was formally known, was organized in 1789 and was the oldest continuous political organization in America, home to Aaron Burr and Boss Tweed. It came to an end in 1961 when DeSapio was defeated for district leader in Greenwich Village. Disgrace enough, yet even further ignominy awaited DeSapio.

He began his political career in 1939 as a leader of the First Assembly District, a post he held until 1946. In July 1949, with the sponsorship of Mafia boss Frank Costello, then an important behind-the-scenes power in city politics, he became boss of Tammany. An astute political kingmaker, he helped guide Robert F. Wagner to the mayor's office, Averell Harriman to the governorship, and numerous other lesser politicos to elective offices and appointments.

But in 1958, when DeSapio's candidates for governor and U.S. Senator were both soundly beaten, a reform movement began to agitate for his removal. The movement was strengthened when Wagner, elected in 1953 with DeSapio's backing, broke with his mentor in the 1960 elections to run on an anti-machine platform. DeSapio could not shake off his reputation as a backroom boss, and his endorsement became a kiss of death. In 1961 he lost his Greenwich Village district leader post, which forced him to resign as leader of Tammany Hall. Tammany had been fading for some time, and DeSapio's departure put the final nail in the coffin. Tammany Hall, after 177 years, was dead.

DeSapio's political career, too, was over, but not his troubles. In 1967, still trying to live off his political connections, he became entwined in the notorious James Marcus scandal. Marcus was a political neophyte appointed to be City Water Commissioner when John Lindsay became mayor in 1965. Although Marcus looked every inch the flush patrician, bad business deals had left him bankrupt. Working with gangster and labor racketeer Anthony "Tony Ducks" Corallo (whom he had met through a labor lawyer friend) and a number of others, he started using his city position to extort money from contractors and utilities doing business with his department. When Con Ed applied for city approval for a huge $200 million dollar hydraulic plant it wanted to build near Storm King Mountain in upstate New York, Marcus and friends saw millions of dollars dancing in front of their misty eyes.

DeSapio, as a political mover and shaker with connections in Con Ed, was approached. Was he interested? Decidedly so. He worked out a scheme in which Marcus would stall on the permit for the Storm King project. When the impatient utility became desperate, DeSapio would ride in like a white knight, and, for a small price, smooth the way.

At the close of November 1967, Marcus was called into the District Attorney's office for questioning about an unrelated incident, and almost immediately broke down. Very soon the whole plot was uncovered. The news that a city commissioner was involved so intimately with a Mafia member shocked even the citizens of New York, and proved a major embarrassment to the Lindsay administration.

Marcus was not indicted in the Con Ed caper, but was sentenced to fifteen months for an earlier extortion scheme. For his part in the Con Ed conspiracy, Corallo was sentenced to four and a half years. Corallo went on to have a successful Mafia career and later became head of the Lucchese organized crime family. In 1986, charged with a huge conspiracy indictment related to his mob activities, he was sentenced to 100 years in prison. DeSapio, once one of the most powerful men in New York City, received a two-year sentence and a $4,500 fine.

Walk up another block to the northeast corner of Ninth Street, once the site of the mansion of Daniel Sickles.

3 Daniel Edgar Sickles, little-known today, was a famous and controversial public figure in the latter half of the nineteenth century. He was a Tammany man who became a U.S. Congressman, a Civil War general who lost a leg at Gettysburg, a foreign minister to Spain, and a confidant of presidents from Pierce to Grant. He was also notorious as a political intriguer, dirty dealer, rogue, and ladies' man.

But he was most famous as the killer of Philip Barton Key, U.S. Attorney and son of anthem-writer Francis Scott Key, whom he shot down on a Washington D.C. street on February 27, 1859. The murder was one of the great American scandals of the antebellum period.

When Sickles arrived in Washington as a newcomer Congressman in 1857 he threw himself lustily into the busy political and social scene, leaving his young wife, Teresa Sickles, to fend for herself, something she did with much success. She commenced a passionate affair with Key that eventually heated up to the point where her paramour rented an entire house for the sole use of their weekly assignations. Neighbors would watch a furtive Key as he unlocked the house, lit a wood fire, and hung a red ribbon as an all-clear sign on one of the upstairs shutters. In a few minutes, Teresa Sickles, with a shawl low over her head, would walk hastily into the house. For months, everyone in the then-provincial town of Washington knew of the affair except Teresa's husband.

He was enlightened in late February 1859, when he received an anonymous note detailing the dalliance. A few days later, anguishing in his study, he glanced out of his window and saw the villain not fifty feet away, walking by Jackson Place across the street from the White House. Sickles grabbed three pistols from his house and rushed across the square. Confronting the startled man, he shouted, "Key, you scoundrel, you have dishonored my bed—you must die!" and shot the U.S. Attorney twice. Key passed away a few minutes later.

At his trial, Sickles claimed temporary insanity, the first time such a defense was made in an American court. As in the Stanford White and the Albert Richardson cases (see pp. 163 and 75), much of the defendant's case was based on the "unwritten law": that a husband has every right to kill a man who copulates with his wife. Amidst a celebrated trial, with public opinion firmly behind him, Sickles was acquitted. The next day he confided to friends: "Of course I intended to kill him. He deserved it."

Although murdering the U.S. Attorney made Sickles something of a pariah, the killing was eventually forgiven, if not forgotten, and he resumed a very public career. Though the odor of scandal always accompanied Sickles, he was considered at the very least a colorful character, a trait New Yorkers appreciate.

Returning to this city at the outbreak of the Civil War, he raised a brigade to fight for the Union and became its general. A controversy erupted over his behavior at the battle of Gettysburg that plagued him perhaps even more than his elimination of Key. Just before the famous battle, he ignored an order from superior officer General Meade and moved his regiment forward from their assigned position. Sickles claimed his presumptuous move saved the day; Meade and others asserted that he nearly threw away the victory. For the rest of his life Sickles vociferously defended his actions that day.

After the war he continued in public service. He was active in local politics, served as minister to Spain from 1872 to 1874, had a hand in breaking Jay Gould's control of the Erie railroad, and was reelected in 1893 to a term in Congress. He moved to 23 Fifth Avenue in 1879 and lived here until his death on May 3, 1914.

ALSO INFAMOUS

One of the most popular incidents in the canon of British crime is the Maybrick affair. In 1889, Florence Maybrick, a transplanted American, was convicted of murdering her husband by arsenic poisoning. James Maybrick definitely met his end through arsenic, but it was revealed at trial that he was an arsenic addict, and swallowed as much as 1/3 a grain a day (a 1/2 grain can be fatal). Her husband seemed quite capable of killing himself. Throughout, she maintained her innocence, and her case became an international cause célèbre. Presidents Grover Cleveland and William McKinley, among many others, appealed to the British authorities for mercy. She was released after fifteen years and returned to her native America, where she died on October 23, 1941. The case has once more become topical: a recently published book purporting to be Jack the Ripper's diary tenders James Maybrick as the famous London murderer. Before her marriage, Florence Maybrick lived for a time at 17 East 14th Street.

Walk up another block to 11th Street, cross Fifth Avenue, and stop in front of 40 Fifth Avenue (the entrance is on 11th Street), where Judge Joseph Force Crater once had an apartment.

4 New Yorkers take a perverse pleasure in recounting taxi horror stories: The driver who took Fifth Avenue at sixty miles an hour; who tried to make a U-turn on the FDR Drive; who knew a shortcut through the Garment District. But surely the taxi ride of Judge Joseph Force Crater on August 6, 1930 must rate among the very worst. He flagged down a cab on the corner of 45th Street and Eighth Avenue, settled down comfortably in the back seat, and rode off toward the Hudson. He was never seen again. From a place of modest renown as a New York State Supreme Court Justice, he skyrocketed to fame as the "missingest man in America." He became a national preoccupation, and the circumstances surrounding his disappearance, the numerous theories to explain his fate, and the countless supposed sightings of him filled newspapers and magazines for years.

Joseph Force Crater was born January 5, 1887 in Easton, Pennsylvania, and came to New York to attend Columbia Law School. In 1917 he married Stella Mance Wheeler, and was soon working as personal secretary to State Supreme Court Justice Robert Wagner, father of the future mayor. In 1927, when Wagner, his employer and mentor, was elected to the Senate in Washington, Crater decided to go into private practice. By 1929 he had worked himself and his wife into a fashionable flat here at 40 Fifth Avenue.

Crater became a player of some stature in city politics. He was President of the Cayuga Democratic Club, an important cog in the Tammany machine, and his connection with Wagner gave him additional power and prestige. His pull was sufficient to snare an appointment to the State Supreme Court from Governor Franklin Roosevelt on April 8, 1930. It was the fulfillment of a long-held ambition for Crater.

In early August Crater and his wife went for a brief vacation in their summer cottage in Maine; the new judge wanted to relax before starting his first term at the end of the month. The couple had hardly settled in, however, when the jurist told his wife that he had to return for a week to New York. He arrived back in the city on August 4 and was last seen two days later. His actions on that fateful day, August 6, were a little suspicious. That morning he went to his downtown office and, along with his assistant Joseph Mara, began packing files into cardboard boxes. At some point in the morning he sent Mara to cash two personal checks totaling $5,150 and stuffed the money into his coat pocket. He and Mara carried the boxes to a taxi and unloaded them here in the judge's apartment. The files were never found.

That evening Crater arranged to have a ticket left at the Belasco Theater for that night's performance of *Dancing Partner.* Just before eight o'clock, he walked into Billy Haas's Restaurant at 332 West 45th Street. There he ran into a friend, who later said the judge appeared in excellent spirits and spoke of returning to Maine for the rest of the month. He drank only orange juice. At 9:15 he left. His friend saw him off at the corner as he settled into the backseat of a taxi heading west on 45th Street. Judge Crater was driven down the block and disappeared into the night.

Somebody picked up the ticket at the Belasco box office, but none of the theater personnel could remember who. Judge Crater's disappearance sparked a massive public response; hundreds provided clues, offered solutions, and reported sightings. The judge was mining in Colorado, motorcycling through Italy, wandering about in San Diego. Such sightings lasted for the next twenty years. The waggish graffito "Judge Crater, call your office!" was long a staple in phone booths and bathrooms.

Part of the unusual attention given to Crater's case was due to the noise made the previous fall by a brash young mayoral candidate, Fiorello La Guardia. The candidate was campaigning on a reform plank, accusing the city and state judiciary of corruption. La Guardia lost the election by a landslide but set in motion several investigations. In March 1930, Magistrate Albert H. Vitale was removed from the bench for fraternizing with known gangsters and for receiving a $20,000 loan from crime boss Arnold Rothstein (see p. 252). On May 7, Judge W. Bernard Vause was indicted and later convicted for mail fraud. The day before Crater's last cab ride, August 5, Magistrate George F. Ewald, Vitale's replacement, was questioned regarding an apparent payment of $10,000 for his new position, a payment that soon led to his removal.

Crater, perhaps, had a reason or two to be nervous about this turn of events. He had a role in a suspicious receivership in which a mortgage company, somehow apprised that the city wanted to buy and condemn a bankrupt hotel to make way for urban improvements, bought it cheap ($75,000) and sold it very dear ($2,850,000) to the city. Another suspicious move came just after his elevation to the State Supreme Court. In late May and early June 1930 he withdrew $7,000 in large bills from his account and sold off stocks and bonds worth $15,799.86. The standard Tammany wisdom held that an appointed office cost a year's salary—in Crater's case, $22,500. Some students of the case conjecture that Crater got nervous about the increasing heat sparked by La Guardia (which led, in September 1930, to the Seabury Investigation) and decided to drop out of sight.

Crater evidently had some dealings with organized crime as well. He met Arnold Rothstein several times and knew Vivian Gordon, a prominent madam later murdered just before she was due to testify in the Seabury Investigation. An alternative theory holds that, like Gordon, Crater was knocked off before he had a chance to testify.

Another possibility is that Crater paid a visit to a blackmailing mistress (remember that $5,150 he stuffed into his coat pocket on August 6) and that a strong-arm friend or two of hers got a bit rough with the judge and inadvertently killed him. Stella Crater's lawyer, Emil Ellis, seemed to think this was the case, and was suspicious of an actress named June Brice. He tracked her down in 1939 but, alas, she was insane and incoherent. The police file on Judge Crater, open for 55 years, was closed in 1985.

Continue west and stop in front of 18 West 11th Street.

⑤ Although it is set amidst nineteenth-century row houses, the angled facade of this house reveals that the structure is modern. The present building was put up in 1978 as a replacement for an 1845 Greek Revival row house, which, while serving as an inappropriate bomb factory for a 1960s revolutionary group called the Weathermen, was blown entirely apart on March 6, 1970.

The Weathermen were a small but prominent group that was originally part of a larger organization called Students for a Democratic Society, a dynamic radical force founded in 1960 and particularly popular on college campuses. At their 1969 convention, a faction advocating a more militant approach broke away from the main group. They dubbed themselves the Weathermen from a line in Bob Dylan's "Subterranean Homesick Blues": "You don't need a weatherman to know which way the wind blows." In other words: the Revolution is obviously imminent; stop talking and hit the streets! They doted on the charisma of handsome Che Guevara, the determination of Mao Tse Tung, and the violent resistance of Ho Chi Minh and other third world guerrillas. Their rhetoric was uncompromising and their methods often violent. The group planned a bombing campaign that would rally the white masses, sustain black revolutionaries, and fracture the establishment.

Founding members included Kathy Boudin and Cathy Wilkerson. The two had similar backgrounds: upper middle class families, political educations in civil rights work and anti-Vietnam War activities. Wilkerson joined SDS while attending Swarthmore College. Boudin, daughter of a prominent left-wing lawyer, was a political activist even in high school. She was involved in civil rights agitation during her college years at staid Bryn Mawr and spent several years after college organizing welfare recipients in Cleveland. By 1969 they were both convinced that the system—capitalism, imperialism, the courts, the police, the universities—had to be smashed and that random violence could jumpstart the revolution.

The plush row house here at 18 West 11th Street was an improbable setting for the birth of class war. It was the home of Cathy's well-to-do father, a businessman and advertising executive. Daughter Cathy, housesitting while her parents were vacationing in the Caribbean, invited a few comrades over: Boudin, Diana Oughton, Ted Gold, and Terry Robbins, all dedicated Weathermen. They set up a bomb factory in the basement workshop normally used by Mr. Wilkerson for restoring antiques. The Weathermen decided that their previous use of firebombs had been ineffective, and they were now intent on a campaign using antipersonnel bombs. On March 6,

1970, Terry Robbins was tinkering downstairs, taping several hundred roofing nails around dozens of sticks of dynamite. At 12:06 in the afternoon, he made a mistake.

The huge explosion blew off the front of the building and sent flames shooting into the street. While smoke and dust billowed from the building, a second explosion rocked the burning structure. Flames shot out the windows and bricks rained on the sidewalk.

Ted Gold, Diana Oughton, and Terry Robbins were killed instantly. The bodies of Oughton and Robbins were blasted apart and almost unidentifiable. All that was left of Robbins was a fragment of his torso; Oughton was identified through a single piece of finger found in the debris. The police later uncovered several unexploded bombs and a cache of 57 sticks of dynamite and 146 blasting caps—enough to blow the whole block apart.

Immediately after the first explosion Kathy Boudin and Cathy Wilkerson emerged, dazed and unclad, from the building. They were taken in by a neighbor and given clothes. As police descended on West 11th Street, the two women thanked their neighbor, quickly left, and disappeared from public view for a decade.

Boudin and Wilkerson went underground, joining a number of other Weathermen who for various reasons (not excluding mere adventure) had done the same. But over the next few years the radical movement withered—many saw the townhouse explosion as a turning point—and young militants moved on to quieter and more complacent concerns. The Weathermen became anachronisms.

Ten years later Wilkerson surrendered, pleaded guilty to illegal possession of dynamite, and was sentenced to three years in prison. The fate of Kathy Boudin, however, was quite different, and will be revealed later in our tour.

Continue down the street to Sixth Avenue. Go left for half block to 446 Sixth Avenue.

6 This was once the unhappy home of securities analyst Joseph Pikul, his wife Diane Pikul (an assistant to a magazine editor), and their two young children. In a celebrated case in 1987, Joseph Pikul killed his wife, and then, in an outrageous turn of events, sued for and was nearly awarded custody of their children.

Joseph Pikul was an odd and violent man, paranoid and brutal. Over the course of three marriages, he had beaten his wives, pistol-whipped his car driver, threatened to kill several friends and strangers, and smashed countless pieces of furniture and dishware. He kept a collection of guns, hired detectives to follow Diane Pikul, and bugged his own home phone. He was also a transvestite who videotaped himself in costume and kept a secret apartment on Rector Street filled with women's clothing.

Diane Pikul was strangely attracted to his violence. On their second date, Joe spat on her during an argument, and Diane later told friends it fascinated her. But such charm proved too much even for Diane after nine years of stormy marriage, and in 1987 she began divorce proceedings.

On the night of October 23, 1987, Diane drove out to meet Joe and the kids at the family's summer home in Amagansett, Long Island, to talk to her husband about divorce arrangements. She arrived in the early morning of the twenty-fourth. Perhaps there was a heated argument; perhaps Joe lay in wait. Sometime around 1:30 AM he beat and strangled Diane while their two children were asleep in the next room. He then wrapped the body up carefully in plastic, packed it in ice, placed it in the trunk of his car, and looked around for a burial spot. After hours of searching unsuccessfully, he drove back to Manhattan that night and parked the car outside this building. Diane's corpse remained overnight in the trunk. The next day he drove to Massachusetts and asked his first wife if he could bury the body in her backyard. She later testified: "I told him it wasn't a good idea to bury anybody on my property because I have a high water table." He ended up dumping her body in a highway drainage ditch upstate and returned to New York to file a missing persons report.

The body was quickly discovered and Pikul, whose actions in the days after the murder were more than a little suspicious, was charged with Diane's death. At this point, Pikul made a move that put his name in the papers: about to be tried for the murder of his wife, he demanded custody of his children. Diane's family, appalled, went to court to block him. Since Pikul enjoyed a presumption of innocence the court was ready to grant his request until it was discovered that, in front of the children, he had assaulted his third wife, a women he had met and married in the several months since his arrest. The children were placed with relatives.

The custody debacle over, the murder trial began. Pikul surprised the courtroom by admitting that he killed his wife and pleading self-defense. He claimed Diane came at him with a knife after he accused her of infidelity. They struggled and he accidently choked her to death while grappling for the weapon. He dumped her body in a drainage ditch because he didn't want their children to see the corpse. And the ten bruises on her head? Those must have come when he dragged her body feet-first to the car. The jury didn't buy it. He was convicted of second-degree murder. In June 1989, while an appeal was still pending, Pikul died of AIDS. Since he passed away before the appeal was decided, his conviction was vacated by the court, and in death, Joseph Pikul is, legally speaking, an innocent man.

Walk another block south, and look across the Avenue to Jefferson Market, the red Gothic building with the clock tower.

7 Described as one of the most beautiful buildings in America at the time it went up, the enchanting façade of Jefferson Market Courthouse belies its original use as a stern courtroom and forbidding prison.

There actually was a market once at Jefferson Market, a miscellaneous collection of low wooden buildings and a tall fire tower that opened in 1832. By 1838 an office of the city watch, precursor to the police department, was located here, and, in 1845, a court was established. In 1877, the present structure was built to house the court and a jail.

The garden on the southern side of the building was the site, from 1933 to 1973, of the New York City House of Detention for Women, a scandal almost from the moment it opened. Reformers objected to the brutal conditions inside while neighbors complained about the constant screaming from the cells. Between 1942 and 1965 there were five investigations into the conditions and administration of the prison. There were tales of corruption, mistreatment of prisoners, overcrowding, and unsanitary conditions. In 1973, to the relief of many, the jail was demolished.

Continue to the next block and pause at 410 Sixth Avenue.

8 The largest Mafia drug case ever conducted in the United States found its most dramatic moment on February 11, 1987, here in front of what was then fittingly named the Black Rock Cafe. The Pizza Connection, as the case was dubbed (because many of the defendants owned pizzerias as fronts to launder money), was a heroin pipeline, staffed by members of the Sicilian Mafia, that stretched from Italy to Illinois. The government estimated that from 1979 to 1984 the Pizza Connection imported $1.6 billion worth of drugs into the country. The investigation that brought it down was the FBI's longest, largest, and most expensive criminal case ever, involving more than a hundred of the Bureau's agents as well as members of the Drug Enforcement Agency, Customs Service, NYPD, and police departments in Italy, Spain, and Brazil. The trial cost $50 million and was the longest federal jury criminal trial on record.

After the French Connection was busted in 1962 (see p. 241), Bonanno family head Carmine Galante (the same man who murdered radical Carlo Tresca in 1943; see p. 48), imported Italian Mafia members to set up a new Sicilian connection to import heroin.

Known as Zips by the American Mafiosi, these foreign gangsters were tough, driven, and, most important, unknown in the States. When Galante was knocked off in Brooklyn in 1979, investigators noticed that his two Sicilian bodyguards had escaped unharmed: the Zips had pulled off a palace coup.

After Galante's exit, one of his imports, Salvatore Catalano, became street boss and number-two man in the Bonanno family. Along with his lieutenant Giuseppe Ganci, he ran the Pizza Connection as something of a separate subsidiary in the Bonanno family. They distributed heroin though pizzerias in the East and Midwest and moved millions of dollars from Manhattan to Switzerland. Profits were not shared with other family members.

Gaetano Badalamenti, at one time Boss of Bosses of the Sicilian Mafia Commission, was the foreign supplier. The main middleman between him and Catalano was Badalamenti's nephew, Pietro Alfano, a middle-aged pizza parlor owner in Oregon, Illinois. Working in this network as wholesalers, retailers, money launderers, and couriers were two to three dozen Sicilian Mafiosi and associates.

After years of probing, bugging, tailing, and other FBI-ish activities, the government busted the Pizza Connection in the spring of 1984. They nabbed Badalamenti (said at the time to be the most wanted narcotics fugitive in the world) and his nephew Alfano in Spain, and brought them back to face trial in Manhattan with twenty other defendants.

The trial lasted seventeen months. Less than one month before the verdicts, on February 11, 1987, Pietro Alfano, his wife, and several other defendants were strolling south along busy Sixth Avenue—the same route you just traveled—after shopping at the popular specialty foodstore Balducci's. As they passed the Black Rock Cafe, two gunmen approached from behind. One put a .38 caliber revolver against Alfano's back and fired three times. As the crowded sidewalk exploded in panic, the assailants ran north and jumped into a waiting van, which darted away down Tenth Street. The government later claimed that the man with the .38 was Philip Ragosta and his partner was Frank Bavosa, but they were never brought to trial.

Whatever the motive for the hit—perhaps to spark a mistrial, perhaps because Alfano was said to be continuing his drug dealing—it was foiled: Alfano lived, though paralyzed from the waist down. He pleaded guilty to narcotics conspiracy and was sentenced to fifteen years.

The 64-year-old Badalamenti was sentenced to forty-five years in prison and fined $125,000. Salvatore Catalano was sentenced to forty-five years and fined $1.15 million. Eighteen of the nineteen defendants present at the end of the trial were found guilty.

Like the French Connection before it, the Pizza Connection is no more; in turn, new sources, most notably the Chinese Connection, have emerged. The supply of heroin has, if anything, increased.

MUG SHOTS

FRANK SERPICO
Honest Cop

Although Frank Serpico served in the New York police department for only thirteen years and never rose above the rank of detective third grade, he may be the most famous cop in New York history. His anticorruption activities were responsible for sparking the Knapp Commission and perhaps the most thorough shakeup ever in the organization and conduct of the police department. A bestselling book and a hit movie chronicled his life.

Serpico wanted to be a policeman from an early age and joined the force at his first opportunity, in March 1960. Although he loved uniforms and guns, he was something of an iconoclast as well. He was attracted to the counterculture of the 1960s and moved to Greenwich Village, settling eventually at 116 Perry Street in a small apartment with a back garden. He grew his hair long, which served him well when he was detailed as a plainclothesman. His fellow cops often thought him a little odd, but, evidently, not odd enough to be honest.

Serpico's career as a whistleblower began in August 1966. While assigned to the 90th Precinct in Brooklyn, a patrolman approached him with a fat envelope. "Here," he said, handing Serpico the envelope, "I've been holding this for you. It's from Jewish Max." Inside was $300 in tens and twenties, protection money from a local gambler. Up to that time, Serpico had been content to ignore the grafting that he saw among his fellow officers. Now he had to put up or shut up: either keep the money or turn it over to a superior with a complaint. After consulting with a fellow cop, David Durk, who was also concerned with corruption in the department, he did the latter, solemnly reporting the incident to the head of the detective squad of the Department of Investigation. Incredibly, the commander told Serpico that to pursue the case meant going before a grand jury. "By the time it's over," he said, "they'll find you face down in the East River." Or, he suggested, you can just forget it happened.

Serpico dropped the matter, but couldn't forget it. He asked for a transfer out of the 90th precinct and ended up in the Seventh Division in the Bronx. Within a month a plainclothesman offered him a cut of some graft money, told him of the protection scheme organized by the division, and introduced him to a gambler who offered him a bribe. Serpico again went to a superior officer to complain; Durk went to a member of Mayor Lindsay's inner circle that he knew. Nothing happened. In May, 1967, the pair spoke to the police Commissioner of Investigation. Again, no action was taken. Meetings with several other officers had the same result.

Finally, in late 1968, an investigation led to charges against officers in the Seventh Division. But Serpico was not satisfied with either the depth or breadth of the housecleaning. Angry and frustrated, he and Durk decided, after nearly four years of dead ends, to go public and arranged an interview with the *New York Times*. The resulting story, published on April 25, 1970, blew the lid off. The allegations of widespread, systemic corruption became a top story in the city's papers and nationwide. In feverish response, Mayor Lindsay formed the Knapp Commission to investigate. In August, Police Commissioner Howard Leary was forced out.

For his integrity, Serpico was rewarded by his fellow officers with scorn and hate. He was, without doubt, the most unpopular man on the force. In the summer of 1970, he was transferred to an undercover narcotics detail and, while making a bust in Williamsburg on February 3, 1971, was shot in the head at close range. The assailant was a low-level heroin dealer named Edgar Echevaria, but Serpico believes he was set up by his comrades in blue. Serpico pulled through, but decided that his days as a cop were over.

He now lives on Long Island on his police disability money. In a 1984 interview he remarked that the NYPD was as corrupt as ever and said bitterly, "The only thing I feel I accomplished is that I did what I had to do."

Cross Sixth Avenue at 8th Street and take the first left down Christopher Street. Proceed another two blocks to 51 Christopher Street and the site of the Stonewall Inn (the present bar of that name here is not the original).

❾ Although Greenwich Village in the 1960s was one of the country's most congenial communities for lesbians and gay men, homosexual life was still severely confined. Nearly all socializing had to be done furtively, for public exposure could mean the loss of a career or apartment, family estrangement, institutionalization, even imprisonment. Physical attacks were not uncommon. There were gay bars and clubs, but they had a precarious existence, subject to raids and shakedowns by the police or seizure of their liquor license by the State Liquor Authority. These conditions caused many gay bars to fall into Mafia hands, since they could operate, with the connivance of the police, without a license. The Stonewall Inn, for instance, was said to be a Gambino bar.

Police raids were common, and, despite its Mob connections, the Stonewall Inn was not exempt. Just after midnight on June 27, 1969, eight officers of the Public Morals Section of the NYPD entered the Stonewall Inn with a warrant charging that the bar had no liquor license. They commenced a standard procedure, probably as well known to the clientele as to the police. Customers with identification were allowed to leave; employees and customers without identification or in drag were to be loaded into a paddywagon and taken to the precinct house for processing. Dutifully, the lesbians and gay men in the bar fell in line for the ordeal.

But that night, those ejected from the bar did not slink away. Rather, a boisterous crowd gathered on the other side of the street, hooting and laughing as their friends emerged from the bar. The crowd was rambunctious, but not angry. However, when a paddywagon rolled up and several people, including the bartender, doorman, and three customers in drag, were marched into the vehicle, the crowd began to boo and yell. Some people began to beat on the paddywagon. Suddenly, the mood changed to anger and resistance.

While most of the cops were inside the Stonewall, the paddywagon pulled away, leaving the street unguarded. At that moment, the crowd charged the bar, heaving bottles, cans, and rocks. A wooden partition behind the window was forced down and a parking meter was used as a battering ram to smash the front door. The cops trapped inside were outnumbered and besieged. Projectiles continued to rain upon them from the cheering and ascendant rioters outside. A trashcan full of lit paper was thrown through the window, setting the bar ablaze. The cops, fighting their way out, turned a fire hose on the crowd. When the sirens of police reinforcements could be heard, the rioters, now swelled to some five hundred, scattered. Thirteen persons were arrested on charges ranging from harassment and resisting arrest to disorderly conduct. A small article on page 33 of the *New York Times* took note of the melee.

Over the next several nights the disorders continued on Christopher Street. Rioting was accompanied by defiant, openly gay behavior. Along with the anger and the high spirits of the crowd was the realization that something significant had occurred, quite spontaneously: a new militant and politicized lesbian and gay male consciousness. A new slogan appeared on the boarded-up window of the Stonewall: Support Gay Power.

A plaque now posted by the entrance of the bar here proudly announces: "Birthplace of the modern Lesbian and Gay Rights Liberation [movement]."

Cross Seventh Avenue South and continue west on West Fourth Street. Walk up four blocks to West 11th, take a left and pause in front of 267 West 11th Street.

LITERARY CRIMINALS OF THE VILLAGE

William Burroughs—206 E. 7th Street. This address was Allen Ginsberg's apartment, which the novelist Burroughs shared with the poet in 1953. Two years earlier, on September 6, 1951, in Mexico City, Burroughs had killed his wife Joan while attempting to shoot a water glass off her head. He pleaded guilty to criminal negligence.

Gregory Corso—190 Bleecker Street. The Beat poet, born at this address, spent his childhood with foster parents and on the streets, often in trouble. He was convicted of robbery in 1947 and spent three years in Clinton Prison in Dannemora, New York. After his release he met Allen Ginsberg and embarked on his successful literary career.

O. Henry—55 Irving Place. Before his arrival and fame in New York, the short-story writer, whose real name was William Sydney Porter, had a career of a different stripe. In 1898 he was convicted of embezzling funds from the First National Bank of Austin, Texas and spent three years in a penitentiary.

Clifford Irving—Chelsea Hotel. In 1971–72, the marginally successful novelist wrote and sold a huge tome purporting to be the autobiography of reclusive billionaire Howard Hughes. The hoax fueled massive media attention as it unravelled; Irving was sentenced to $2\frac{1}{2}$ years.

Norman Mailer—73 Perry Street. In the early morning hours of November 20, 1960, after a long night of drinking, novelist Norman Mailer stabbed his wife Adele several times with a penknife. She was hospitalized but did not press charges.

Ezra Pound—164 Waverly Place. Pound spent time here during a two-year sojourn in New York in 1910–11. After World War II he was indicted on nineteen counts of treason for his vociferous support of Italy and the Axis powers. He pleaded insanity and spent twelve years in St. Elizabeths Hospital in Washington, D.C.

John Reed—42 Washington Square South. Not counting many arrests without convictions, the radical bohemian and author of *Ten Days That Shook the World* spent four days in the Passaic County Jail in 1913 for his participation in the Paterson silk workers strike and three months in solitary confinement in 1920 in Finland for sedition.

Oscar Wilde—48 West Eleventh Street. The English writer lived here for several weeks after an 1882 lecture tour through the United States. In a notorious series of trials in 1895, Wilde was convicted of "gross indecency" (as the English court delicately termed homosexual acts) and sentenced to two years in prison.

10 Murder is almost always a nasty business, yet some murderers seem more pathetic than malevolent. One of these was Dr. Robert W. Buchanan, who made a long run of stupid moves when dispatching his second wife Anna Sutherland on April 23, 1892 and managed to bungle himself into the electric chair.

Buchanan, born in Nova Scotia in 1862, came to New York twenty-four years later with his first wife and daughter and set up a medical practice here in the building before you. Business appeared to be modest, for the doctor spent a great deal of time at Macomber's bar on Sixth Avenue.

In early November 1890, Buchanan told his barkeeper friend that he had divorced his wife. A week or two later he asked Macomber to accompany him to Newark, New Jersey to witness the will of a widowed patient, Anna Sutherland. She left her estate (some property and capital amassed as the proprietor of a bordello) to any future husband, or, if she had none at the time of her death, to her friend and physician Robert Buchanan. Sutherland was, according to descriptions, no great beauty (Buchanan referred to her as "an old hag"), but, evidently to cinch things up, Buchanan married his patient in late November.

The doctor had mercenary motives all along, no doubt, but he soon found himself unable to abide his new wife. And she, after a period of infatuation, came to feel likewise about her husband. After a year or so, she threatened to return to Newark and her former profession and take her property with her.

In January 1891, a medical student, Carlyle Harris, murdered his young wife with a dose of morphine (see p. 184). The sensational trial was discussed and debated all over town, including in Macomber's bar. Among the smoke and spirits, witnesses later testified, Buchanan had declared that Harris's deed would have gone undetected if he had only added a little atropine to his dose of morphine. This would have prevented the telltale contraction of his victim's pupils that had alerted the police. At the same time Buchanan mentioned that his wife was feeling a little ill herself.

On April 23, after a sudden sickness of three days, Anna Sutherland passed away. The doctors called in listed the cause of death as a cerebral hemorrhage, although Buchanan had told his friends she suffered from kidney trouble. A few days after the funeral, Buchanan returned to Nova Scotia, where, three weeks after Sutherland's death, he remarried his first wife and brought her back to his home here. In his absence, however, the suspicions of the coroner had been aroused and the newspapers began sniffing. The body of his second wife was exhumed. On June 6, Buchanan was arrested for murder in the first degree, the indictment charging him with poisoning Anna Sutherland with morphine.

Much of the trial was occupied with expert witnesses and long discourses on chemistry and biology. The prosecution chemists claimed tests had shown morphine—and atropine—in the body; the defense chemists claimed the results could as easily be due to ptomaines formed in the organs after death. The jury listened day after day to intricate and exhaustive discussions of leucomains, molybolic acids, aquatafina, the Pallagri test, the Atto method, the Stars method, and the Dragendorf method. They were nonplussed. If the trial had gone no further, Buchanan might have been acquitted. But the doctor, against the wishes of his lawyers, insisted on taking the stand. Still a student of the Harris case, he thought the young man had been undone by not testifying. He refused to make the same mistake, and ended up making a different one.

The prosecutor Francis Wellman, began the questioning thus:

> Q: When you married your wife, had you fallen in love with her?
> A: I decline to answer that question.
> Q: Why?
> A: Because I don't think it's a proper question.
> Q: Why?
> A: I decline to answer.
> Q: Did you even like her?
> A: Before marriage I liked her.
> Q: Did you love her?
> A: I don't know what you call love.
> Q: By what you yourself call love, did you fall in love with her?
> A: I liked her. That's the best I can answer.
> Q: Well, if you can't answer that question, suppose you tell us whether you knew exactly how much money she had before you asked her to marry you?
> A: Yes, I knew about that, but I deny marrying her for her money. Maybe it had a little to do with it.

Buchanan made a very poor impression on the jury. Most damaging however, was a letter he had written to Macomber from Nova Scotia just two weeks after Sutherland's death. It did not reveal any murderous plot, but rather discussed, too indecently for any contemporary account to reprint, his lusty desires for the young country girls he was encountering. The jury, appalled at the callousness of such a libertine, needed no further evidence, and brought back a guilty verdict. After two years of unsuccessful appeals, Robert

---

ALSO INFAMOUS

Another block up, at 63 Bank Street, punk rocker Sid Vicious, bassist for the short-lived but influential English band The Sex Pistols, died of a heroin overdose on February 2, 1979. He was under indictment for having murdered his girlfriend Nancy Spungen in the Chelsea Hotel on October 12, 1978.

Buchanan died in the electric chair at Sing Sing on July 2, 1895. Loose talk—and loose morals—confounded his elaborate plot.

Return to Seventh Avenue South and walk south a block past Christopher to Grove Street to the building on the corner, 61 Grove Street.

11 Elia Kazan and Budd Schulberg's *On the Waterfront*, now considered a classic of American film, was based on a series of articles entitled "Crime on the Waterfront" written by *New York Sun* reporter Malcolm Johnson in 1948. Johnson won the Pulitzer Prize for his investigative work on crime and corruption in the port of New York. The articles centered on the killing of stevedore Anthony Hintz, who was shot to death in January 1948 here in this building. Unlike the movie, the real story does not have a heartening ending.

Once the world's greatest port, the New York piers were also long one of the city's richest sources of illicit lucre. Organized criminal activity was a way of life on the waterfront. Extortion, theft, smuggling, hijacking, kickbacks, payroll padding, embezzlement, and murder were commonplace. In 1950, losses due to theft were estimated at $140 million, three times greater than in all other American ports combined. The corrupt International Longshoremen's Association, headed by the notorious Joe Ryan, was the main organizer and enforcer of much of the racketeering. Ryan, a rough and tumble longshoreman who was also a skillful organizer and politician, became president of the union in 1927. His presidential tenure lasted twenty-six years, and was characterized by self-enrichment and sweetheart contracts.

One of Ryan's cronies was an ex-gangster named John "Cockeye" Dunn. Despite a long criminal record, in 1937 Dunn obtained a charter for the Motor and Bus Terminal Checkers, Platform and Office Workers Union, a creation that provided him with a power base on the waterfront. By the early '40s Dunn and his brother-in-law Ed McGrath, considered the brains of the outfit, controlled all the piers from 14th Street down to Cedar Street with one exception: Pier 51, whose hiring boss was Anthony Hintz. Though he was evidently an honest man, Hintz was not a crusading reformer; he just wanted to keep Dunn from taking over his pier. He and his brother Willie, also a stevedore, resisted Dunn but lived according to the waterfront code: they didn't make waves and they didn't talk to the police.

Even so, Hintz knew he was in a precarious position. The docks were not a healthy place to disagree, or be disagreeable. Years earlier, on March 14, 1936, Joe Butler, a loader, was shot and killed. On June 15, 1937, longshoreman Johnny Costello was shot to death.

On December 9, 1939, union boss Dave Beadle was shot and killed. Richard Gregory, an ILA delegate, was murdered on November 16, 1940. The two suspects in the Gregory murder, Thomas Cunniff and Emil Nizich, were themselves killed within the year. A checker in Dunn's local, Joseph Moran, was shot on February 7, 1941. In the thirty years before Hintz breathed his last, several dozen dockworkers had been murdered. An assistant district attorney at the time, William Keating, estimated that Johnny Dunn was responsible for at least fifteen. Not one case had been solved.

On January 8, 1947, three men walked into 61 Grove Street: Dunn, Andrew Sheridan (nominally the business agent for Dunn's union but actually a gunman and strong-arm), and Danny Gentile, a friend of Hintz who had joined the Dunn forces. Dunn and Sheridan carried guns; Gentile was there to distract Hintz if necessary. Just as Hintz was leaving his third-floor apartment for work, the three men ambushed him on the landing. Dunn shouted, "Kill the rat, kill him and kill that rat brother of his!" and let loose with six shots. Hintz fell to the stairs, while the trio made their escape, Dunn and Sheridan over the roof, Gentile out the front door.

If the shots had killed their target instantly, Hintz would no doubt have joined the long list of unavenged victims. At least fifteen people saw the three gunmen in and around the building, but not one ever came forward and not one ever testified. But Hintz hung on for three weeks and in that time, after mulling over the event and the waterfront's traditional code of silence, made a dying declaration that named his killers: "Johnny Dunn," he replied when asked who shot him. "He done well, too." Hintz's wife and brother also provided information implicating Dunn.

By trial time, the case was front-page news, and the courtroom was packed. On December 31, 1947, the jury found John Dunn, Andrew Sheridan, and Daniel Gentile guilty of murder in the first degree. Gentile's sentence was later commuted to twenty years to life, but Dunn and Sheridan were executed on July 7, 1949.

These first successful convictions in a waterfront rackets killing helped to make crime and corruption in the port a national issue and led to several investigations. Revelations of graft and embezzlement forced Ryan out of the International Longshoremen's Association in 1953, and the same year its parent union, the American Federation of Labor, expelled the union. But what really brought an end to the criminal rackets on the docks was the end of the waterfront itself. The port failed to adapt to containerization, a method of shipping in sealed railroad cars, and trade slowed, stalled, and died. There are no longer any commercial piers on Manhattan, a staggering fact given the size and power of the port up until the 1960s. The New York port, once the world's richest and greatest, has vanished. The huge font of crime has simply evaporated. *On the Waterfront,* once biting social commentary, is now a period piece.

Walk down Grove Street two blocks until Bedford, and then take a left.
Continue to 86 Bedford Street.

12 The unmarked door here leads to Chumley's, a former speakeasy that has clung proudly to its Prohibition roots. Alone among its many peers, Chumley's has survived much as it did during the dry days of the 1920s.

The original structure was built in 1831 and was at one time a blacksmith's shop. In 1926 Lee Chumley bought the structure and remodeled it into a speakeasy, fixing the front to look like a garage. The place soon attracted a literary crowd, including John Dos Passos, Edna St. Vincent Millay, and Theodore Dreiser, and Chumley began to display the book jackets of his published patrons—a tradition that continues to this day. Chumley died in 1933, but his wife, Henrietta Chumley, took over the place and ran it unchanged until her death in 1960. Since then a number of equally reverent owners have kept the bar looking much the same.

Chumley's is one of the last survivors of a huge number of bars that slaked the thirst of New York during Prohibition. In 1929, Police Commissioner Grover Whalen estimated that there were 32,000 bars in the city, double the pre-Prohibition count, but many consider his figure too low. The largest concentration of illegal clubs and saloons in Manhattan was in midtown, and 52nd Street between Fifth and Sixth Avenues in particular was known to be well blessed. The humorist Robert Benchley, of Algonquin Round Table fame, once counted 38 speakeasies on the block. The midtown clubs were the most expensive and well known, among them Club 21 (still in existence at 21 West 52nd Street), Leon & Eddie's (33 West 52nd Street), the Stork Club (132 West 58th Street), and the El Fey (107 West 45th Street).

Here in the Village, in addition to Chumley's, drinkers were especially attracted to the Fonton, at 88 Washington Place (owned by Charlie Berns and Jack Kriendler, who later opened the more famous Club 21), Barney's (85 West Third Street), Julius's (West 10th Street and Waverly Place), and many others. Painter and Villager John Sloan remarked during Prohibition, "When I first came here there was a saloon on every corner. Now there are ten speakeasies on every block."

Supplying these joints took a huge effort that involved both top-level smuggling and simple brewing, elaborate laboratories and kitchen stills, denatured alcohol and homemade wine, and gangsters, cops, politicians, and housewives. The leading bootleggers in New York included William "Big Bill" Dwyer, who built an empire smuggling liquor from Europe to Long Island; Waxey Gordon, the leader of a group of bootleggers that controlled thirteen large breweries in New York, New Jersey, and Pennsylvania; Owney Madden, who supplied spirits to hundreds of speakeasies and restaurants; Frank Costello, who worked with Dwyer and eventually took over his operation; and Lucky Luciano, coordinator of the "Big Seven Group" of East Coast bootleggers.

Take the next right, on Barrow Street, and walk a block down to 85 Barrow, where the story of Kathy Boudin, last seen stumbling out of the bombed-out Weatherman townhouse on West 11th Street, is continued. Unlikely as it seems, this staid apartment building is a small landmark of revolutionary Black nationalism.

13 Although mass protest and the middle-class radical movement had collapsed by the early 1970s, not every revolutionary had retired. From the embers of the Black Panther Party a number of militant black nationalist groups formed, still dedicated to war against the white capitalist system.

Mutulu Shakur was the linchpin of one such group, organized in the mid-1970s, called the New Afrikan Freedom Fighters, or sometimes the Revolutionary Armed Task Force, or, among themselves, the Family. The small cadre—the core group consisted of less than a dozen people—considered themselves a clandestine army fighting to establish an independent black state in the South. The Family, though committed to black separatism, was joined by a handful of whites, most of them Weathermen veterans (see p. 125).

Their ambitious plans required a large war chest, so the group commenced to rob stores and armored cars, robberies that they characterized as "expropriations." Over the course of about five years the Family attempted some twenty robberies, about a third of them successfully. Among these was a stickup on October 12, 1978 of the Chase Manhattan Bank branch on Ninth Avenue near Thirteenth Street. Other actions took place in New Jersey and upstate New York. They also succeeded in freeing black revolutionary Joanne Chesimard (also known as Assata Shakur), from Clinton Correctional Institution for Women in New Jersey on November 2, 1979. Shakur was bundled off to exile in Cuba, where she remains. Daring and flawless, the escape gave the Family attention and confidence.

On October 20, 1981, twelve members, including Mutulu Shakur, took on their most ambitious project: the robbery of a Brink's armored car in Nyack, New York. The attempt, carefully planned and rehearsed, nevertheless turned into a murderous bungle. During the holdup a Brink's guard was shot and killed. A switch in getaway cars was spotted and the police had time to set up a roadblock. Trying to shoot their way through, the gang killed two Nyack police officers. Four members of the group were captured immediately and almost all their comrades were arrested over the next few months. The Brink's robbery attempt brought the Family nationwide attention at the same time that it destroyed them.

It also brought fugitive Kathy Boudin back into public view. She was arrested in one of the getaway cars.

The fugitive had been living quietly on the Upper West Side of Manhattan since 1978. The Weathermen had long since disintegrated, and Boudin was not particularly politically active. Most of the charges against her had been dropped and she was toying with the idea of surfacing. Though not an active member of the Family, she was in contact with them and occasionally helped out. The Brink's job was apparently the first robbery in which she had participated.

On April 26, 1984, Kathy Boudin pleaded guilty to one count of murder and one count of robbery and was sentenced to twenty years to life. She is now incarcerated in the Bedford Hills Correctional Institution.

The story comes to 85 Barrow Street because Mutulu Shakur, the driving force of the Family and mastermind of the Brink's robbery, hid out here following the debacle. He stayed for six weeks, before, with the FBI closing in, he slipped away and made good his escape. He eluded the police until 1986, when he was captured in Los Angeles. He was convicted on eight counts, one of which was for the Brink's robbery, and sentenced to sixty years in prison.

Yet another resident gives this building a place on our tour. The apartment used by Shakur belonged to Edward Lawrence Joseph. Twelve years before, Joseph had been a defendant in the Panther 21 trial, one of the notable trials of the 1960s radical movement. Nearly two dozen members of the New York chapter of the Black Panther Party were brought to trial in September 1970 on a huge indictment. The main count charged them with conspiring to blow up the 44th Police Precinct station house and, from a vantage point on a hill above Harlem River Drive, snipe at the survivors who emerged. None of this happened: dynamite hidden at the precinct house had been replaced by a harmless mixture of clay and oatmeal by one of the several undercover agents that the NYPD had placed in the Black Panther Party. Two Panthers were discovered on Harlem River Drive with several rifles, but they were not among those tried with the Panther 21.

The jurors, appalled by the extensive use of undercover agents and apparent political persecution of the Black Panther Party, acquitted the defendants of every one of the 156 charges. But the strain and expense of the trial permanently crippled the New York chapter of the party. Edward Lawrence Joseph, at 18 years old the youngest of the Panther 21 defendants, eventually settled in this apartment building.

Continue down Barrow Street and turn left on Hudson Street. Walk another two blocks to St. Luke's Place and go left. Continue to 6 St. Luke's Place.

14 Dapper James Walker was the very popular Mayor of New York from 1926 to 1932. Dubbed "the Night Mayor," he was known more for his easy manner, quick wit, nightclubbing, and accommodating ethics than for any political or managerial skill. The famous Seabury investigations of 1932 revealed just how accommodating his ethics were.

James John Walker was born on June 19, 1881 and grew up in this house from the age of five. His father was a city alderman who pushed his reluctant son, who preferred theater and songwriting, into a political career. With his father's Tammany connections and his own good looks, Walker made a smooth and successful go of it. He was elected assemblyman when only twenty-eight years old, moved to the State Senate in 1915, and became Senate Democratic leader in 1918. He was viewed as a sharp and liberal young man with a promising political future and an unfortunate weakness for show girls. Despite his affairs, which he did little to conceal, and his lack of seriousness, which he turned to his advantage in a city enjoying the roaring '20s, he ran for mayor in 1925 and won easily.

Walker's flamboyance could not hide the problems caused by his lack of leadership. By his second term, which began in 1930, the corruption in his city government was too great to conceal. On August 21, 1930, Governor Franklin Roosevelt ordered an investigation into the magistrates' court, and launched the famous Seabury investigations, the most extensive and effective inquiry into political corruption in New York City history.

Samuel Seabury, the straight-arrow lawyer appointed as referee, was initially charged with investigating only the magistrates' court, but his snooping turned up such treasure that he ended up managing three inquiries, the second addressing the New York county district attorney, Thomas C. T. Crain (resulting in his resignation) and the third, and most dramatic, aimed at the city government.

The latter stretched from April 8, 1931 to December 8, 1932. More than 2,260 witnesses were examined privately; another 175 appeared in public hearings; and some 52,000 pages of testimony recorded. The results were damning, and made obvious that the playboy Mayor's administration was riddled with graft. Payments for political offices, judgeships, and contracts were standard practice; kickbacks were commonplace; protection of gamblers and gangsters routine.

Meticulous detective work by Seabury's staff had uncovered several instances of suspicious financial dealings by Walker. Several investors promoting the Equitable Coach Company had set up a slush fund for the mayor that provided him with more than $10,000 during a 1927 European vacation. Later, Walker facilitated the granting of a franchise for the bus company. J. A. Sisto, an investment banker with a large interest in the Checker Cab Corporation, had sent Walker an envelope with $26,000 in bonds, which supposedly represented the Mayor's profits on a stock deal in which he had invested absolutely no money. After receiving the bonds, Walker pushed through legislation favorable to Checker. Paul Block, owner of the *Brooklyn Standard Union*, set up a joint brokerage account with Walker in 1927. Again, without investing a dime, Walker turned a profit, making $246,693 in two years. Block had a share of a company hoping to sell tiles for the subways. Seabury's assistants also turned up evidence of a secret account opened by Russell Sherwood, a bookkeeper in Walker's old law office. Between January 1, 1926, and August 5, 1931, Sherwood deposited nearly a million dollars in the account for Walker, $750,000 of it in cash. Sherwood fled to Mexico City to avoid Seabury's subpoena.

The high point of the investigation came in May 1932 when Seabury put Walker on the stand. The mayor remained unruffled and the public, unaware of the corruption that Seabury had uncovered, cheered him on. Walker replied to his interrogator's probing with jokes and jabs, and avoided direct answers. Typical was his response when Seabury asked if he remembered shaking hands with J. A. Sisto: "Due to the activity that I have been in since 1910, I do shake hands with a great many people I don't know, and try to make them believe I do, but please don't tell them about it." When confronted with the existence of Sherwood's secret account he replied, "I hope he proves it as mine. I will try to collect."

Despite what he thought was a good performance, Walker's days were numbered: the committee's revelations had been devastating. James Walker resigned as mayor of New York on September 1, 1932. In the following mayoral election, reformer Fiorello LaGuardia took over the administration of the country's largest city. James Walker died on November 18, 1946.

Stroll a few houses down to 12 St. Luke's Place.

15 On the morning of June 8, 1931 the body of a young woman— good-looking, well-preserved, still smartly clothed in a silk dress—

was found on a desolate stretch of Long Beach, Long Island. She had died by drowning, but whether death was accidental, self-inflicted, or homicidal was not apparent. The mystery of Starr Faithfull had commenced.

The newspapers were enthralled with the case, and it filled their pages throughout the summer of 1931. The reasons were simple. Foremost, of course, was her unbeatable name. Starr Faithfull was real, although she had been christened Starr Wyman at her birth in 1906. Her parents divorced in 1924 and less than a year later her mother, Helen MacGregor Pierce, married Stanley Faithfull, both wife and daughters (Starr had a sister named Tucker) taking his name. More attractive still was her character, for Starr Faithfull seemed to have jumped out of a Scott Fitzgerald book. She wore her hair bobbed, partied energetically, drank too much, and indulged in sex. She was an emblem of the rebellious, frantic era of speakeasies and flappers: a perfect symbol, cast in a tragic role.

She lived with her eccentric family here at 12 St. Luke's Place. Her father, Stanley Faithfull, was a particularly odd character who throughout the furor that followed the discovery of her body, lied to investigators and newspapers and tried to profit from his daughter's death, first by selling his story to the tabloids, then by suing the same papers for libel. His actions at times seem so puzzling and suspicious that some accounts of the case have implicated him in the tragedy. The Faithfulls maintained that Starr was a model daughter, dutiful and honest, sober and chaste. They were, her father said, a close and happy family with no secrets. Wishful thinking, perhaps, but an absolute lie.

Starr Faithfull was neither sober, chaste, nor obedient. She drank to excess, swallowed barbiturates and sniffed ether, and often failed to return home at night. Her diary revealed many trysts and one-night stands. She had a particular liking for cruise ships, and enjoyed stateroom parties and the company of crew members. The idea that her family life was genial is disposed of succinctly in her diary, where she referred to her stepfather as "that insufferable ass!" and wrote "God damn our home."

Her diary also reveals a deeply troubled woman, by turns withdrawn and animated, listless and stubborn. She would probably be labeled a manic-depressive today. Much of her maladjustment can be traced to a startling episode of her youth that forms a subplot to the case. Beginning when Starr was eleven years old, and continuing for many years, she was sexually abused by a family friend; her parents learned of the abuse only years later, in June 1926. The perpetrator was the prominent and wealthy Andrew J. Peters, a former congressman and a former mayor of Boston. In a move subject to a number of interpretations, the Faithfulls pursued an "agreement" in which they kept the episode a secret and Peters paid them at least $20,000. When news of this pact came out after Faithfull's death, her parents piously claimed that every penny and more of the money went for psychiatric care for their daughter.

Starr Faithfull was last seen alive on the night of Friday, June 5. Dr. Charles Roberts, a ship's surgeon on the Cunard line, accompanied Faithfull to a couple of bon voyage parties on board the *Mauretania* and the *Carmania,* two cruise ships docked at Pier 56 at the foot of West 16th Street. She left at approximately 10:30 P.M., quite drunk. Where she was and what she did for the next two days remains a complete mystery. There are no clues and no witnesses. Starr Faithfull just vanished.

But there are some clues to her state of mind in the days prior to her death. These are evident in letters that Starr had written to Dr. George Jameson Carr on May 30, June 2, and June 4. When finally revealed, these dramatic letters turned the investigation on its head.

Dr. Jameson Carr was a ship's surgeon for the Cunard line that Faithfull had met on a cruise to England in 1927. She was madly in love with him, but the affection was not returned. Said the doctor, "You don't become romantic about a girl on whom you used a stomach pump the first time you saw her." Still, he remained a friend and confidant. Faithfull last saw the doctor on May 29, when Jameson Carr left New York on the Cunard liner *Franconia.* Faithfull had come on board to toast his departure, which she did, as usual, with too much enthusiasm. She got falling-down drunk and the doctor asked her to leave. She tried to stowaway but was discovered. The ship had already cast off and the hapless young woman was lowered by rope, kicking and screaming, to a passing tug.

Jameson Carr learned of Faithfull's death when he arrived in England and immediately shoved off again to return to New York with the three letters he had received from her en route. The letter of June 2 was a formal note of apology for her behavior on the *Franconia.* But the first and last were desperate suicide notes. "I am going (definitely now—I've been thinking of it for a long time) to end my worthless, disorderly bore of an existence—before I ruin anyone else's life as well. I certainly have made a sordid, futureless mess of it all. I am dead, dead sick of it," she wrote on May 30. The third letter, written the day before she disappeared, reiterates her intention, "If one wants to get away with murder one has to jolly well keep one's wits about one. It's the same way with suicide. If I don't watch out I shall wake up in a psychopathic ward, but I intend to watch out and accomplish my end this time."

These revelations, seemingly so explicit, put an end to the official murder investigation. Starr Faithfull's death was ruled a suicide. But over the years, doubts have persisted.

Some have suggested that the unfortunate Faithfull (perhaps drugged: 10 grains of veronal, a barbiturate, were found in her body) fell in a stupor or was flung from a passing cruise ship. Another theory posits that she was killed on the beach by a one-night stand or a rapist. Stanley Faithfull claimed that his daughter was kidnapped and killed by agents of Andrew J. Peters.

But these theories all display serious flaws. If she had floated to the beach from a cruise ship, her body would have been battered or bloated (instead it was found in surprisingly pristine condition). No one saw her on any ships. The autopsy showed no sign of sexual activity in the twenty-four hours before her death. And there is no evidence at all behind Stanley Faithfull's fanciful and paranoid theory.

The most sensible solution points to suicide. The letters to Jameson Carr indicate her clear intent. Some years before she had attempted suicide with an overdose of barbiturates. It seems likely that the bruises found on her body—the cause of much dark speculation—were caused when she leapt off a stone jetty that jutted into the water close to where her body was found.

ALSO INFAMOUS

Theodore Dreiser lived at 16 St. Luke's Place when writing *An American Tragedy*, his classic novel based on the Chester Gillette murder case. Gillette impregnated nineteen-year old Grace Brown when both were working in a clothing factory in Cortland, New York in 1906. Uncomfortable with matrimony or fatherhood, Gillette drowned Brown while they were out rowing on Big Moose Lake on July 11, 1906. He was found guilty and electrocuted the next year.

Continue on St. Luke's to the corner of Seventh Avenue and turn right. Pause at the next block, Clarkson Street.

16 "The worst civil disorder the United States has ever known," the New York Draft Riots, turned the city into a battleground for four days in July 1863. This street witnessed one of its most horrific incidents, the gruesome murder of William Jones.

The Union cause was not an especially popular one in New York. The Civil War had meant the end of business with the South, the city's major trading partner. Unemployment and inflation had followed. City Hall was controlled by Democrats antagonistic to the Republicans' war. Abolitionism was scorned by much of the white working class, who feared free blacks as competition.

Draft rioters hang and burn William Jones in Clarkson Street.

Lincoln's promulgation of the first federal draft in the nation's history sparked resentment and cries for resistance. Especially galling to the working class was the bill's stipulation that exemptions to military service could be bought for $300, turning the struggle into a poor man's war. The drawing of names for the new draft began on Saturday, July 11, 1863, without incident, but over the weekend the mood of the city grew increasingly tense. Groups began to form on street corners and outside bars throughout town. Amid the swearing and speechmaking, the crowds bristled and resistance stiffened. When the lottery resumed on Monday, July 13, a mob led by members of the Black Joke volunteer fire company attacked and destroyed a draft office at Third Avenue and West 46th Street. This was the spark that set the city on fire.

Roiling mobs fanned out across the city, filling Broadway, Fifth, Third, and First Avenues; marching to City Hall Park and Park Row; and heading toward black residential enclaves in Greenwich Village. One witness described First Avenue full of thousands of rioters:

> The rush and roar grew every moment more terrific. Up came fresh hordes faster and more furious; bareheaded men, with red, swollen faces, brandishing sticks and clubs, or carrying heavy poles and beams; and boys, women and children hurrying on and joining with them in this mad chase up the avenue like a company of raging fiends.

Over the next four days, roaming crowds of rioters attacked property, police, the army, and civilians. After attacking an armory at West 21st Street and Second Avenue, one thousand carbines passed into the hands of rioters. Several draft offices were sacked, the Colored Orphan Asylum was destroyed, the *New York Tribune* offices were stormed, dozens of homes were looted. Nearly 120 people were killed. The police and nearby army units found themselves hopelessly outmanned and outgunned, and five Union Army regiments had to be pulled back from Gettysburg to quell the uprising. The New York Draft Riots were finally put down by Thursday, July 16.

The riot reached Clarkson Street on the first day. About six o'clock that evening, three white laborers led by John Nicholson, a bricklayer, were chasing a black man up Varick Street. The pursued man turned into Clarkson Street, pulled out a pistol, and, firing at and wounding Nicholson, made good an escape. Unfortunately, William Jones, a black laborer, was walking down the street at that moment after shopping for a loaf of bread. The enraged whites seized Jones, beat him, and then hanged him from a tree. While a crowd gathered, a fire was set beneath his body, which burned until put out by a rainstorm at eleven that night. Wrote contemporary historian Joel Tyler Headley, "He was literally roasted as he hung, the mob revelling in their demoniac act." It took a force of 100 policemen to disperse the crowd, take control of the street, and recover the body. Headley lamented: "All this was in the nineteenth century, and in the metropolis of the freest and most enlightened nation on earth."

John Nicholson was indicted for the murder of William Jones, but was never brought to trial. Two others, Patrick Coffee and Thomas Quinn, were accused of complicity but never formally charged.

NOTABLE RIOTS IN NEW YORK CITY

Liberty Pole Violence, 1766–70—Patriots and British soldiers tussled over the rise and fall of several Liberty Poles—masts erected as symbols of the revolutionaries' cause—from 1766 to 1770. The Liberty Pole now standing in the City Hall Park was placed there in 1921 in the same spot as its sanguinary predecessors.

Spring Election Riots, April 8–11, 1834—Mobs of warring Democrats and Whigs, totaling some 10,000–15,000, battled it out at election time in several parts of the city. The Mayor was wounded and the riots finally put down by the military.

Police Riot, June 16, 1857—New York's most unusual riot, one that featured two rival police departments bashing it out for control of the city! When the Republican-dominated State government created a new Metropolitan Police force under Albany control,

Democratic Mayor Fernando Wood declared the legislation unconstitutional and refused to disband the city-controlled Municipal Police force. On June 16, Metropolitan police attempting to serve the Mayor with a warrant in City Hall were met with a force of Municipal police, and a huge brawl between the two forces engulfed the park. Twelve policemen were injured. Throughout that summer the city hosted two police departments, both of which spent at least as much time battling each other as catching lawbreakers. In the autumn Mayor Wood conceded defeat and disbanded the Municipals.

Orange Riot, July 16, 1871—Tensions were high as Protestant Irish marched to gloat on the anniversary of the Battle of Boyne and the victory of the Prince of Orange over the Catholic James II. Well protected by several hundred police and military units, the Orangemen marched down an Eighth Avenue thick with both angry and curious Catholics. As they passed 25th Street a shot was heard and the military panicked, leveling their rifles at the crowd. In the melee that followed, two policemen and thirty-one civilians were killed.

Race Riot, Aug. 15–16, 1910—When Arthur Harris, who was black, saw his wife accosted by Robert Thorpe, who was white, on the corner of Eighth Avenue and West 41st Street, he fought to rescue her, in the process fatally stabbing the interloper. Thorpe turned out to be a plainclothes police officer who claimed he was arresting Mrs. Harris for soliciting. Thorpe died from his wounds, and several days later, gangs of white toughs, enraged by the officer's death, rioted throughout the Tenderloin, targeting blacks for beating. The police did nothing.

Harlem Riot, Aug. 1, 1943—A disturbance at the Hotel Braddock on 126th Street resulted in the wounding of soldier Robert Bandy by a white policeman. The rumor that Bandy had been killed sparked massive rioting throughout the area. Six people were killed and 185 injured before things cooled down.

Cross Seventh Avenue and walk up Carmine Street two blocks to Bleecker Street. Turn right, cross Sixth Avenue, and then head left into Minetta Street.

17 The calm environs of Minetta Lane and Minetta Street, now so charming and picturesque, were among the most notorious and dangerous blocks in the whole city in the late nineteenth and early twentieth centuries.

Novelist Stephen Crane described the scene and the mood in the 1890s when he was a newspaper reporter:

> One wonders how such an insignificant alley could get such an absurdly large reputation, but, as a matter of fact, Minetta Lane, and

Minetta Street, which leads from it southward to Bleecker Street, MacDougal Street, and nearly all the streets thereabouts were most unmistakably bad, but when the Minettas started out the other streets went away and hid. To gain a reputation in Minetta Lane, in those days, a man was obliged to commit a number of furious crimes, and no celebrity was more important than the man who had a good honest killing to his credit. The inhabitants, for the most part, were negroes, and they represented the very worst elements of their race. The razor habit clung to them with the tenacity of an epidemic, and every night the uneven cobbles felt blood. Minetta Lane was not a public thoroughfare at this period. It was a street set apart, a refuge for criminals. Thieves came here preferably with their gains, and almost any day peculiar sentences passed among the inhabitants: "Big Jim turned a thousand last night." "No-Toe's made another haul." And the worshipful citizens would make haste to be present at the consequent revel.

Notorious criminals who lived and worked here included No-Toe Charley, Bloodthirsty, Black Cat, Old Man Spriggs, Jeff Saunders, and Jube Tyler.

Walk through Minetta Street, turn right on Minetta Lane, and then take a left on MacDougal. Walk one block to West Third Street and look left.

(18) West Third Street was the hub of a small but bustling red-light district in the last two decades of the nineteenth century that appears to have specialized in what were then fringe sexual tastes. Although this block was once thick with brothels, the only original building remaining that saw service as a disorderly house is 133 West Third, once owned and operated by the famous Matilda Hermann, known as "the French Madam" (she was from Alsace, which accounts for the disparity between her name and her monicker) and one of the star witnesses at the Lexow Investigation into police corruption.

On this block stood one of the city's (and probably the country's) first male homosexual brothels, The Golden Rule Pleasure Club, run by a woman known as Scotch Ann. A visitor described it:

> The basement was fitted up into little rooms, by means of cheap partitions, which ran to the top of the ceiling from the floor. Each room contained a table and a couple of chairs, for the use of customers of the vile den. In each room sat a youth, whose face was painted, eyebrows blackened, and whose airs were those of a young girl. Each person talked in a high falsetto voice, and called the others by women's names.

Thompson Street between Houston and West Third Streets was notorious for black prostitutes that catered to a trade in interracial sex. One resident lamented: " . . . after nightfall it is absolutely dangerous to pass this locality. In the daytime it is very little better."

The bagnio of Marie Andreas, at 42 West 4th Street, specialized in theatrical sex performances. It was the scene of a famous incident during the vice tour of reformer Charles Parkhurst (see p. 170) known as "Dr. Parkhurst's Circus," in which the employees of the house gave him a show, though the Reverend was too demure to say specifically what it was.

MUG SHOTS

MAXWELL BODENHEIM
Bohemian victim

Maxwell Bodenheim—a brilliant poet, a roguish ladies' man, an irascible iconoclast—seemed the quintessential bohemian and the embodiment of Greenwich Village almost from the moment he first arrived in the city in 1915. He lived in garrets, edited small literary journals, enjoyed casual affairs, and poured forth an impressive stream of poems, novels, and plays. Years later, when Bodenheim slipped into alcoholism and became, literally, a Bowery bum, some read into his life a metaphor for the decay and death of the Village itself.

Born on May 26, 1892, in Hermanville, Mississippi, Bodenheim was expelled from high school, jailed for deserting the army, and arrested for vagrancy several times while bumming about in the Southwest. Yet somehow he managed to write and do it well. When he was still in his early twenties, his poetry was ranked by some with Wallace Stevens, Carl Sandburg, and Edgar Lee Masters. He also wrote plays for the Provincetown Playhouse and more than a dozen novels, including the bestselling and scandalous *Replenishing Jessica*.

The handsome writer cultivated a reputation as a womanizer and a cynic. In an odd and grotesque streak lasting from spring to fall 1928, two women committed suicide, ostensibly after affairs with him, another lover attempted suicide, and a fourth was killed in a subway accident that left Bodenheim's love letters strewn all over Times Square station. These events brought him more notoriety than any of his writings.

Bodenheim's irascibility eventually became more irritating than charming, his cynicism broadened into meanness, and he drank too much. By the '30s he was a barfly at the San Remo and the Minetta Tavern, cadging drinks and selling bits of poetry on scraps of paper for a buck. Once a first-rate talent, he became a Village character. In another decade, he had descended to the flophouses and wine bottles of the Bowery.

Along the way he picked up two companions. One was Ruth Fagan, who, like Bodenheim, was brilliant and wounded and an alcoholic. She became his wife in the spring of 1951. The other was a

Bowery bum and ex-mental patient named Harold Weinberg.
Though Bodenheim evidently hated Weinberg he made no great
effort to lose him. Men in Bodenheim's condition often cling to
companions that they don't like.

On the night of February 6, 1954, the three shared a room at a
flophouse at 97 Third Avenue. They were drinking heavily. Evidently
Weinberg began making sexual advances toward Fagan, and
Bodenheim attempted to intervene. Weinberg picked up a .22 and
fatally shot the poet. He then attacked and killed Fagan with a knife
and fled the room.

In an eerie passage from an early poem, Bodenheim seemed to
envisage the grisly scene:

He sits now in a vapid rooming-house
And spies a form upon the empty bed.
One spot of dread moves slowly on his head,
Like some invisible, resistless louse.

Weinberg was found four days later and eventually committed to
the Matteawan State Hospital for the Criminally Insane.

Walk east (away from Sixth Avenue) a block to Sullivan Street and turn
right. Continue to 225 Sullivan Street.

19 In a more than modest tenement apartment here at 225 Sullivan
Street, the reputed boss of the Genovese family, Vincent Gigante,
lives with his mother. Gigante has his headquarters down the street
in the Triangle Civic Improvement Association at 208 Sullivan. He
spends most of his nights, though, at a town house at 67 East 77th
Street.

Gigante is a strange Godfather: he walks outside in pajamas and
slippers, sometimes muttering; he hasn't left the city in years; he
spends no time out on the town and rarely eats at restaurants. His
family says Vincent Gigante is mentally ill; the police claim that he
feigns insanity to avoid prosecution.

Gigante, born in 1928, grew up in the neighborhood and embarked early on a life of crime, but he first attracted attention as the
gunman in the famous attempted murder of Frank Costello in 1957.

Frank Costello, often dubbed "the prime minister of the underworld," was an immensely powerful figure in the New York underworld and city politics. A street thug in East Harlem at a tender age,
he became a protégé of Arnold Rothstein and made a fortune in
bootlegging, slot machines, and other rackets. When Lucky Luciano
was deported in 1946, Costello assumed the leadership of his Mafia
family. At the apogee of his power in the 1940s, he was a major

power broker in the city's machine politics, with strong ties to Tammany boss Jimmy Hines and Mayor William O'Dwyer.

The power of Costello eventually became an impediment to the ambitious Vito Genovese, who wanted control of the Luciano family, and it is thought that he put out a contract on Costello. The contractee was the young Gigante.

On the night of May 2, 1957, at about 9:30 P.M., a limousine containing Gigante and driven by, it is believed, Tommy Eboli, parked across the street from the Majestic Apartments at 115 Central Park West. The two waited patiently (although nervously) for nearly an hour and a half, until they saw a cab with Costello pull up outside the building. Gigante quickly got out of the limo and dashed into the lobby ahead of Costello, who, rushing inside, didn't notice the husky gunman.

"This is for you, Frank!" snarled Gigante, in perfect gangster fashion. Costello whirled as the assassin fired his pistol at point-blank range. The bullet entered just behind Costello's right ear and exited by the left, but, incredibly, it traveled around the back of his head, only piercing the skin. Costello received no more than a flesh wound.

Gigante dashed out and made his getaway but surrendered to the authorities a few weeks later. Since Costello could not or would not identify him in the ensuing trial, Gigante was acquitted of attempted murder.

Neither flamboyant nor smart, Gigante seems to have reached the top through attrition. Genovese died in 1969 while in prison. His successor, Tommy Eboli, was murdered in Crown Heights, Brooklyn in 1972. Anthony "Fat Tony" Salerno then assumed the crown and served until 1986, when he was imprisoned on racketeering charges. He died on July 27, 1992. Gigante took over when Salerno was "sent up the river."

The Genovese crime family has an estimated 400–500 members and is involved in construction unions, garbage removal companies, New Jersey waterfront rackets, gambling, and loan-sharking.

Continue to Bleecker Street and turn left. At the next street, Thompson, take a right and cross Bleecker Street. At the southeast corner is 184 Thompson Street.

20 Now a modern apartment building, this was, from 1925 to 1936, the site of the Genovese Trading Co., a scrap dealership with a junkyard next door and the place of business (legal and illegal) for Vincent Gigante's boss, Vito Genovese. One of the most famous—and, reputedly, most ruthless—Mafia bosses of all time, Genovese directed his extensive interests in narcotics, numbers, slot machines, racketeering, and the like from this address.

Born in Risigliano, Italy in 1897, Genovese arrived in New York and this neighborhood in 1913 and seems to have gone bad with alacrity. He was still a teenager when he met Charles "Lucky" Luciano, and the two became partners in robberies, burglaries, bootlegging, and narcotics smuggling. They rose together through Mafia ranks in Joe "the Boss" Masseria's crew, Luciano serving as the boss's right-hand man. But in a power struggle between Masseria and Salvatore Maranzano, known as the Castellammarese War (so-called because Maranzano and most of his minions hailed from Castellammare del Golfo in Sicily), the two young gangsters sided with Maranzano and double-crossed their employer. Genovese was said to be one of the four gunmen who shot Masseria in Scarpato's Restaurant in Coney Island on April 15, 1931. However, they soon chafed under the autocratic leadership of Maranzano, and within five months, turned against their boss yet again. Maranzano was killed in his offices in the New York Central Building at 230 Park Avenue (now the Helmsley Building) on September 10, 1931 by gunmen hired by the ambitious friends (see p. 247). Luciano, after ten years, was on top; Genovese served as underboss.

Genovese then set up one of the strangest Mafia killings on record, a hit carried out not for power, money, or revenge, but for love. Sometime in the early 1930s, Genovese met Anna Petillo Vernotico, fell deeply in love, and decided upon marriage. That she already had a husband seemed to Genovese only an inconvenience and he contracted gunmen Peter Mione and Michael Barrese to clear the aisle for him. On March 16, 1932, the body of Gerard Vernotico was found, tied and strangled, on the roof of 124 Thompson Street. (The building still stands, two blocks down, on the northeast corner of Thompson and Prince Streets.) Twelve days later Genovese and Petillo were wed. The famous Mafia informer Joe Valachi said, "I remember when we—Vito and me—were in Atlanta [Penitentiary] together later on, he would sometimes talk about her, and I would see the tears rolling down his cheeks. I couldn't believe it." The couple were divorced in 1950, and even though Petillo testified extensively in divorce court about her husband's criminal activities and assets, he never attempted to stop her.

Luciano and Genovese's stay at the top did not last long. On July 17, 1936, Luciano was sentenced to thirty to fifty years for enforced prostitution. In 1937, hearing that an associate had tied him to a killing, Genovese fled to Italy. There he reportedly became chummy with Mussolini and, according to one theory, did the Duce a favor by having anarchist Carlo Tresca killed in New York (see p. 48). When the Americans invaded, Genovese somehow ended up serving as an interpreter for the Allied Military Government. At the same time he was also a major figure in the country's thriving postwar black market. Amid some embarrassment, the government took him off the payroll and brought him back to New York in 1945 to face an indictment for the murder of Ferdinand "The Shadow" Boccia, who had been gunned down eleven years earlier. But the Brooklyn District Attorney's office showed a curious lack of interest in receiving and prosecuting Genovese, a reluctance that raised questions about the extent of corruption—and the reach of the Mob—in the D.A.'s office. These suspicions would later rebound upon Mayor William O'Dwyer, who was Brooklyn District Attorney from 1940–42. O'Dwyer's connections with organized crime would lead to his forced resignation as mayor in 1950.

Genovese did stand trial, but the key witness, a gangster named Pete LaTempa, was mysteriously poisoned in his cell before the proceedings. The trial ended with a directed verdict of acquittal. After this close call Genovese went to work to consolidate his power. He evidently had a hand in the murders of Willie Moretti on October 4, 1951 and Steven Franse on June 19, 1953, both of whom were lined up behind Frank Costello, the man who had taken over when Genovese fled to Italy. In May 1957, Genovese told Vincent Gigante to take a ride uptown.

Although Gigante bungled his assignment, Costello magnanimously stepped aside. But Genovese had little time to enjoy his bloodless coup. On July 8, 1958, he was indicted for narcotics violations and was later sentenced to 15 years in Atlanta Penitentiary. In prison, Genovese made one more mistake. He turned on his cellmate and old associate Joseph "Cago" Valachi and threatened to kill him. Valachi, understandably upset, sought protection from the federal government, in return becoming the most famous and valuable Mafia informant ever. Much of what is known about Genovese, and the Mafia in general, comes from Valachi.

Vito Genovese died of a heart ailment on February 14, 1969 in the federal prison medical center in Springfield, Missouri.

Nearest subway: West 4th Street Washington Square A B C D E F Q
Nearest bus line: M 5; M 6; M 21

5

The Tenderloin and Times Square

A Criminal Sketch of the Tenderloin

> I wish I could give my readers something like a decent picture of the
> New York of the [eighteen-]eighties, and especially of its underworld.
> What a red-hot game it was! Life was fierce! Faro banks and poker
> joints by night, bed at five o'clock in the morning, up for the night's
> work at five o'clock in the evening, sometimes winning, more often
> losing. You could find in the Tenderloin the biggest toughs in
> creation, murderers, burglars, con men, boxmen, and the ordinary
> common or garden gunman on hire like the Italian bravo.

So enthused thief Eddie Guerin about this neighborhood in his memoirs.

The Tenderloin was New York's premier vice district, the most notorious and most sinful of the many bad neighborhoods and wicked quarters that have graced or despoiled the city in its long history. From the 1870s to World War I, the district—roughly the area between 23rd and 42nd Streets and Sixth and Eighth Avenues—was saturated with brothels, gambling halls, betting shops, and saloons in concentrations never seen before or since. The Tenderloin was so famous for being so bad that its name has become a generic term for any urban district devoted to vice.

Until the Civil War, Manhattan island above 23rd Street was largely undeveloped. When the Fifth Avenue Hotel was built on the northwest corner of Fifth Avenue and 23rd Street in 1857, it was so far uptown that New Yorkers thought the establishment could survive only as a summer resort. Its unexpected year-round success encouraged further development. Other hotels followed, theaters

The Tenderloin and Times Square

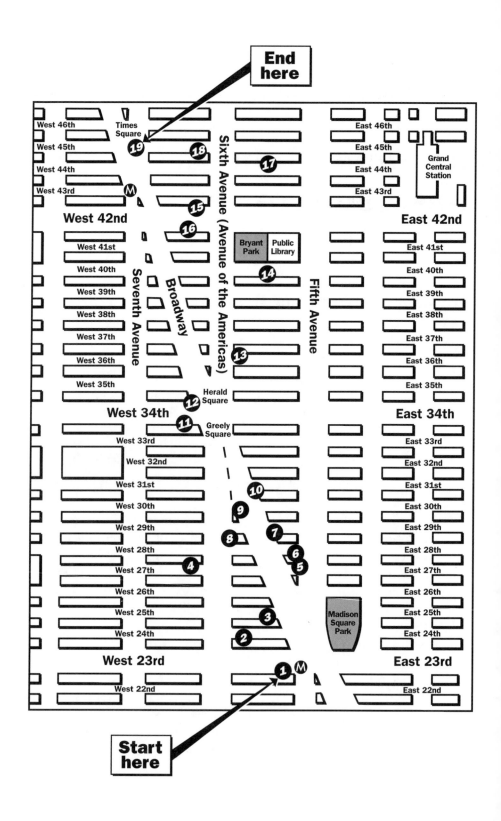

continued their crawl up Broadway, and restaurants and saloons popped up to serve the new clientele. With plenty of space and an accommodating city administration, brothels, gambling halls, gaming rooms, and low dens of vice soon took up residence with enthusiasm. By the 1870s the sinfulness was going full blast.

The area—the twenty-ninth police district—was dubbed the Tenderloin about 1876. The circumstances were recorded in testimony by Policeman Alexander "Clubber" Williams during the later Lexow Committee investigation into police corruption:

> Q: How did [the name "The Tenderloin"] originate?
> A: Through a newspaper reporter, a man that was on the *Sun* that used to call on me in the Fourth precinct; when I was transferred to the Twenty-ninth [in 1876] he came up there and asked me how I liked the change: I said, I have been living on rump steak in the Fourth district, I will have some tenderloin now; he picked it up and it has been named that ever since . . . .
> Q: This is the first time a waiting and anxious public has had an opportunity to hear from your lips your understanding and your reason [for] calling the Fourth precinct the "rump steak."
> A: No; I said I had been living on rump steak.
> Q: What did you mean by that?
> A: Well, I got better living in the Twenty-ninth.
> Q: Why?
> A: Better saloons; better hotels.

Prostitution—unchecked and even fashionable—flourished in the Tenderloin as never before in the city's history. In the 1870s, in the block between Sixth and Seventh Avenues, there were twelve brothels on 26th Street and twenty-two on 27th Street. Nearby streets hosted many others. The most famous houses of ill repute were owned by the "Seven Sisters," siblings from a New England family whose expensive and well-known establishments lined 25th Street west of Sixth Avenue. The best brothel was reputed to be that of Mrs. Kate Woods at 105 W. 25th Street. An 1870s guidebook to New York brothels entitled *The Gentleman's Companion* described her sumptuous palace: "Her gallery of oil paintings alone cost $10,000. Rosewood furniture, immense mirrors, Parisian figures etc. The house is furnished at the cost of $70,000."

By the turn of the century, prostitution, along with the rest of the vice district, had migrated north, and the main streets for vice became West 31st (with fourteen bordellos) and West 32nd (with sixteen) Streets. The going price in most houses was $1 to $2 for a fifteen-minute tryst. Big spenders could shell out $10 or $20 and spend the night.

The extent of prostitution at this time is staggering. The Society for the Prevention of Crime, observing brothels on West 40th Street

Blades and bawds enjoy a late night on Sixth Avenue.

from 8:20 to 11:00 P.M. on a November night in 1911, reported that at least 556 men entered the establishments during that time. One house attracted over 100 customers in less than three hours.

Gambling, too, was in the midst of a boom in popularity and extravagance, and houses were, in the words of one reformer, "as thick as the roses in Sharon." The extent and locations of this vice are explored a little later in this chapter.

Saloons and dance halls—which in addition to offering the sinful pleasures of drink and dancing were rendezvous for prostitutes—were numerous and popular. The most famous included the Cremorne at 108 West 32nd Street, the Haymarket at the southeast corner of West 30th Street and Sixth Avenue, the Star & Garter at 504 (now 860) Sixth Avenue, the Alhambra at 37 West 28th Street, the Cairo at 34 West 29th Street, the Savoy Music Hall at 28 West 39th Street, and Koster & Bial's at 115–17 West 23rd Street.

The lamps of the Tenderloin began to dim around the turn of the century, the victim of a number of forces: several reform campaigns, including those of the Reverend Charles Parkhurst and District Attorney William Travers Jerome; a Navy clampdown on prostitution conducted near ports; the encroachment of garment manufacturing; and changing social patterns and sexual habits.

In 1931, Detective Cornelius Willemse commented, with a note of nostalgia, about the lost Tenderloin: "Any cop who knew the

Tenderloin laughs when he hears the New York of to-day called a wicked city. One block of the Tenderloin provided more vice than exists in the whole area of the present 'White Light' district."

Crime did not, however, wholly abandon the neighborhood. When the garment industry came to dominate the streets, wrongdoing adapted. That development is discussed later in the tour.

Stalking the Tenderloin

> Nearest subway: 23rd Street R
> Nearest bus lines: M 2; M 3; M 5; M 6; M 7; M 23

The tour begins at 12 West 23rd Street, just a few feet west of the southwest corner of 23rd and Fifth Avenue.

1 It was a dark and stormy night—and therefore a thoroughly appropriate setting for one of New York's greatest and most enduring criminal mysteries, the murder of Benjamin Nathan. Thundershowers poured over the city on the night of July 28, 1870, falling too on the Nathan mansion, which still survives here at 12 West 23rd Street.

In the morning, Washington Nathan descended the stairs from his bedroom to discover the lifeless body of his father Benjamin sprawled in the parlor in a puddle of blood. He yelled to his brother Frederick, who rushed down, stooped over his father's body to check for life (and in so doing drenched his nightshirt in blood, a fact that cast initial suspicion on him), and then, with his brother, rushed outside to call for help.

Nathan lay on his back in the parlor with his feet extending into a small room that was used as a study, although there were signs that the body had been moved. It appeared that he had been struck a blow while writing at his desk, and that a struggle then ensued. There were five head wounds, one of which had crushed the skull near the temple. There were other wounds on the arms, chest, and back, and three fingers on the right hand had been crushed. Blood soaked the floors and covered the walls.

Inside the study was an open and empty safe. In addition, two watches, three diamond studs, and a gold medal were missing. The murder weapon was soon found on the first floor by the front door. All accounts call it a carpenter's "dog," a piece of wrought iron about sixteen inches long with both ends turned down at right angles and sharpened at the ends, something like a huge staple. It was

Kaddish for Benjamin Nathan.

smeared with blood and hair. By the doorframe between the two rooms was a perfectly formed handprint in blood, the signature, as it were, of the murderer. But fingerprints meant nothing to the police of the day, and the solution to the mystery was washed off the wall the next day.

Benjamin Nathan was a well-known stockbroker and member of a prominent Portuguese-Jewish family (The famous Judge Benjamin Nathan Cardozo was not only a namesake but also a relative). He was born in New York City in 1813 and enjoyed a successful career in finance and business, sitting on many corporate boards and serving as the vice president of the New York Stock Exchange in 1851. He was president of Shearith Israel, the city's oldest and most prestigious synagogue.

He had retired a few years previously and turned his brokerage firm over to his two eldest sons. During the summer Nathan normally stayed at his summer estate in Morristown, New Jersey. But July 29 was the anniversary of his mother's death, and, intending to go to synagogue to recite the *Kaddish* (the Jewish prayer for the dead) he stayed in the city. He told the housekeeper, Mrs. Kelley, to pile up a few mattresses in the parlor.

Five people spent the night in the house: Benjamin Nathan; his older son Frederick; another son, Washington (something of a black sheep); the housekeeper Anne Kelly; and her son William, who acted as a general handyman around the house.

Frederick Nathan had gone to dinner in Brooklyn, returned about midnight, exchanged a few words with his father, and went upstairs to sleep. Washington Nathan had spent a less sober night. He admitted that, from 9:00 PM to midnight, he had sojourned in the brothel of Irene Macready at 104 East 14th Street and dallied with her employee Clara Dale (who substantiated his story). He arrived back home at twenty minutes after midnight, noticed that his father was asleep, and passed up the stairs to bed. Anne Kelly had been the housekeeper in the Nathan house for four years. Sometime after 10:00 PM, she carried ice water to his room, arranged the bedding, fastened the doors and windows, and retired to her room. She heard, she said, nothing. Her son William slept that night in the attic. He awoke at 5:00 in the morning, and was engaged in shining the Nathan shoes in his room when he heard the cries of Washington Nathan. He heard nothing during the night.

These facts were elicited at the coroner's inquest held the week following Nathan's death. It was the sum of the investigation, for there was never a trial, nor the arrest of any suspects. The police investigation, in fact, was miserable. One account of the case laments:

> Few murder mysteries can be cited which exhibit such a lack of detective instinct on the part of the police as the Nathan tragedy. If they discerned a clue anywhere, they failed to act on it. They were unable to trace a single stolen article. They were baffled in their attempts—if they made any—to find out the truth about William Kelly. The big reward of 45,000 dollars offered for the discovery and capture of the murderer did not stimulate them. They allowed the blood-marked garment of Frederick Nathan and the stained carpet in the room where the murder was committed to be taken away—the first to the laundry and the second to the cleaners—a few hours after the tragedy, and offered no explanation for their remissness.

But there are two theories and at least four suspects.

It was either an inside job or an outside job. If an inside job, then the likely suspect is Washington Nathan. He had a reputation as a wastrel who did not always get along with his father. He was the last person to see his father in the evening and the first one to encounter him in the morning. Perhaps Washington needed money for his high living and was discovered by his father while cleaning out the safe.

But it's a weak case, and few give it much credence. Washington and his father were not on particularly bad terms, there's no evidence that he was in need of money, and no physical evidence— bloody clothes, bruises or scrapes, sudden riches—that connect him to the crime.

The outside job theory is more plausible. Here we have three suspects: William Kelly, and two professional thieves, John T. Irving and Billy Forrester. Kelly proponents posit that he admitted confederates

Probable culprit Billy Forrester.

into the house for robbery, but that they were surprised in the act and forced to dispatch Nathan. Others counter that Kelly, evidently something of a dimwit, just wasn't the type.

John T. Irving, while serving a term in San Quentin prison in California some three years after the murder, confessed to being an accomplice. But it appears that he did so only to get off for two outstanding burglary charges and, since no corroborating evidence could be unearthed, he was never charged with the deed.

Billy Forrester emerges as the likeliest candidate. Shortly after the killing, a convict in Sing Sing, George Ellis, said that he and Billy Forrester had discussed robbing the Nathan manse. He was brought down to New York and passed a test by identifying the murder weapon, the carpenter's dog, from among a pile of twenty-five similar instruments. Forrester was discovered a year and a half later in Texas and hauled back to the city, where he was represented by the infamous law firm of Howe & Hummel (see pp. 83). Since Ellis was a convict, he was not produced to testify against his onetime partner, and the case collapsed. But Abe Hummel delivered a tantalizing morsel when he later said, "In regard to Forrester I cannot speak fully without violating professional honor, for the man was a client of my office; but I can say this, that from what I learned of him, Washington Nathan had no more to do with the killing of his father than I."

Unlikely suspect John T. Irving.

ALSO INFAMOUS

A nineteenth-century landmark in New York was the Edwin Booth Theater, built by the famous actor (now overshadowed by his infamous brother John Wilkes) in 1869 on the corner of 23rd Street and Sixth Avenue. The basement saloon under the theater, owned by Ivan Siscovitch, was "headquarters for all the noted forgers in America," according to Chief of Detectives Byrnes. Such underground luminaries as Charles Becker, George Wilkes, and George Engles (famous for his attempt to defraud the Bank of England) were known as customers.

Walk north on Broadway a block and turn left on West 24th Street. Continue over to the humble building at 22 West 24th Street, a site connected with New York's most famous murders.

2 This building, when prouder, was the office and bachelor's den of the great architect Stanford White and the site of his infamous "Red Velvet Swing," in which he used to send his paramours sweeping toward the ceiling. Of the landmarks associated with the murder of White, only this one remains.

On the warm summer evening of June 25, 1906, opening night for the otherwise forgotten musical, *Mamzelle Champagne*, the famous architect was shot three times in the crowded Madison Square Garden rooftop theater, one bullet fatally piercing his left eye. The assassin was Harry Thaw, errant son of a Pittsburgh coal baron. As White fell to the floor, bringing down the table with a clatter, Thaw walked calmly to the elevator and informed his shocked wife, the young Evelyn Nesbit, that he had just saved her life. He put up no struggle when disarmed, and was soon in custody. By the next day the stunning murder was a national sensation.

At the time of his death, Stanford White was America's premier architect. Working with partners Charles McKim and William Mead, he adorned New York with some of its finest buildings— many of them bold and controversial for their time. The Metropolitan Club, the Players' Club, the Washington Square Arch, were all his. Pennsylvania Station, torn down in 1963 and now much mourned, was his masterpiece. One of his most successful designs was the scene of his demise, Madison Square Garden. The culture, the energy, the sophistication, and the decadence we associate with New York all found some degree of repose in White. He was a successful architect, designer, and photographer with a restless taste for beautiful young women. The top floor of this building was his bachelor's pad (although he had a wife in another town), which was outfitted with mirrors, indirect lighting (unusual at the time), a huge bed, and a red velvet swing.

Harry Thaw was a different story altogether. His own mother once wrote that "his mind is more or less unbalanced." His father wrote him out of his will (though his more tender-hearted mother later fixed that). He was a paranoiac and prone to fly into unpredictable and uncontrollable rages. He was a cocaine addict and a sadist who hired prostitutes to whip.

He also had mountains of money, which seems to be the only plausible reason that Evelyn Nesbit would willingly submit to marriage. In 1898 the poor Nesbit family—mother, brother and fourteen-year-old Evelyn—moved from Pittsburgh to try their luck in New York, taking a room in a modest boardinghouse at 249 West 22nd Street. Nesbit soon got work as a model, posing for, among others, Charles Dana Gibson.

Her face gave her a quick entree to the theater, and not long after her arrival in the city she landed a spot as a chorus girl in the hottest show in town, *Florodora*. Word was that millionaires were falling all over themselves to marry a *Florodora* girl. Nesbit came to the attention of two; White, sadly already married, and Thaw, sadly not.

Stanford White wooed Nesbit for awhile, and in late 1901, on an unchaperoned date, took advantage of the young girl when she had passed out on champagne. Despite this brute behavior, Nesbit became White's mistress, and admitted, long after the trial, that she was head over heels in love with the architect. But a liaison with White could never be more than a fling—not only was he married, but he possessed an irrepressible roving eye. So Nesbit threw in her lot with a man who had been doggedly beseeching her for years, the strange but rich Harry Thaw. They were married on April 5, 1905, in Pittsburgh.

Nesbit had a weapon she thought would keep the erratic Thaw in line: his obsessive, psychopathic hatred of White. A mention of her ex-lover's name would set Thaw to cursing and shaking. He called White a beast, a blackguard, "Blank the Pimp," and a "wholesale ravisher of pure American virgins." For years he had fumed. He wrote hysterical letters to Anthony Comstock, informing that guardian of public morality, with a marvelous precision, that White had "ravished 387 girls." Though Comstock dutifully followed up on these red-hot stories, the smutbuster later testified that he "thought [Thaw's] mind was unbalanced." Nesbit's strategy kept her sugar daddy in line for awhile, but not forever.

On June 25, 1906, the Thaws and Stanford White found themselves sharing the Madison Square Garden rooftop terrace for *Mamzelle Champagne*. This was an unpleasant surprise for White, but Thaw knew his nemesis would be there and was quite prepared. Halfway through the show the Thaws and their guests decided to leave and made their way toward the elevator. Thaw lagged behind. "I had looked at the stage," he later recounted,

> and now I looked to my left to see if there were any I knew, a thing I always did. I saw the "B" [the Beast, Thaw's term for White] . . . . I saw a path from the stage to his table; going directly he would not have seen me. I walked to the stage and turned towards him so that he must see me coming.
>
> There I saw him thirty feet in front of me, and as he watched the stage he saw me. I walked towards him and about fifteen feet away I took out my revolver. He knew me and he was rising and held his right hand towards, I think, his gun and I wanted to let him try, but who was next? A man, a dozen men might have maimed me, cut off the light, allowed him to escape and rape more American girls as he had; too many, too many as he ruined Evelyn.
>
> Half-rising he gazed at me malignantly. I shot him 12 feet away. I felt sure he was dead. But I wanted to take no chances, I walked toward him, and fired two more shots. He dropped.

Thaw was actually about three feet away and Stanford White was unarmed.

Malcolm Langford, a writer on the case, notes that the prosecution of Thaw was "the most sensational trial ever held in an American court." It made the front pages of newspapers around the world. The courtroom was always packed. On the first day of Nesbit's testimony, 10,000 people jammed Broadway. All of Manhattan was ablaze with "the Thaw Affair."

Interestingly, the public and the papers of the time held precisely opposite opinions of the principals than we do today. Thaw, the violent paranoiac, was seen as the gallant defender of virginity; White, creative genius, was an evil voluptuary; Nesbit, enthusiastic mistress, was viewed as a pure blossom plucked and despoiled.

Thaw's lawyers and family pushed for an insanity defense, but Thaw was adamantly opposed, insisting that he was sane and fully justified. "I believe the community owes me a debt of thanks for what I have done," he maintained.

The defense compromised on his demands, pleading formally that Thaw had been temporarily insane between the time Nesbit first told him of her deflowering by White in November 1903, and the time nearly a year and a half later when he fired the three shots that brought him back to his senses. But defense lawyer Delphin Michael Delmas threw in, for good measure, the old exculpatory "unwritten law," that natural imperative that endows every man with the right to save his honor and his wife, by violence if necessary. The plea, then, was something like justifiable insanity.

District Attorney William Travers Jerome considered Thaw as crazy as a loon, but was forced to try and prove him sane. "Will you acquit a cold-blooded deliberate, cowardly murderer," he asked the jury in his summation, "because his lying wife has a pretty girl's face?"

When Nesbit took the stand, the whole country paused to listen. Delmas unveiled a brilliant legal move that devastated the prosecution. He asked Nesbit not about her relationship with White per se, but rather about what she had told her husband about that relationship—the terrible saga that had driven Thaw mad. Her testimony was made unassailable. Cross-examination to test the veracity of her testimony was inadmissible; the question was not whether what she said was true, but only whether she actually told her husband what she claimed. Who was to know? Thaw, of course, was kept well away from the stand. Jerome was stymied.

Crowds fought to get into the standing-room-only courtroom when Nesbit delivered her painful, tear-drenched testimony. Grown men held their breath in rapt terror. Grown women were admonished to leave the courtroom. Thaw buried his face in his hands, and wept. Through three days her history poured from Nesbit's lips: White drugged her and traduced her, she hated and feared the brute, her husband had saved her life. By all accounts, she gave the performance of her life.

They may have been applauding in the aisles, but the jurors brought back mixed reviews. The first trial ended in a hung jury. A second trial, eight months later—with the defense abandoning any mention of the unwritten law—and with Nesbit giving a nearly word-for-word repeat performance—found the defendant not guilty on grounds of insanity.

In 1915, Thaw received a third trial and was declared sane and acquitted of all charges. His first act was to divorce the long-estranged Nesbit. His strange career continued. In 1917 he was indicted for kidnapping and whipping nineteen-year-old Frederick Gump Jr. In 1927, he was sued by nightclub hostess Marcia Estars, who claimed he beat her up at a party. In 1933, headwaiter Paul Jaeck brought suit for a beating. Harry Thaw died of a heart attack in Miami on February 22, 1947, rich and unrepentant.

Nesbit, cast off from Thaw and his limitless cash, had to make do for the rest of her days in modest circumstances. She went back to the theater and a long succession of decreasingly lucrative engagements as a dancer and lounge singer. She opened a few clubs herself, including Chez Evelyn on West 52nd, but they all went under. She became a heroin addict for a time and lost the beauty that a man had killed for. She died in 1961 in Los Angeles.

Double back to Broadway and walk to 25th Street. Turn left and stop in front of the Arlington Hotel, still open for business at 18 West 25th Street.

3 This hotel was once the headquarters for Louis "Lepke" Buchalter and Jacob "Gurrah" Shapiro, in their prime the undisputed bosses of the garment industry and the city's most notorious racketeers.

The involved but fascinating history of crime in the garment district actually begins further south, on the Lower East Side, around the 1890s. The manufacture of preassembled, ready-to-fit clothing got its start there by putting the huddled masses to work doing piecework at home in the tenements. Such work was the backbone of the Lower East Side's economy. In the fevered pace of the crowded streets, manufacturers struggled to survive and workers struggled to organize. To cut out competition, break strikes, maintain strikes, or stop rival unions, these folk sometimes needed help. They turned to the tough strong-arm men—*shtarkes* in Yiddish—of the Jewish criminal gangs.

Around the time of the First World War, consolidation in the industry, population loss in the Lower East Side, and a need for loft space impelled the needle trades to migrate from the Jewish quarter on the east side to this neighborhood. By the 1920s the blocks between 24th and 41st Streets and Sixth and Ninth Avenues sheltered thousands of shops. Garment manufacturing became one of New York's leading industries, employing tens of thousands and clothing much of America. When it moved uptown, the racketeers, extortionists, and *shtarkes* marched in lockstep right along.

In those early days, two rivals—Louis "Kid Dropper" Kaplan and Jacob "Little Augie" Orgen—vied for supremacy in the rackets. A long war between the two gang leaders culminated in the dramatic murder of Kid Dropper on August 28, 1923.

He had been arraigned at the Essex Market Court and told—Wild-West style—to get out of town. A contingent of eighty policemen were provided to guard him on his way to Grand Central Station and a train to take him to forced retirement out west. The street was cleared and Kid Dropper surrounded as he was escorted to a taxi by several burly cops. He no sooner settled in the back seat, however, when shots rang out and a bullet caught him in the head. A seventeen-year-old novice gunmen from Orgen's gang named Louis Cohen had smuggled a pistol through the police cordon in a newspaper and pressed it against the taxi's rear window. Cohen who was defended by none other than soon-to-be-mayor Jimmy Walker, drew a twenty-years-to-life sentence. Upon release, Cohen returned to the streets.

But Orgen's victory was brief. Not long after consolidating his position he was challenged by two soldiers in his own gang, Louis "Lepke" Buchalter and Jacob "Gurrah" Shapiro.

Like their racketeering predecessors, Buchalter and Shapiro grew up in poverty on the Lower East Side, the sons of immigrants (Shapiro was an immigrant himself, brought here from Odessa at the age of two), and like them, turned to delinquency at a young age. Around 1922 they began working with Little Augie Orgen's gang, but were scheming even then.

In 1927 painters in Brooklyn's Local 102 of the International Brotherhood of Painters, Decorators and Paperhangers went on strike. The local was controlled by an ally of Buchalter and Shapiro's named Hyman "Little Hymie" or "Curly" Holtz. But a group of contractors turned to Orgen and Jack "Legs Diamond" Noland for muscle to break the work stoppage. Buchalter and Shapiro found themselves at odds with their boss, and decided it was a good moment to break out on their own. On October 15, 1927, Buchalter, Shapiro, and Holtz piled in a car and swung by Orgen's headquarters at the corner of Norfolk and Delancey Streets and, spying Orgen and Diamond on the sidewalk outside, opened fire. Orgen was killed instantly; Diamond was wounded and retired from the labor field. No witnesses were willing to testify, no charges were ever filed.

Buchalter and Shapiro were now absolute rulers of their feifdom: the ten blocks of the garment district. They were called "the gold dust twins of the underworld" and were always referred to as one unit, usually as "L and G" (for their nicknames Lepke and Gurrah) or simply "the boys." At the height of their power, around 1935, they had substantial influence in the fur, men's garments, women's garments, and baking industries. They made a fortune from dues, assessments, extortion, sweetheart contracts, exclusive buyer and seller arrangements, payroll looting, and outright theft. They even owned several garment companies and made a bit of money legitimately. Buchalter and Shapiro had their hands in several unions and manufacturers' associations, but the key to their power was control of the Five Borough Truckmen's Association, which had a stranglehold on the shipping of garments and components in and out of the garment district. The uninterrupted flow of trucking was essential to every manufacturer, and they paid Buchalter and Shapiro dearly for it.

In 1936, the pair were tried by the federal government for violating the Sherman Antitrust Act and drew sentences of two years. But facing additional, more serious charges from New York Special Prosecuter Thomas Dewey, they jumped bail. A huge manhunt ensued while the pair hid out quietly across the river in Brooklyn. Ailing, Jacob Shapiro surrendered to the authorities on April 14, 1938. Louis Buchalter remained in hiding, systematically eliminating potential witnesses—nine cronies and several innocent bystanders were murdered between August 1938 and November 1939, including Louis Cohen, Kid Dropper's assassin. After taking care of this business, and thinking that a deal had been negotiated on his behalf, Buchalter surrendered to newspaper columnist and radio gossiper Walter Winchell at Madison Avenue and 23rd Street on August 24, 1939. Buchalter was wrong about a deal, and after a series of trials involving drug dealing, labor racketeering, and murder, he was sentenced to death and electrocuted March 4, 1944. Shapiro pleaded guilty to several counts of extortion and was sentenced to fifteen years to life. He died in prison.

The departure of "the boys" changed little in the garment district. Labor racketeering and extortion continued. In 1991, federal charges were brought against Thomas and Joseph Gambino, sons of crime boss Carlo Gambino. They were accused of using their control of the trucking business to extort money from garment-industry contractors, much as Buchalter and Shapiro had done half a century before. In a plea bargain, the brothers agreed to pay a $12 million fine and remove themselves from the business of trucking goods from manufacturers to contractors (though not from manufacturers to retailers).

MUG SHOTS

CHARLES PARKHURST
Reformer

Crusading reformers are in short supply these days: Most people have come to the conclusion that government is beyond rehabilitation. Before such cynicism grew pervasive, however, reform movements played a prominent role in the United States. One of those was the anticorruption and antipolice movement spearheaded by New York's most famous reformer, Rev. Dr. Charles Henry Parkhurst.

In 1880, Parkhurst became the pastor of Madison Square Presbyterian Church, which once stood on the east side of the square on the site now occupied by the Metropolitan Life Insurance Building Tower. For eleven years he was a conventional shepherd, dispensing quiet homilies at sermontime. But in 1891 he became president of the Society for the Prevention of Crime, and perhaps it set him to thinking. On February 14, 1892, he delivered a now-famous sermon, "the echoes of which," according to the *New York Times,* "reverberated throughout the English-speaking world," attacking Tammany Hall and the police department. He was not a man to mince words: He charged that New York was in the hands of ". . . polluted harpies that, under the pretense of governing this city, are feeding day and night on its quivering vitals. They are a lying, perjured, rum-soaked, and libidinous lot." The reverend declared that Mayor Hugh J. Grant, District Attorney De Lancy Nicoll, Tammany Hall, and the police department were linked in an "official and administrative criminality that is filthifying our entire municipal life, making New York a very hotbed of knavery, debauchery and bestiality." Parkhurst was immediately called before a grand jury to substantiate his charges and was forced to admit that he had no proof.

Rebuked, Parkhurst decided to fight back by proving his assertions. He hired a private detective and, along with another parishioner, made a now-celebrated creep through the vile grog shops and loathsome brothels of Sodom. Disguised as scamps, the three visited saloons in the slums by South Street Seaport; whorehouses on West Third Street, including a male brothel known as The Golden Rule Pleasure Club; and dancehalls in the Tenderloin. His slumming produced headlines and, more important for Parkhurst, affidavits for the grand jury, testimony that addressed not principally the existence of these spots, but rather their payoffs to, and protection by, the police. As he later said, "My campaign in New York was not directed against prostitutes or prostitution, against gambling or gamblers, against drunkenness nor drinkers. . . . my whole battle was waged against the hypocrisy and collusion of our city government."

On March 13, Parkhurst was back in church with a sermon that backed up his original charges. This time, the accusations could not be ignored nor the public clamor stilled. Parkhurst's efforts spearheaded the creation of the Lexow committee by the State legislature (see p. 81) and a reform ticket that defeated Tammany's mayoral candidate in 1894. Richard Croker, Tammany's leader, left for Europe and Theodore Roosevelt became head of the city's police force. But the appeal of goodness quickly faded, and in the municipal elections of 1897, Tammany bounced back.

In 1908, Parkhurst resigned as head of the Society for the Prevention of Crime and ten years later retired from his long and watchful post at the Madison Square Presbyterian Church. In 1927, at the age of 85, he married his secretary. He died on September 8, 1933, under unusual circumstances. While sleepwalking, a condition he had suffered all his life, he plunged from a second-story porch roof and was fatally injured.

Continue to Sixth Avenue (Avenue of the Americas), turn right and walk another two blocks to West 27th Street, the center of the vice trade during the heyday of the Tenderloin. Proceed to 107 West 27th Street.

4 *The Gentleman's Companion*, an underground guide to the brothels of New York published in the 1870s, lists the following brothels, and their owners, on 27th Street between Sixth and Seventh Avenues: Mrs. Disbrow, 101; Mrs. Emma Brown, 103; Miss Maggie Pierce, 104; Joe Fisher, 105; Miss Dow, 106; Mrs. Standly, 107; Miss Fanny Harvey, 108; Mrs. Edgarton, 109; (no name listed), 111; Clara Middleton, 119; Mary Dennison, 121; Georgia Allen, 122; Miss Anna Manzoe, 123; Miss Blanchard, 126; Mrs. Lizzie Goodrich, 128; Mrs. Hattie Phillips, 130; Mrs. Kate Heath, 132; Kate Davis, 134; Miss Lou St. Clair, 138; Mrs. Cutler, 140; Mrs. Lucas, 142; and Mrs. Ellis, 146; a grand total of 22 brothels on this block alone.

The only original building remaining is this one at 107. Evidently, the author of *The Gentleman's Companion* didn't think too much of the place, since his only comment is: "The Ladies boarding-house at 107 West 27th St. is kept by Mrs. Standly and is very quiet." Not much of an endorsement, but better than the review received by her next-door neighbor at 109, Joe Fisher's place, of which he warns that "the landlady and her servants are as sour as her wine."

Turn back and walk the two blocks to Fifth Avenue. Pause on the northwest corner.

5 In a city the size of New York it's inevitable that a few people fall through the cracks now and again. Next to Judge Crater (see p. 122), the city's most famous missing-person case is that of Dorothy

Harriet Camille Arnold, a seemingly proper woman from an assuredly rich family living at 108 East 79th Street. On December 12, 1910, the twenty-five-year-old heiress went out shopping, starting from her home and working her way through stores and emporiums until she reached this corner. Here she ran into a friend. They chatted and promised to meet again the next week at the society debut of Dorothy's younger sister. They bid adieu and Dorothy Arnold crossed Fifth Avenue and vanished.

Dorothy Arnold was not an uncontrollable or moody daughter. She was not the type to take off on a whim or a tryst. She lived with her parents, and though she had a secret or two, there was little rebellion. On that December day, she had on a very fashionable fringed skirt, high-button shoes, a waist-length coat, and a silver-fox muff. She wore the latest in haute couture on her head—an oversized black velvet hat called a Baker, decorated by an equally oversized rose. Dorothy Arnold would be hard to miss.

The Arnold family, eager to avoid scandal, kept the disappearance a secret from both press and police for six weeks, drafting private detectives instead. Finally they relented, and on January 22, 1911, New York became aware that Dorothy Arnold was gone.

Upon the news, the city's journalists went burrowing in their tireless fashion and discovered that Arnold had a wild streak, manifested in a discreet affair with a portly forty-year-old from Philadelphia, George Griscom, Jr. Griscom was wintering in Naples, but cabled back that he knew nothing of the disappearance, and made his way quickly back to the States. He was never considered a suspect. Despite a long search and massive publicity, Dorothy Arnold never came home.

Various rumors claim that she died during an abortion, that she fell overboard from a ferryboat, or that her parents had banished their pregnant daughter to Switzerland. Her disappearance remains a complete mystery.

Continuing on Fifth Avenue, walk up to 28th Street and stop in front of 6 West 28th Street.

6 The gaming houses of the Tenderloin were hosts to the golden age of gambling in this country. The costliest, fanciest houses were located here. The best of them were lavishly decorated, served full dinners and expensive wines, and ran a square game. There was John Daly's place at 39 West 29th Street, the leading house in the city from 1885 to 1895. Its food and wine were said to rival Delmonico's, the city's best restaurant. Frank Farrell took an average gambling den at 33 West 33rd Street and turned it, with the help of Stanford White and half a million dollars, into "The House With the Bronze Doors." He

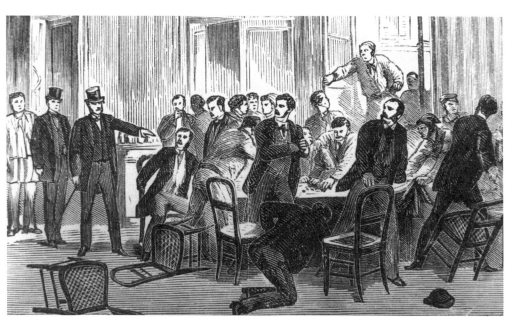

Who forgot the payoff? Bust in a gambling hell.

filled the rooms with European paintings and Persian rugs. The doors came from a doge's palace in Venice.

Then there was Richard Canfield, America's greatest gambler. His establishment at 5 East 44th, opened in 1899, superseded John Morrissey's "818 Broadway" (see p. 46) as the most famous and most luxurious gambling house in the country. Canfield spent a million dollars to refit and furnish the townhouse. The *New York Times* wrote:

> It is the finest place of its kind in this country if not in the world, and the nightly play there is enormous. It draws its patrons from the wealthiest men in the country, and while it is not hard for a man whose appearance denotes a fair measure of affluence to pass its portals, the 'shoe-string gambler' does not long remain its guest.
>
> The entire big brownstone house is fitted throughout with extreme magnificence. The rarest Eastern carpets are upon its floors, and masterpieces of art adorn its walls. The furniture, consisting mainly of divans and davenports, are marvels of beauty and luxuriousness.
>
> Servants throughout the house attend to the wants of the players and the place is conducted much like one of the most exclusive clubs. Entertainment is free to the guests. The costliest dishes—game, pates and the rarest wines—are served throughout the night. Everything is conducted with the utmost decorum. There are no loud words or heated arguments, all being quietly but firmly stopped at their incipiency.

Canfield closed his club on the last day of 1901, fearing the forces of reform that were elected the previous November. A year later it was raided by the famous crusading district attorney William Travers Jerome, who found some gambling paraphernalia stored in a secret room. Canfield was arrested and eventually forced to pay the stern penalty of $1,000.

The building at 6 West 28th Street once housed the well-known and high-class gambling club of Thomas Darden and Willard Fitzgerald and stood on a street thick with such dens. Darden was a Washington banker who found that his money circulated a little faster in a gambling house than in a bank. He went into business with gambler Fitzgerald in this building around 1890 and for a time it was one of the top clubs in the city. Fitzgerald died in 1894 and Darden retired the next year. The place was later run by the notorious Shang Draper, whom we shall run into later on in this tour. The building of another well-known gambling house survives, that of William "Dink" Davis, at 57 West 28th Street.

Continuing on West 28th, proceed to Broadway and pause on the corner of West 29th Street.

7 An obscure but interesting affair, the Walworth parricide, occurred here at the southeast corner of Broadway and West 29th Street in 1873, when the site was occupied by the Sturtevant House.

Mansfield Walworth was a novelist of little note or success. His most popular book, the now-forgotten *Warwick*, published in 1869. His lack of literary success seemed to addle him, and he began to write threatening letters to his ex-wife in Saratoga about visitation rights and money: "Prepare yourself for the inevitable. . . . two pistol shots will ring about your house—one slaying you, the other, myself."

Frank H. Walworth was, by all accounts, a sober and dutiful son, much attached to his mother. On June 2, 1873, he came into the city and checked into the Sturtevant House here. He sent a note to his father to come see him in his hotel room to discuss family matters, and the senior Walworth complied the following morning. A few moments later, four shots rang out. Mansfield Walworth had been shot twice in the breast, once in the arm, and once in the face. He died within minutes. Frank Walworth walked calmly down to the front desk and announced, "I have shot my father." He later made a statement in which he said that, "I told him that there were bounds which I would not allow any man to go beyond with impunity, especially when my mother was being insulted," but also claimed he fired in self defense.

The jury took four hours to find the younger Walworth guilty of murder in the second degree. He was sentenced to life in prison.

Walk on West 29th Street to Sixth Avenue. Just to your left, at 822 Sixth
Avenue (then 466) was the saloon of Tom "Shang" Draper.

8 There were many well-known rogues prowling the streets, bars,
brothels, and gambling halls of the Tenderloin in its prime. Among
the most notorious members of the criminal underworld of the time
were Westley Allen (called by Chief of Detectives Thomas Byrnes
"the most notorious criminal in America"); Ned Lyons (admired by
fellow thief Eddie Guerin as "one of the greatest burglars and bank
robbers ever known in America") and his wife, the con artist Sophie
Lyon; William Sharkey (dubbed by Police Chief George Walling
"one of the biggest rascals in New York"); Max Shinburn, who retired to Europe and bought the title of Baron of Monaco on his proceeds from bank burglaries; John "Red" Leary, who pulled off a
celebrated escape from the Ludlow Street Jail; Joseph Lewis, alias
"Hungry Joe," who swindled Oscar Wilde when the writer was visiting the city; and "Little Joe" Elliot, forger and bank robber. These
were familiar names to the New Yorkers of the last few decades of the
nineteenth century.

One of the most famous of the lot was Tom "Shang" Draper,
thief, gambler, and barkeep. Eddie Guerin recalled that he was
". . . notorious throughout America as the king of New York's underworld." He was a member of the George Leonidas Leslie gang—
according to Chief of Detectives Byrnes "one of the strongest bands
of burglars and thieves that ever existed"—and helped to pull off
their robbery of the Manhattan Savings Institution, the largest haul
of its day (see pp. 33). In the 1880s Draper gave up the risky business of bank robbery and established a saloon and gambling hall here
at 822 (then 466) Sixth Avenue. Later on, as his prominence and
capital grew, he bought several gambling houses, including the one
you just passed at 6 West 28th Street.

His saloon on Sixth Avenue was the sight of a famous and fatal
shootout on October 16, 1883. A thieves' quarrel over the division
of booty had fomented a murderous hatred between bank burglars
John "Johnnie the Mick" Walsh and John Irving (not the John T.
Irving who falsely confessed to the Nathan murder; see pp. 159). On
the night of the 16th, long after closing time, Walsh sat drinking
here in Draper's saloon with some underworld cronies. The lights
were low and the place was deserted except for this surly crew. Suddenly, they heard the sidedoor creak and turned to see Irving creep-
ing in with a revolver at the ready. Irving raised his pistol, fired a
bullet into Walsh's chest, and then dashed inside the saloon to a bil-
liard room in the back. Though wounded, Walsh jumped after his assailant and got off a shot that hit Irving squarely in the heart, killing

Shootout victim John Walsh.

him instantly. But the carnage was not over. Into the fray dove William O'Brien, alias Billy Porter, a safe cracker and confederate of Irving. He shot Walsh in the head, mortally wounding him. With two men sprawled on the bloody floor, Porter ran out of the saloon and directly into the hands of a policeman.

Defended by the ubiquitous Abe Hummel of Howe & Hummel fame, Porter was acquitted of the murder of Walsh. Shang Draper happened to be eating oysters next door with Red Leary. He didn't see a thing.

Continue up to West 30th Street, turn right and head to Broadway again. Just to the right of the corner of Broadway and West 30th, 1217 Broadway once stood on a site now occupied by 1225 Broadway.

9 Another famous barroom shootout, with a different cast of Tenderloin toughs, took place here, once Dick Darling's saloon. This is where Charles P. Miller, "king of the bunco men," was assassinated in 1881.

Miller was a suave and popular underworld character. Police Chief Walling, in his memoirs, describes him with admiration:

> In person he was slim, fair, polished, agreeable and one of the best conversationalists that ever frequented the first-class resorts of the Twenty-ninth Precinct. He was invariably well-dressed, clean-shaven and good-looking, liberal to a fault, slow in making confidential friends, equally slow in making enemies. . . . It is within reason to say that he had a shake-hands acquaintance with a thousand men who

never dreamed he was a rascal. He knew every police officer by sight, at least, every politician, every man and nearly every woman about town. He lived like one of the "gilded youths" of Uppertendom, disdaining whiskey, strong drinks and cheap cigars, and taking his meals in none other than first-class restaurants.

One enemy he did make was Billy Tracy, a thief and forger who owned a saloon at 33 West 29th Street. The enmity between the two had led to an earlier shooting in Tracy's bar, when Miller wounded the saloonkeeper. On November 7, 1881, Miller was sitting at a table in the saloon here, exercising his conversational skills with a number of friends. Tracy entered, walked to the bar, and ordered a whiskey. He then turned to Miller (after, no doubt, dramatically emptying his glass in one go and slamming the shot glass on the bar) and snarled, "I came in here to kill you!" He produced a revolver and shot Miller once in the stomach. The wounded man fell to the floor unconscious and died soon after.

Like Porter in the Walsh shooting, Tracy was acquitted of murder. He went back to the sawdust and spittoons of his saloon.

Walk a block up Broadway and cross the street to the southeast corner of West 31st Street. The corner building was once the Grand Hotel, built in 1869 and one of the preeminent hostelries during its day.

10 New York has always drawn the talented and creative from the home-towns of America, idealistic youths yearning for success in the culture capital of the country. Dolly Reynolds, an aspiring actress, was apparently neither talented nor creative, but she came nevertheless. And though her charms proved insufficient for the stage, they were ample enough to achieve some success in the big city: a rich and generous lover. Her sugar daddy was Maurice B. Mendham, a financial broker from Long Branch, Long Island, who set her up in a eight-room apartment on West 58th Street and showered her with expensive jewelry.

On August 15, 1898, around noon, Dolly Reynolds checked into the Grand Hotel, registering as "E. Maxwell & wife, Brooklyn." At half past five, she returned to the hotel with the pseudonymous Mr. Maxwell and the couple proceeded to Room 84 on the fourth floor. The hotel staff described Reynolds' companion as a handsome man, just under medium height, with dark hair and a dark mustache. At 7:00 that evening the couple went out; at 11:30 they returned. The desk clerk saw "Mr. Maxwell" once more, walking through the lobby, alone, sometime between 2:00 and 2:30 in the morning. He had come down by the stairs, not by the elevator, and departed through the front door. He did not return.

Dolly Reynolds was discovered dead the next morning. Her head had been crushed by an iron pipe curiously amended: one end had been folded down to form a cudgel and tape had been wrapped around the other.

A handbag nearby had been sliced open and was empty of money (this is interesting since the knife used to cut the purse would presumably have made a more efficient murder weapon than the lead pipe). Reynolds' diamond ring and earrings, gifts of Mendham, had been wrenched from her body. It was later discovered that, perhaps not incidentally, there was another robbery in the hotel on the same floor the same night.

An odd clue was discovered. Tucked beneath Reynolds' corset was a $13,000 check from the Garfield National Bank made out to her by Dudley Gideon and endorsed on the back by S. J. Kennedy. The check turned out to be worthless: there was no Dudley Gideon. But there was a Dr. Samuel J. Kennedy. He was a dentist with offices on West 22nd Street, and Reynolds was his patient. Since the first obvious suspect, Mendham, produced a rock-ribbed alibi, Kennedy was arrested and eventually put on trial for her murder.

The state claimed that Kennedy was having an affair with Reynolds and dispatched her before she found that his gift of a $13,000 check was phony. Reynolds' mother told the court that her daughter had been home in Mount Vernon the day before her murder and mentioned her dentist. She said that Kennedy had offered to put a $500 bet on a horse that was a sure winner. The trusting Reynolds drew out the sum from her account, telling her mother she would hand it over to Kennedy at their next meeting, 6:00 P.M. on August 15. This story is particularly intriguing because, although there was no Dudley Gideon doing business at the Garfield National Bank, there was among the bank's customers a David Gideon, a well-known horse player and gambler. Could Reynolds have hit a 26-1 longshot?

The check business is puzzling. If Kennedy was the murderer, why would he put his signature on the check? Would he take $500 from her and immediately give her a check for $13,000? And what was the point of a check she would soon find out was worthless? The prosecution claimed that Kennedy had written the check the week before to entice Reynolds to give him the money for the horseracing scheme. That night he demanded it back, and when she refused, he killed her in a vain attempt to reclaim it.

In court, Kennedy, handsome, darkhaired and mustachioed—much like, take note, the mysterious Mr. Maxwell—replied that he had met Reynolds only at his office, that the signature on the back of the check was a forgery, and that someone was impersonating him. He said that on the night Reynolds was trysting with Mr.

Maxwell, he had been by himself at Proctor's Theater on 23rd Street watching vaudeville. He afterwards took a streetcar to the Battery and embarked on the 12:25 A.M. Staten Island ferry on his way home to New Dorp. He produced several witnesses to corroborate his version, including his parents, who claimed they saw their child in bed asleep at 3:00 A.M. (the quickest trip between the Grand Hotel and New Dorp would have taken two hours). Kennedy's wife and child, who lived in the same house with the in-laws, were—conveniently, if one suspects Kennedy—vacationing in Maine.

The jury found Kennedy guilty in eight hours, but a new trial was ordered when it became clear that the police had fabricated some evidence. A second and a third trial ended in deadlocks. After seven years (three of which Kennedy had spent in prison) the charges were dropped. No one else was ever indicted, and the murder of Dolly Reynolds remains a mystery.

Continue up Broadway to West 34th Street and Herald Square. On the other side of the intersection, at 116 West 34th Street, opposite Macy's, once stood the Herald Square Hotel.

11 In 1907 Ida E. W. Wood checked into suite 551–52 of the Herald Square Hotel and did not emerge for twenty-five years. In early 1931, when she was ninety-three years old, debilitation forced her out of seclusion, and from that time until her death on March 11, 1932, she became known in New York newspapers as "The Recluse of Herald Square." Reporters and readers delighted in stories of her eccentric life in the hotel, her rediscovered past as a society belle in postbellum New York, and, especially, the size and fate of her large fortune. As a mere recluse Wood would not merit mention in a book of crime, but she earns inclusion as one of America's greatest impostors.

During and just after the Civil War, Wood was a member of the city's elite. She was known in society circles as the rich daughter of Thomas Henry Mayfield, prominent sugar planter of Louisiana. In 1867 she married Benjamin Wood, a state senator and U.S. congressman, publisher of the *New York Daily News*, one of the city's major papers (unrelated to the present paper of the same name), and the brother of Fernando Wood, twice the mayor of the city. She met President Lincoln, danced with the Prince of Wales during his visit to the city in 1860, and became editor-in-chief and publisher of the *Daily News* upon her husband's death. Intelligent, poised, and successful, she was, to all appearances, an example of the best of high society.

But the well-bred Ida E. W. Mayfield Wood was a fiction, the creation of a poor young Irish maid, Ellen Walsh from Massachusetts. She was able to come to New York, create a new identity out of whole cloth, marry into the top echelon of the power elite, and fool the most educated and sophisticated slice of the big city. Not only that, but she brought along her mother, brother, and two sisters, one of whom she camouflaged as her daughter. They were, for all of New York, the charming southern Mayfield family, their Boston Irish accents somehow muted, transformed, or passed off as southern lilts. Wood/Walsh played this charade perfectly from the time of her arrival in New York in 1857 as a 19-year-old domestic until her death, and parlayed her deception into a fortune of over a million dollars. After the death of Benjamin Wood in 1900 (who probably knew at least part of Wood's real past), Wood gradually withdrew from public life. Seven years later, she took rooms with her two sisters in the Herald Square Hotel, and there, amid growing piles of clutter and dust, spent the rest of her life. Necessities were brought up by the elevator operator and passed quickly through the doorway. Food was cooked on a small electric burner. Her youngest sister Emma died in 1928 and her other sibling, Mary, passed away in 1931.

The true identity of Wood came to light only after her death the following year during tireless research necessitated by the execution of her will.

Now turn your attention to the famous Macy's.

12 New Yorkers love to hate Con Edison, the huge, unfriendly electrical utility. None, however, have become quite so consumed as George Metesky. His gripe against Con Ed turned into an explosive vendetta that panicked the city for years.

On July 24, 1956, a small bomb exploded in a telephone booth here in the world's largest department store. A terse article in the *New York Times* noted that "similar explosions have occurred in dozens of public places here in recent years." The explosion was an early rumbling of what was soon to become a wave of bombings and panic in the city. Before it was over, some thirty-seven bombs would go off without warning around the city, the work of the terrifying "Mad Bomber."

The first explosive device traced to the bomber had been found—unexploded—years earlier in a Con Ed building on West 64th Street. Through the early '50s he was hard at work, planting three or four bombs a year, but the police released little information and the press did not connect the incidents. By 1956, however, the year of the Macy's episode, the explosions were becoming more frequent, the devices were getting larger and more powerful, and the bomber was becoming more brazen. Explosions rocked Grand Central Station, Penn Station, Port Authority, Radio City Music Hall, Con Ed buildings, theaters. At the same time, the bomber, a prolific letter writer, was dashing off communiqués to the press, accusing Con Edison of "dastardly deeds" and "ghoulish acts" and swearing revenge on the utility. They were neatly written in capital letters, with an odd telegraphic manner. A typical one read, in part:

> THESE BOMBINGS WILL CONTINUE UNTIL CON EDISON IS BROUGHT
> TO JUSTICE—MY LIFE IS DEDICATED TO THIS TASK—EXPECT NO CALLS
> ABOUT BOMBS IN THEATERS AS YOUR ACTIONS—NO LONGER
> WARRANT THE EFFORT OR DIME—ALL MY SUFFERINGS—ALL MY
> FINANCIAL LOSS—WILL HAVE TO BE PAID IN FULL.

No one had yet been killed, but it seemed only a matter of time. The city was terrified. (And adding to the panic was an epidemic of copycat callers and pranksters.) When the Macy's bomb blew up, reporters could refer only vaguely to "the mysterious 'bomb terrorist.'" But a sensation like this demanded a lively tabloid label, and the press soon delivered with the accurate, if unimaginative, moniker, "The Mad Bomber."

While the public fretted about some berserk, salivating Tom o' Bedlam, the truth was more surprising. The Mad Bomber was an otherwise mild and polite man named George Metesky. Later, after he was nabbed, the *New York Times* would write that he looked like "the man who passes the collection plate in a small-town church." A bachelor, he was cared for by his two spinster sisters in a modest house in Waterbury, Connecticut. He went to church regularly, never drank, and was neat in appearance. Unfortunately, he was also a delusional paranoiac with a dangerously sophisticated knowledge of bombmaking.

On September 5, 1931, while employed as a generator wiper for the United Electric & Power Company (a firm that later merged with Con Ed), a backdraft of hot gas from a boiler knocked Metesky down. He complained of headaches and promptly went home. But the company doctors could find no physical symptoms, and after several months' absence, he was dropped from the payroll. He later claimed that the accident had given him tuberculosis and asked for compensation, but the company denied responsibility. This was the injustice that sparked Metesky's long, hateful obsession with the utility.

After a lengthy search through thousands of old and dog-eared company claims files, Metesky's case came to light. A secretary going through the old folders at the behest of the police came across a claim form with the term "dastardly deeds." She recalled it as one of the Mad Bomber's pet phrases. She read on, and the language throughout the case file seemed to echo the bomber's writing style and inflections. And his description seemed to fit a psychological profile that had been drawn up for the police. The identification was clinched when The Mad Bomber dropped the date of his accident in a letter to the press: it was the same date as the accident in Metesky's file.

When arrested on September 21, 1957, Metesky freely and proudly admitted to the bombings. Obviously insane, he was sentenced to Matteawan State Hospital. Released in 1973 after seventeen years, he went home to Waterbury, Connecticut. When asked how he felt about Con Edison, he merely replied, "I think it's best not to talk about that just now."

MUG SHOTS

MABEL PARKER
Master Forger

A wave of check forgeries that had been plaguing the city in the summer of 1903 seemed to end with the arrest of James Parker. He was nabbed when he tried to pick up a suit that he had paid for with a forged check and was sent to the Tombs for arraignment. It soon became apparent, however, that Parker (whose real name was James Singerly) was only the utterer, that is, the person presenting a forgery, and not the penman himself. In the hope of finding his coworkers, a plainclothes detective trailed a young woman who had visited Parker in the Tombs. She turned out to be Mabel Parker, the inmate's young wife.

The detective, impersonating a burglar and reform-school friend of her husband, eventually obtained Parker's confidence. To his surprise, she revealed that she was the forger, and to prove it, took out a sheet of paper and began to copy, freehand, his signature and several others. Her hand was steady and expert—Mabel Parker was a natural. The detective later said admiringly, "She's the most wonderful person with a pen I've ever seen. She's turned out forgeries that positively cannot be told from the originals. She wrote my name for me so that I positively couldn't tell it from my own signature."

Mabel Parker was raised by foster parents in Minneapolis, but proved unruly as a teenager and was trundled off to a convent close to New York. She later claimed that she was intent on taking vows until Singerly wooed her away. They were married on June 28, 1899 at the "Little Church Around the Corner," the Manhattan landmark at 1 East 29th Street, and went to live a very secular life together at 110 West 38th Street in the Tenderloin. James Singerly was a professional crook from Pittsburgh and it was not long before he brought his wife into the criminal fold.

The detective immediately confiscated the page and arrested Parker. At her trial, she dressed demurely and said shyly that she had signed her name to a page already full of forged signatures. Her gallant husband went on the stand and claimed that he was the forger and that his wife knew nothing of his criminal activities. The jury was unable to reach an agreement. During the entire trial, in full view of the jury, she sat at the defense table copying signatures for the newspaper reporters sitting behind her!

A second trial ensued, and again, despite strong evidence, the jury could not bring itself to convict Parker for forgery (perhaps all that time among the nuns had given her an angelic glow). They had to do something with all the evidence, however, so they convicted her of uttering, appending an appeal for mercy. She was sentenced to the Bedford Hills Correctional Facility. Her husband, in addition to being found guilty of forgery, had to bear the censure of enticing his pure bride into a life of crime. He was sentenced to ten years in Sing Sing.

Continue up to the northeast corner of Sixth Avenue and West 36th Street.

13 Sixty-nine West 36th Street no longer exists, having been swallowed and digested by the large and ugly building occupying this end of the block. It stood approximately at the entrance of the parking garage to your right. The address is a landmark in American criminal history: it was once Henry's Restaurant, where on a summer day in 1925, Ruth Snyder and Henry Judd Gray met for the first time and kicked off one of the country's most famous murder cases.

After that meeting, the pair pounced into a torrid and adulterous affair. After two years of secret rendezvous, they hatched a plan to dispense with Snyder's husband, a distracted magazine editor who ignored his wife. Later, during the trial, each blamed the other for coming up with the idea and delivering the death blows. In all likelihood, Snyder was the instigator: she was the dominant partner in the relationship (Gray called her "Momsie"), had taken out two large life insurance policies in her husband's name, and evidently had tried to poison him on six or seven previous occasions.

After careful preparation, the night of March 19, 1927 was chosen. Gray was in Syracuse selling corsets, but, after arranging an inept alibi (he asked a friend to rumple his hotel bed and hang a "Do Not Disturb" sign on the doorknob), he took a train to Grand Central and then a bus out to the Snyder home in Queen's Village. He arrived at about 10:30 PM. The house was empty; he entered through a side door that Snyder had left open. He found, under a pillow, several utensils his lover had left: a sash weight, chloroform, and, to keep up his pluck, a bottle of bootleg whiskey. Gray hid in a bedroom and waited for his lover and her husband to return from a party.

Mr. Snyder was beaten with the sash weight, smothered with a pillow soaked in chloroform, suffocated with cotton stuffed in his mouth, and strangled with curtain wire. Who did what was the subject of later disagreement between the two. Their efforts were quickly confessed to under police questioning, and their bonds of love soon clipped by the law. In court, she said:

> I tried to plead with him . . . to change his mind. Then I went upstairs to the bathroom. I had been there five or ten minutes when I heard this terrific thud. I immediately opened the bathroom door and ran down the hall and I saw Mr. Gray leaning over my husband. I ran in and I grabbed Mr. Gray by the neck . . . he pushed me to the floor and I fainted and remembered nothing until I came to and saw my husband all piled up with blankets and blood all over the place.

He said:

> She took me by the hand and we went into the hall; the door of her husband's room was closed. She opened the door and I followed her. I don't know how long I stood there trying to get my bearings and I struck him on the head, just one blow. He got me by the necktie and I hollered, Momsie, Momsie, for God's sake, help me! I had dropped the weight and she picked it up and hit him on the head . . . the next thing I remember was being upright on the floor again.

The jury believed them both and brought in verdicts of guilty of first degree murder. They were executed in the electric chair at Sing Sing prison on January 12, 1928.

ALSO INFAMOUS

Belly dancer Little Egypt, perhaps the country's first sex symbol, gained nationwide notoriety by dancing naked—or at least in very suggestive veils—at an infamous society stag party give by Herbert Barnum Seeley in 1895. Legend maintains that she introduced the hoochy-koochy dance at the World's Columbian Exposition in Chicago in 1893, but there's no proof that she was, in fact, ever there. On January 5, 1908, Catherine Devine, a.k.a. Little Egypt, having descended from dancing to prostitution for her keep, was found strangled to death in her bed in a cheap flat at 226 West 37th Street. She was apparently killed by a customer, but there were no suspects nor arrests. The siren, once so fervently desired, had lain forgotten for at least two days.

Continue to West 40th Street and take a right. Walk to the middle of the block on the south side to 32 West 40th Street.

14 "In the spring of 1891 there occurred one of the most distressing criminal tragedies that ever aroused the sympathy of the people of

New York, or indeed, of the entire country," wrote District Attorney Francis Wellman not long after. "Indeed," he continued, "it would have been hard to find a man or woman at the time who was not more or less familiar with some of the details, or who had not formed some opinion or impression as to the guilt or innocence of the defendant."

That defendant was Carlyle W. Harris, accused of poisoning Mary Helen Neilson Potts, a nineteen-year-old woman who attended the Comstock School for Young Ladies in a building here that preceded the present structure. Wellman was the prosecuting attorney.

On the night of January 31, 1891, Potts was found by schoolmates nearly comatose in her bed. "I've had a wonderful dream," she said, "but please watch over me, as I think I am going to die. I never felt like this before. Carl said I could take one of those pills for twelve nights in succession. He said he had taken them himself. If anybody but Carl had given them to me I would think I was going to die, but of course Carl would not give me anything but what was right." This long-winded soliloquy, which delivers Harris to the electric chair on a silver platter, sounds a tad overdone. Another version, which rings truer, has her saying merely, "I feel numb all over. I feel so queer. I wish you would come and see what's the matter with me."

Nevertheless, whether her sleep was wonderful or uncomfortable, it was deep, and when she could not be roused from slumber, the students called in the school's doctor. He found a patient with the classic symptoms of morphine poisoning: lack of muscle control, extremely shallow breathing (twice a minute), a body pale and bathed in perspiration, and a contraction of both pupils to pinpoints. Despite the efforts of the school doctor and several others, Potts died the next morning.

In the somber room the doctor found an empty box with the inscription "C. W. H.—One before retiring." The initials were those of Harris, of course, and he was sent for. The young man, a medical student, admitted prescribing six headache capsules for her, each of four and a half grains of quinine and one sixth of a grain of morphine, and having them made up at a local druggist's store. He had ordered six, but given Potts only four. He later produced the two remaining capsules, both of which contained the correct ratio of quinine to morphine.

The doctor assumed that some mistake had been made by the druggist or by the patient, and listed the death as an accidental poisoning.

But Potts's mother had a different opinion from the doctor's, and she knew Harris better. She had first met him eighteen months earlier, in 1889, when he began to court her daughter. Harris was at that time a twenty-two-year-old finishing his first year at the College

of Physicians and Surgeons on 23rd Street. Though slight, with a
thin mustache and glasses, he was self-assured, suave, and intelligent,
and Helen Potts was smitten. The mother did not like this suitor and
tried to end the romance, but the rebellious young couple were secretly married in City Hall under false names. It appears in retrospect
that the groom's primary motivation was to get Potts in the sack.
During the trial rumors arose that he had married two other women
under similar circumstances, and that he had bragged to friends of
this successful seduction technique. It seemed to work with Potts,
for four months later, the first-year medical student attempted to
perform an abortion on his wife. He failed, and she went to stay with
an uncle who was a doctor to recover and was delivered of a stillborn
fetus. It was after this ghastly episode that Mrs. Potts learned of the
secret marriage, and needless to say, her opinion of Harris was not
improved by it. Still, if the couple were married, the mother at least
wanted things proper, public, and Christian. But Harris stalled again
and again at announcing their union—at the trial the prosecution
claimed that a public marriage would cut him off from a grandfather's inheritance. Finally, Mrs. Harris laid down an ultimatum:
Harris must publicly wed her daughter by February 8, 1891, the first
anniversary of their surreptitious vows. The day he received this demand, he had a druggist fill out a prescription for six capsules.

Helen Potts was buried quietly and no doubt would have
moldered quietly without the persistence of her mother. Unsatisfied
with the lack of an investigation, she went to the *New York World*
with her suspicions. The resulting press attention forced an investigation and an indictment against Harris for murder. The trail began
on January 15, 1892.

The prosecution maintained that Potts had died after ingesting a
doctored capsule containing 3–5 grains of morphine. The motive
was Harris's fear of the imminent disclosure of his marriage. The
morphine he had obtained at school, when Professor George
Peabody gave a timely lecture in early January on the toxicology and
pharmacology of morphine and had passed around samples. Peabody
later testified at the trial to the presence of morphine in Potts's body,
thereby both opening and closing the last chapter in Harris's life.

The prosecution tried to maintain that the young woman's symptoms were compatible with kidney disease or uremic poisoning,
though they couldn't quite explain away the contraction of her
pupils, an invariable accompaniment to morphine overdose. The two
capsules that Harris had kept, with an idea that their untampered
state would prove an alibi, actually hurt him, since they showed that
the druggist had prepared the prescription correctly. The jury took
only two hours to find the defendant guilty. An appeal was denied,
as was a petition sent to the governor, signed by 60,000 people, for

a pardon. Harris was executed on May 8, 1893. His last words were, "I can have no motive for concealment now. I die absolutely innocent of the crime of which I have been convicted."

Double back to Sixth Avenue and continue to 42nd Street. Just to your left, on the north side of the street, at 113 West 42nd Street (now a pornographic bookstore), the Murray Hill Turkish Baths once stood.

15 In late June of 1897, news wire reporter Joseph Gavan went to the Baths for his weekly rubdown. But his regular masseur, William Guldensuppe, was not there. "Where's Billy?" he asked. "He got a day off on Friday to go with some skirt to Long Island and we haven't seen him since," a coworker answered. "I guess he'll be back to work tomorrow or the next day."

Gavan was disappointed. He had been looking forward to a good rub; he was working long and hard on a case making huge headlines in the city's papers. Diverse parts of a man's body, carefully dissected and wrapped in oilcloth, had been turning up in the past week. An upper torso was found bobbing in the East River. The lower portion was uncovered in Highbridge. In Brooklyn, by the Navy Yard, a pair of legs were discovered. All were wrapped up in the same distinctive red and gold material. The lack of a head fueled the mystery.

William Randolph Hearst had just brought his yellow journalism techniques to New York with the purchase of the *New York Journal,* and was now engaged in a furious circulation war with the *New York World.* The mystery of the headless torso became fodder for the battle, and was making the front pages of several tabloids with speculation, misinformation, and falsehoods. Gavan, upon hearing of the unusual disappearance of his favorite masseur, shared his suspicions with a policeman friend. By the next day, the corpse was identified as Guldensuppe's.

Detectives learned that Guldensuppe had lived for the past eighteen months with Augusta Nack, a stout German midwife who had abandoned her husband to shack up with the masseur at 439 Ninth Avenue. Of late, however, the fierce ardor had cooled somewhat, at least on Nack's part, since a new boarder, Martin Thorn, had moved into a room in their home. Guldensuppe and Thorn found themselves rivals for the affections of their flatmate.

At the same time that the macabre packages were appearing, Long Island police discovered an empty house in Woodside, Queens that showed clear signs of foul play. The walls of the bathroom were streaked with blood, and a drainage ditch in the back yard was full of red water. The couple who rented the cottage fit the description of Nack and Thorn. A trail of evidence began to surface. A telegram from Guldensuppe to Nack, telling her to inform his supervisor at the Murray Hill Turkish Baths that he would not soon return to work, turned out to be written in Thorn's hand. A stable owner identified Nack as the woman to whom he had rented a horse and carriage on June 28, the day before bits of Guldensuppe began to show up, and Thorn as the man who had returned them. A shopkeeper was found in Long Island who remembered selling the red and gold cloth to a woman fitting Nack's description. Augusta Nack was taken into custody; Thorn went on the lam.

In July, amidst a huge manhunt, Thorn secretly made contact with a friend to whom he revealed the grisly truth. Nack had no hand in actually dispatching Guldensuppe, he said, but she had lured the victim to the Woodside cottage. Thorn continued:

> I went to the cottage early on Friday, June 28, bringing with me my revolver, razor, stiletto and a saw. . . . It was in [a] clothes closet I was hidden. It was also on this upstairs floor that the bathroom was located. When Guldensuppe opened the closet, I fired my revolver just as he caught sight of me. The bullet entered his skull next to the right temple and down he went. I then ran downstairs and said to Mrs. Nack:
>
> "It is done!"
>
> "I know it is," she said, "because I heard the shot."
>
> I then told Mrs. Nack to beat it to New York and to return at five o'clock when the body would be ready for removal. She did. I returned to Guldensuppe and heard the death rattle in his throat. He was still breathing. A stab of my stiletto through his back soon croaked him.
>
> Before Mrs. Nack returned from New York, I had stripped the body of all the clothes, bought five pounds of plaster of Paris from a grocer in Woodside and threw the body into the bathtub where I cut off the head with my razor and the legs with my razor and saw. When the plaster of Paris was moistened, I inclosed the head in it and wrapped the other parts of the body in an oilcloth which Mrs. Nack had purchased from a woman in Dutch Hills.
>
> When Mrs. Nack showed up a five o'clock everything was ready for a getaway, but we decided to leave the bundles containing the body in the house until the following morning which was Saturday. It was then that we took the upper part of the body over to Greenpoint. We crossed over to New York on the Tenth Street ferry. We stood on the stern of the boat and when the passengers and the deckhands had gone forward as the boat entered her slip on the New York side, I threw the bundle overboard. Later I carried the head in my lap on a street car and threw it into the river."

When Thorn set up another meeting with his friend, the latter, fearing he would be killed, notified the police and Thorn was captured at their rendezvous.

He did not repeat this confession at his trial. Despite a valiant effort by defense attorney William Howe that sought to cast doubt not only on the identity of the torso but also on the very existence of Guldensuppe (during the trial Howe referred to the deceased as Gildersleeve, Goldensoup, Gludensop, Goldielocks, Silverslippers, and "a creature as imaginary as Rosencrantz's friend Gildenstern"), Thorn was convicted. He was strapped into the electric chair on August 1, 1898. Nack pleaded guilty to first degree manslaughter and was sentenced to ten years. When she was released it is said that she returned to Ninth Avenue and opened a delicatessen.

Walk a little farther down the block, and look across the street to 140 West 42nd Street.

16 The murder of Jane Lawrence De Forest Hull by Chastine Cox was, although a completely forgotten crime today, once, "the talk of all America for months," according to police historian Augustine Costello. It received widespread coverage in the newspapers and magazines of the day, in which it was compared to the Nathan murder mystery.

Hull came from a prominent family but was known for more than her pedigree: a contemporary account of the case says she "was a lady noted, not only for her great beauty, but also her magnificent form." That was not enough to pay the bills, however, and in middle age Hull had been forced to rent out rooms in her mansion here at 140 West 42nd Street.

On June 11, 1879, Hull was found dead in her bedroom, tied to her bed with a sheet stuffed in her mouth, upon which she had suffocated. A few items of jewelry were missing, but many more valuable pieces were untouched. There was no sign of forced entry.

Initially, police suspected the victim's husband, Dr. Alonzo Grandison Hull, of the crime. In addition to the peculiar circumstances just mentioned, he seemed to exhibit little emotion or even concern over his wife's violent death. But several days later, some of her jewelry was discovered pawned in Boston, and the police matched the description of the pawner to Chastine Cox, at one time a servant in the Hull boarding house. A week later Cox was spotted praying in a church in Boston and, called outside, was arrested and sent back to New York.

Cox initially confessed that, while burgling the house, he had been discovered by Hull. He overpowered her, tied her to the bed, and gagged her to keep her from crying out. Cox was tried, found guilty, and sentenced to death. He then gave a second and more truthful account. He and Hull were actually longtime lovers and he often spent the night with her in the boardinghouse. In fact, she had given him the keys to the house and her apartment. On the night of June 10, he had let himself in as usual. Cox recently had been gambling heavily and losing, and he asked Hull for some money. When she refused, he took some jewelry from her dressing table and told her he would pawn them and bring her the tickets. She tried to grab her valuables back, a struggle ensued, and, as he related in his first confession, he tied her up to silence her. He did not, he said, intend to kill her. Cox was hanged in the Tombs on July 16, 1880.

Return to Sixth Avenue and turn left. Go two blocks up to West 44th Street, turn right and walk to the Hotel Iroquois, at 49 West 44th Street.

17 This was the scene of the murder of William Henry Jackson, a septuagenarian broker found brutally beaten in his suite on the tenth floor on July 27, 1911. A bottle of chloroform was discovered on the bathroom floor and soon traced to seventeen-year-old Paul Geidel, who had worked as a bellboy in the hotel but been discharged a few weeks before. He had sneaked back into the Iroquois to rob Jackson, but had botched the chloroforming and instead beaten the man to death. The teenager made away with $7, a gold watch, and a pair of cufflinks. Geidel was convicted of second-degree murder and sentenced to twenty years to life. A thoroughly sordid crime, but notable in one respect: Geidel, entering prison at the age of seventeen, did not emerge again until the age of eighty-five, earning him a place in the Guinness Book of World Records for the longest prison sentence ever served: sixty-eight years, eight months, and two days. He enjoyed seven years of freedom before he died in 1987.

Head back to Sixth Avenue and walk another block up to West 45th Street. Just off of the southwest corner, on a spot now taken over by the big black skyscraper at 1155 Sixth Avenue, stood, in 1912, a brownstone that held the home and gambling den of Herman Rosenthal. (104 West 45th Street, Rosenthal's address, is gone, but row houses much like his are still standing, though altered, at 133 and 135 West 45th Street.)

18 Without benefit of a love triangle, celebrity stars, or even deviant sex, the Becker-Rosenthal case has managed to become one of New York's most famous criminal incidents. The affair was an obsession for years, and appeared almost daily in city papers during its three-year course, often on the front page. The Becker-Rosenthal case helped elect a governor and sent five people to the electric chair.

"I am signing my own death warrant,"
Herman Rosenthal.

1912 had been a bad year for gambler Herman Rosenthal. He was once a protégé of Tammany kingpin Big Tim Sullivan and the owner of several casinos, but by that year his empire had contracted to one modest gambling house at 104 West 45th Street. By April, even that was gone: the place had been raided, the equipment destroyed, and a twenty-four-hour police guard posted inside to prevent reopening. The raid was ordered by Lt. Charles Becker, head of the police department's Special Squad 1, which was charged with breaking up gambling in the city. The raid so incensed Rosenthal that he decided to make public a little secret he knew about Becker, and on July 14, a long front page story in the muckraking *New York World* featured his bombshell: Becker was a grafter and a thief whose raids on gambling houses were fakes carried out to please his superiors; far from ridding the city of gambling, Becker promoted it, taking his cut in profits, payoffs, and protection money; Becker was actually a partner in Rosenthal's gambling house; he fronted the gambler $1,500 and took a twenty percent cut of the profits. The charges swept the city like wildfire, and the next day District Attorney Charles Whitman called on Rosenthal to give his story to the Grand Jury.

When Rosenthal accepted the invitation of the district attorney to testify he said, "I am signing my own death warrant." He was right. The voluble gambler left Whitman's office at 11:00 on the evening

A grafting policeman, but also a killer
cop? Police Lt. Charles Becker.

of July 15 and took a taxi uptown to his regular hangout, the cafe in
the Metropole Hotel, which once stood here on 43rd Street just east
of Broadway. It was a favorite of many in the sporting and gambling
fraternity of the Runyonesque Times Square of the day. Rosenthal
settled behind a table with a ginger ale and several newspapers and
began to read about himself. Others in the restaurant pointed and
whispered; few dared to talk to him.

At about 1:50 A.M., a man, never identified, walked up to his
table. "Can you come outside a minute, Herman? I got somebody
out here wants to see you." Rosenthal obligingly arose, walked out
of the lobby, and, on the sidewalk outside, encountered four men
standing opposite him in a row. Without a word they drew pistols
and fired. One shot hit him in the neck, one in the nose; two bullets
tore into Rosenthal's head and before he fell to the sidewalk he was
dead. The gunmen trotted across the street, got into a waiting car,
and made their getaway. Despite the presence of several cops on the
street at the time, none engaged the assassins or got the license number of the getaway car.

District Attorney Whitman immediately put the blame on Becker
and pursued the case against the police lieutenant with intense energy, his mouth speaking of reform but his eyes clearly on the governorship of New York and, perhaps in moments of reverie, the
presidency of the United States. In the trial that followed, a strange

assortment of colorful (but deadly) characters emerged, gamblers and pimps and drug pushers, most of them Jewish gangsters from the Lower East Side and denizens of the underground world of Rosenthal and Becker.

Whitman charged that Becker had instructed his collector, a gambler named Bald Jack Rose (né Jacob Rosenzweig), to round up some friends and silence Rosenthal. (Jack Rose soon had a cocktail named after him: 1½ oz. apple jack, ½ oz. grenadine, 1½ tablespoons lime juice; shake vigorously with ice and strain). Rose hired four young gunmen from the gang of Big Jack Zelig (see pp. 208) to do the actual dirty work, the wonderfully nicknamed Whitey Lewis (Jacob Seidenschner), Lefty Louie (Louis Rosenberg), Gyp the Blood (Harry Horowitz), and Dago Frank (Frank Cirofici).

On the stand, Rose related his conspiracy with Becker. He revealed the heart of it in this testimony:

> Q: Prior to the killing of Rosenthal, had Becker spoken to you about him?
> Rose: I had several conversations with Becker about Rosenthal. He said, "Rosenthal was going to the District Attorney and he means to stop me if he can and I must stop him."
> Q: What else did he say?
> Rose: "There is only one thing to do with a fellow like Rosenthal and just stop him so that he will not bother any one for all time." I said, "What do you mean?" and he said, "Well, there is a fellow that ought to be put off the earth."

It was a weak case that hung on the testimony of a group of sly thieves and gamblers, all of whom received immunity for their admitted roles in the death of Rosenthal only by implicating Becker. The *Evening Post* observed dryly that "the mechanical similarity of their stories was so marked that it inevitably suggested rehearsal."

The defense claimed that Rosenthal was a victim of a gambler's war, that Becker had much more to lose with Rosenthal dead than alive, and that the testimony of Rose and his cohort was designed both to exculpate the real killers and eliminate their vice-fighting nemesis on the police force. The defense was weakened by its insistence that Becker was an honest cop, which he was not. But his lawyers were afraid, perhaps with good reason, that the jury would not be willing to distinguish between a grafting policeman and a killer cop.

On October 22, 1912, Becker was found guilty of first-degree murder. Although that verdict was set aside by the Court of Appeals, a second jury, presented with a slightly different cast of witnesses, came to the same conclusion. A huge public campaign called for a pardon from the governor—none other than the man who prosecuted Becker in his first trial, Charles Whitman. Pardon denied.

Charles Becker went to the electric chair on July 30, 1915. The four gunmen—Whitey Lewis, Lefty Louie, Gyp the Blood, and Dago Frank—had been convicted in a separate trial and were executed by the state in April 1914.

Why did this sordid case of lowlife gamblers and a grafting cop capture so much attention?

Part of it seems to stem from the very dramatic exit of Rosenthal. He had captured the city's attention while still alive, and his execution, at high noon on main street, as it were, seemed both shocking and inevitable: the chronicle of a death foretold.

And there was something more here too. The case indicated that the anti-society of the criminal underground was becoming so powerful, so bold and audacious, that it threatened to overpower and replace legitimate society entirely. If a crooked cop could so boldly shoot down a gambler in front of the eyes of the entire city, it meant that nothing could be trusted: neither the police, the courts, the government, nor one's fellow citizens. "This crime," declared the well-known clergyman Lyman Abbot, "is a challenge to our very civilization." The contemporary reaction to the Becker-Rosenthal case seems very much like our own obsession with the dark intrigues and mysteries of the JFK assassination.

Continue down West 45th Street to Broadway, Seventh Avenue, and the infamous, inimitable Times Square.

19 Even before Times Square existed, when this intersection cradled an isolated shantytown of squatters, the neighborhood had a disreputable reputation, its character revealed in such nearby landmarks as the Thieves' Lair and Rascal Rock. The place was eyed with suspicion and the denizens were considered "the most degraded of our population." The neighborhood has clung tenaciously to this heritage throughout a long history of economic upheavals, wars and depression, reform movements and urban renewals.

In the last decade of the nineteenth century, the theater district arrived here and the intersection enjoyed a brief period of elegance. Longacre Square, renamed Times Square in 1904, was a district of ornate and expensive restaurants, theaters, and hotels. Appropriately tucked among such establishments were the high-toned gambling houses of Richard Canfield, John Daly, Dave Busteed, and Lou Ludlum, discreet and classy places where rich gentleman gambled.

Soon vaudeville establishments and music halls joined the legitimate theaters, and in a corresponding development, cheaper gambling joints sprouted alongside high-class houses. In 1911 Louis "Bridgey" Webber, a gambler from the Lower East Side, opened up a faro house at 117 West 45th Street, the first plebeian gambling establishment in these parts. Soon, Herman Rosenthal, whom we met earlier, opened up his place across the street. Prostitution, spilling north from the Tenderloin, was long present here, but was given a great boost during World War I when restless and rambunctious servicemen landed in Times Square for a fling before or after battle.

But the most dramatic change came with Prohibition. It meant not just the end of the fancy restaurants and saloons, but also the birth of speakeasies and night clubs, a more egalitarian clientele, a flood of gangsters, and a new frenetic, garish sensibility. Times Square became Runyonesque.

The whole underworld, it seemed, took up here. Kid Dropper (see p. 168) established a headquarters in the Putnam building on Broadway between West 43rd and West 44th, where the Paramount Theatre Building now stands; Big Bill Dwyer kept an office in the Loew's State Theater Building; Larry Fay ran a number of joints, including the Club El Fey at 107 West 44th Street; Dutch Schultz had a piece of the Embassy Club on East 57th Street. Arnold Rothstein, called Mr. Big and often considered the mastermind behind much of New York's organized crime in the 1920s (see p. 252) held court in Lindy's Restaurant. Lucky Luciano made Dave's Blue Room, on Seventh Avenue above 51st Street, a regular hangout in the '30s.

The glamor and glitz of the square began to dim when the Depression hit. Legitimate theaters, unable to survive, became movie theaters, radio studios, or burlesque houses (Minsky's arrived in 1931). Cheap amusements such as dime dance halls and penny arcades came to dominate. World War II brought another great wave of soldiers and sailors and prostitutes.

Burlesque houses gave the square a salacious reputation, but after Mayor La Guardia's ban in 1937, New York was more demure than most other big cities. "There is nothing approaching the nudity permitted in other cities in our midtown clubs," explained one 1948 guidebook. "Navels must be covered up."

That changed in a big way in 1966, when Martin Hodas installed the first pornographic peep shows in a magazine shop at 259 West 42nd Street and ignited an explosion of sex-related business in Times Square and particularly on "the Strip," 42nd Street between Sixth and Eighth Avenues. The peep shows took off like wild fire, breeding X-rated movie houses and bookstores, leading to live sex shows, and fomenting a huge influx of prostitution. Times Square became a sexual emporium. By 1972, an estimated 1,200 prostitutes lined Eighth Avenue every night, while the several hundred young male hustlers, called "chicken hawks" in street vernacular, preferred Broadway.

Drug dealing was widespread here as early as the 1940s. (In 1942 an investigator reported that "on any street corner—if you knew the pushers—you could buy heroin. Teen-agers bought marijuana openly, mostly in the washrooms of restaurants.") By the '70s drugs overwhelmed the neighborhood, and the drug dealers and prostitutes stood practically shoulder to shoulder. By then 42nd Street between Seventh and Eighth Avenues had earned a reputation as the worst block in the city, with the rest of Times Square trailing not far behind.

The neighbohood has improved a bit since its worst days two decades ago. In an attempt to polish up the district and clear out the vice trade, a number of skyscrapers have been built in the area. Times Square has risen, but only physically. On the street level, the same old unruliness remains. The Disney Corporation now proposes to move in and redevelop. Whether it can remake Times Square in its squeaky clean image remains to be seen.

FAMOUS CRIMES OF TIMES SQUARE

The Car Hook Tragedy—A quarrel on April 27, 1871 on a streetcar at Seventh Avenue between 46th and 47th Streets turned fatal when William Foster struck Avery D. Putnam with a large iron hook. Foster was executed on March 21, 1873. This was one of the first crimes to bring home to New Yorkers the randomness of violence in the modern big city.

Charles Chapin case—Chapin, the gruff city editor of the *New York Evening World* who was the model for the editor in the well-known Broadway show and movie *The Front Page*, shot and killed his wife on September 16, 1918 in the apartment they shared in the Hotel Cumberland at West 55th Street and Broadway. He died in Sing Sing in 1930.

Hotsy Totsy Club murders—This speakeasy, at 1721 Broadway between 54th and 55th Streets, was owned by gangster Jack "Legs Diamond" Noland. An early morning rumble on July 13, 1929 left longshoreman William "Red" Cassidy and ex-convict Simon Walker dead of gunshot wounds. Diamond was thought to be involved, but, due to a lack of witnesses, at least five of whom were killed or went into hiding, he was never tried.

Willie Sutton heist—America's most famous bank robber graced this intersection on October 28, 1930, when he robbed the M. Rosenthal and Sons jewelry store on Broadway between 50th and 51st Streets. In an elaborate and well-timed operation, Sutton, in disguise, made off with $150,000 worth of merchandise in the middle of busy Times Square. The judge told Sutton, "I doubt very much that there could be a recital of a crime so daring in New York City" and gave him thirty years.

Victor Riesel assault—While leaving Lindy's Restaurant at Broadway and 51st Street on April 5, 1956, the labor columnist was attacked with sulfuric acid, which left him permanently blinded. The assailant, Abraham Telvi, was whacked two weeks later. The mastermind was said to be labor racketeer Johnny Dioguardia, who wanted to keep Riesel from testifying before a grand jury. Dioguardia was never formally charged.

Nearest subway: Times Square N R S 1 2 3 7 9
Nearest bus lines: M 6; M 7; M 10; M 27; M 42; M 104

The East Village

A Criminal Sketch of the East Village _____

The *bouwerie* that Peter Stuyvesant bought here in 1651, an estate that ran from present-day Fourth Avenue to the East River and from 17th Street down to Fifth Street, was a picturesque farm of gentle fields, apple and pear orchards, herb and flower gardens. Not at all a promising place for crime.

Fortunately, at least for our present purposes, the neighborhood eventually became overbuilt, overcrowded (at the turn of the century it was part of the most densely populated area in the world), and the scene of many interesting misdeeds.

Urbanization began here in earnest in the 1860s when developers filled the streets with cheap tenements to house New York's burgeoning immigrant population of Irish and German workers. In almost no time at all the area around Tompkins Square Park presented, in the contemporary words of the *New York Herald*, "that indescribably dusty, dirty, seedy, and 'all used up' appearance peculiar to the East Side of town"—a look the neighborhood has nimbly managed to maintain to the present day.

Charles Loring Brace, in his 1872 *The Dangerous Classes of New York*, wrote that in this tenement district "congregate some of the worst of the destitute population of the city—vagrants, beggars, nondescript thieves, broken-down drunken vagabonds who manage as yet to keep out of the station-houses, and the lowest and most bungling of the 'sharpers.'"

The Dutch Mob of Johnny Irving, Mike "Sheeny Mike" Kurtz, Dutch Chris (né John Wilson), and Billy Porter (né William O'Brien), were active in the blocks from Houston to Fifth Street east of the Bowery until they were broken up in 1877. Farther up, between 11th and 13th Streets and First Avenue and Avenue A, a small

The East Village

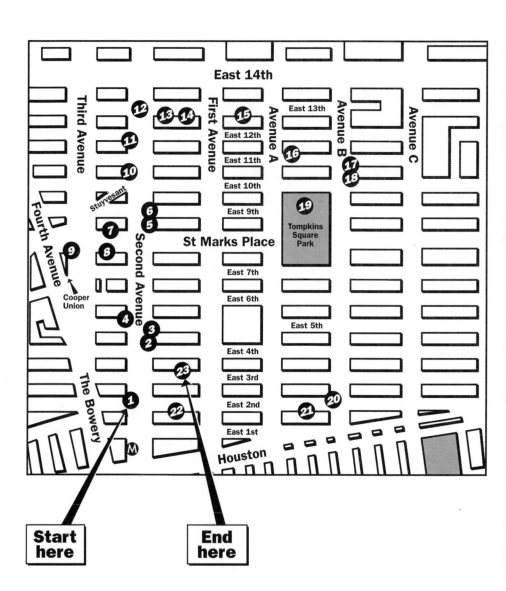

Gangster and *goniff* Monk Eastman.

gang of roughs dubbed the Mackerelville Crowd caused trouble. And the Gas House Gang, natives of the Gas House District east of First Avenue from 34th to 14th Streets, is said to have ranged as low as 11th Street on Third Avenue.

But despite these ruffians, this neighborhood was no match for such truly notorious areas as Five Points, the Tenderloin, or the East River docks. An 1885 survey found that in the eleventh precinct, the streets east of Avenue B, "crimes of note are rare."

It was between the 1890s and the 1920s that East Village crime really came into its own. The huge influx of Eastern European Jewry that began in the 1880s made the Lower East Side the most densely populated area on earth. Spurred by poverty, isolation, and opportunity, an extensive Jewish criminal underground emerged. In 1913, city authorities estimated that in a district here of only one square mile stood 200 brothels, over 200 pool halls (betting joints), and 336 gang hangouts.

Monk Eastman, whose real name was Edward Osterman, is probably the best known of the early Jewish criminals. His gang—the Eastmans—was organized as early as the 1890s, and though his home turf was Chrystie Street, his domain stretched as far north as 14th Street. He had strong political ties to Big Tim Sullivan, the Tammany boss of the ward, and took care of the many strong-arm political and electioneering tasks for the Irish politician.

Other famous alumni from the East Village and Lower East Side include Nathan "Kid Dropper" Kaplan, Jacob "Little Augie" Orgen, Big Jack Zelig, Dopey Benny Fein, Louis "Lepke" Buchalter, Jacob

Dopey Benny Fein, gangster with a class conscience.

"Gurrah" Shapiro, Meyer Lansky, and Charles "Lucky" Luciano. Craig Thompson and Allen Raymond's *Gang Rule in New York*, published in 1940, reported that "the lower East Side of Manhattan in the first twenty years of the twentieth century was the greatest breeding ground for gunmen and racketeers . . . that this country has ever seen."

Prostitution flourished as well, and streetwalkers were found in droves on Allen Street, Chrystie Street, Second Avenue and Fourteenth Street. Second Avenue was so thick with the trade that it earned the nickname "pimp row." And there was gambling, drug dealing, labor racketeering, and many other crooked lines of business. Much of our inside information on the Jewish criminal underworld of those days comes from the voluminous, detailed, and colorful notes of a private detective, Abe Shoenfeld. Hired by a Jewish charitable organization to investigate the haunts and habits of neighborhood criminals, his unpublished record is a priceless source of material, and he is often quoted in the following tour.

By the 1930s the golden age of East Side crime was over. Strict immigration quotas had cut off fresh supplies of thieves and victims alike. As the population shrank, so did the profitability of prostitution and gambling, and the practice of these vices diminished. Those able to raise a stake left the ghetto and moved out to the suburbs of Harlem, Brooklyn (where Murder, Inc. set up business), and places farther afield. In the ensuing decades, the poor and deteriorating neighborhood has retained a higher-than-average crime rate, but, once again, crimes of note are rare.

Drugs are the leitmotif of current criminal activity in this neighborhood. Although a drug trade existed here as early as the turn of the century (see p. 226), it was miniscule compared to the dealing and consumption that first erupted in the late 1960s. Trafficking has shifted around in the succeeding quarter century: during the 1960s heroin dealing was centered on Avenue C and Fifth Street; twenty years later, the trade hovered around Avenue B and Second Street (see p. 231); in the '80s, marijuana was especially easy to find on Tenth Street between First and Second Avenues, and St. Marks Place; crack, which arrived in New York in 1986, was sold in especially heavy quantities on 13th and 14th Streets. However, drugs of all kinds are easy to find throughout the East Village, and narcotics trafficking and drug abuse continue to sap the neighborhood of vitality and growth.

Stalking the East Village

Nearest subway: Second Avenue F
Nearest bus line: M 15; M 21

Our tour starts on the northwest corner of Second Avenue and East First Street, at 19 Second Avenue.

1 Jon Wheiler, "well known in gang circles on the east side as 'Johnny Spanish,'" according to the *New York Times,* was shot down in front of a restaurant here on July 29, 1919. The murderer, probably rival gang leader Nathan "Kid Dropper" Kaplan, calmly walked away, accompanied by two companions. Among his many criminal occupations, Spanish was involved in labor racketeering, and it was evidently a squabble during a garment strike, when he and Kaplan backed opposing sides, that caused the rift between the two. Kaplan was arrested for the murder but discharged for lack of evidence. No one was ever brought to justice for the homicide.

Johnny Spanish was typical in many ways of the wiseguys and gangsters that inhabited the crowded Lower East Side. He moved up the criminal ladder from juvenile delinquent to pickpocket to, while still in his teens, armed robber. Spanish distinguished himself from his lesser-known peers with a reputation for ruthlessness. Policeman Cornelius Willemse wrote that "he was remorseless in his treatment of foes."

In addition to robbing and extorting, Spanish was also a drug dealer, and moved cocaine out of the restaurant here, which served as a base of operations for a gang headed by himself and his brother, named, appropriately, Joe Spanish. Just two years before his murder, he was arrested here for possession of cocaine.

There is a curious story told of Spanish. It's said that once, in a jealous rage, he shot his pregnant girlfriend in the stomach. Some months later, her child was born with several fingers missing.

The Johnny Spanish hit should not be confused with the Spanish Louis hit, which took place earlier and farther up Second Avenue. Although it is little known, the rubout deserves mention, for it evidently involved the first use of an automobile in connection with a murder. Gang leader Spanish Louis, whose real name was probably John C. Lewis, was killed outside 303 East 11th Street, just off Second Avenue, on April 2, 1910. The killers escaped in a Pierce Arrow.

MUG SHOTS

ROSIE HERTZ
Famous Madam

Though Rosie Hertz was known in the Lower East Side as Mother Hertz, wore a *sheitel* (the traditional wig of orthodox Jewish women), and was reserved in her dress, she was anything but maternal or modest. Rosie Hertz was a notorious brothel owner and former prostitute. Working with her husband and several brothers and cousins, she was, in her prime—the decades around the turn of the century—the most successful and famous madam in the city. Detective Abe Shoenfeld, writing of her in 1912, reported that "Rosie Hertz has been the teacher and mother of more prostitutes, whores, madams, etc., than any other individual woman in the world." Judge Joseph E. Corrigan said that she was "for a generation a kind of general godmother for the prostitutes of the East Side" and declared that her brothel "was as much a public feature on the lower East Side as the Brooklyn Bridge."

Rosie Hertz, née Rosenbach, came to the business naturally. Her mother Gittel, with whom Rosie arrived in the city from Hungary in the early 1880s, was said to be the very first Jewish madam in New York. Her daughter got her start as a freelance streetwalker, servicing customers in coal cellars and basements. Like a bawdy Horatio Alger hero, Hertz worked hard for her success.

In the course of her thirty-year career she ran brothels at 9, 13, 15, 17, 20, 22, and 24 East First Street; 4 East Second Street; 218 East Ninth Street, the Dry Dock Hotel at the northeast corner of East Third Street and The Bowery; and the New England Hotel at 39 Third Avenue. But her most famous address was 7 East First Street. Detective Shoenfeld reported with grudging admiration that it had the reputation of having delivered " . . . the wisest and cleverest and also the very best prostitutes and Madams this city can boast of."

In her long career, Hertz cleared around a million dollars. She was able to leave the crowded streets where she got her start and purchase a home in Borough Park, Brooklyn complete with a horse and buggy.

Part of her success was due to her generosity with protection money. She had several local politicians and policemen on her payroll and remained unmolested for her first twenty years of business. In one notable coup, she finagled a judge—none other than William Jay Gaynor, later to serve as mayor—into issuing an injunction to prevent the police from posting a patrolman outside her brothel door. (This is not to imply that Gaynor was corrupt; he was merely an ardent civil libertarian.) Shoenfeld reported that " . . . her station has been impregnable. She has withstood the onslaughts of raids . . . animosity directed against her and her business [and] the attacks of the invincible [reforming district attorney William Travers] Jerome."

In the fall of 1912, however, the murder of Herman Rosenthal (see p. 190) and publicity from a magazine article sparked intense police harassment that caused her to close up shop. Though she retired from Manhattan, she did not surrender: two years later she was reportedly back in business with a disorderly house in Norfolk, Virginia.

Walk up two blocks, cross the avenue, and pause at 76 Second Avenue, the former location of Segal's Cafe.

2 Back in the golden age of the Jewish gangster (roughly the first two decades of the century), Segal's Cafe was a popular hangout for the local underworld. Owned by two brothel keepers, Louis "Little" Segal and Aaron "Big Aleck" Horlig, it catered to the neighborhood's hungry pickpockets, con men, gamblers, and pimps. Detective Shoenfeld declared that "It is without a doubt one of the best hangout joints in the city of New York, also in the country." Schoenfeld's colorful account of its patrons and their avocations, in contemporary slang, includes Patsye Keegan, "gun–pipe fiend–mack"; Sadie Chink, "ex-prostitute–owner disorderly house"; Little Mikie Newman, "gangster"; Candy Kid Phil, "gun"; Sam Boston, "gambler–owner–former fagin–fence–commission bettor"; Jennie Morris, "alias Jennie The Factory—former prostitute and at present disorderly house owner"; Bessie London, "best gun-mol in the world"; and Birdie Pomerantz, "gun-mol–married to Philly Furst, a gun, now out of town working the rattlers and shorts and towns out west." (A brief glossary: a gun is a pickpocket and thief, from the Yiddish *goniff*; a pipefiend is a opium smoker; a mack is a pimp; a fagin is a teacher and leader of a gang of young pickpockets; a gun-mol is a female pickpocket; a rattler is a train; a short is a street car.)

As if in amends for past behavior, the site now houses a church.

Take a few steps up the street to 80 Second Avenue.

❸ By the early 1920s, Joe "the Boss" Masseria had scraped and scrapped his way to the top of the Italian underworld. His power centered around his domination of "the curb exchange," the informal market at Mulberry and Kenmare streets in Little Italy where criminals bought and sold bootleg liquor, drugs, and other contraband (see p. 106). Working under him were such later mob stars as Lucky Luciano, Vito Genovese, Frank Costello, and Thomas "Three-Finger Brown" Lucchese. Masseria was what the younger gangsters called a "Mustache Pete"—an old-style crime boss, unostentatious, hardworking, socially conservative, and wedded to a particular neighborhood and a particular criminal specialty. Oddly, he lived not in Little Italy but here in this humble building at 80 Second Avenue.

In 1922 he was in the midst of a power struggle with Umberto Valenti, and the two had already (literally) exchanged shots (see p. 105). On August 9 of that year, Masseria left his home here and began walking up Second Avenue. Two of Valenti's gunmen were waiting across the street, and when they saw their quarry start out, rushed into the street firing. Caught off guard, Masseria ducked into a millinery shop at 82 Second Avenue, the men right behind, still emptying their revolvers. The boss was able, somehow, to duck their point-blank shooting. Pistols empty and pride deflated, the hapless assassins rushed into a waiting getaway car, only to encounter more trouble. As they sped around the corner, they ran smack into a crowd of members of the International Ladies' Garment Workers' Union, just out of a meeting. When some unionists tried to stop the car, the gangsters began shooting into the crowd. They wounded seven altogether, one fatally.

Masseria gained confidence and increased stature from his good luck in surviving the assassination attempt, and when it was his turn to strike back at Valenti, he did so successfully. That story takes place a bit farther on in the tour.

Masseria became a victim some years later in a legendary hit at the Nuova Villa Tammaro Restaurant in Coney Island, betrayed by his trusted lieutenant Lucky Luciano (see p. 248). On that day (April 15, 1931), Luciano met his boss right here before suggesting a drive to their favorite spaghetti joint.

Cross back to the west side of Second Avenue at the corner of 5th
Street. Pause at the northwest corner, 87 Second Avenue (now the
Cooper Square Restaurant).

④ The *New York Times Book Review* of July 19, 1981 contained a glow-
ing review of a first book, *In the Belly of the Beast*, by an unknown
writer, Jack Henry Abbott. "Out of nowhere comes an exceptional
man with an exceptional literary gift. His voice is like no other, his
language is sharp-edged and hurling with rage." The review might
have been enough to launch a successful career; instead it is remembered only as an example of massively bad timing.

The paper hit the street on the evening of July 18, but by that
time the city knew who Abbott was, and not because of his skill with
a pen. That morning, while the *New York Times* was being folded
and bundled, Abbott had killed a man and fled town.

Abbott was not a typical author. He wrote his book while a convict in a federal penitentiary, and his work is a searing indictment of
the horrors, both extraordinary and routine, of the American penal
system. Abbott had spent nearly his entire life in the grim grip of this
system. He was sent to the Utah State Industrial School for Boys, a
reform school, at the age of twelve. Released at eighteen, he was in
prison within six months for passing bad checks. From that time
until his release in 1981 at the age of thirty-seven, he spent only six
weeks on the windy side of the bars, all of them on the run after an
escape from the Utah State Penitentiary. During one prison stint, he
knifed an inmate to death in a fight.

Soon after his book was published, Abbott was paroled. He came
under the wing of novelist Norman Mailer (see p. 133), who found
him a job in New York and gave him an entree into the New York
writing scene.

Early in the morning of July 18, 1981, Abbott was eating breakfast at Binibon's, a small eatery now replaced by the Cooper Square
Restaurant. Binibon's was a quiet, unpretentious coffee shop catering to the young artists, actors, writers, and hangers-on of the neighborhood. Holding down shop that morning was Richard Adan,
twenty-two-year-old son-in-law of the owner, and, like so many of
his customers, an aspiring writer. His first play had just been accepted
by La Mama, the well-known experimental theater located just down
the block. He had been married five months.

According to the later prosecution version, Abbott walked to the
back of the restaurant and asked Adan for the location of the bathroom. Adan replied that the place had none and walked Abbott outside to the corner to show him where he could relieve himself.
Abbott apparently misunderstood the young man's actions and, used

to the belligerent and violent intercourse of prison, assumed Adan was taking him outside for a fight. He pulled out a knife and stabbed Adan, killing him almost instantly.

Abbott's version is, of course, a bit different. He says Adan was truculent from the moment Abbott walked in with two friends, that he tried to kick Abbott out of the restaurant, and that, before stepping outside, he grabbed a kitchen knife. Abbott asserts he was only defending himself. No other knife was ever found ("lost among the debris on the sidewalk" says Abbott), and his version was unconvincing.

Abbott took flight (although he managed to keep a brunch date several hours after the knifing). In a few weeks the fugitive was tracked down in Louisiana. Amid a great deal of publicity, with many barbs directed at Norman Mailer's role, Abbott was found guilty of first-degree manslaughter and sent back to prison. Two brief literary careers were over.

Continue up to St. Marks Place, cross the avenue, and walk to 140 Second Avenue.

5 Now the Ukrainian National Home and suffering under an ungainly aluminum-foil facade, this building was, eighty years ago, the Stuyvesant Casino, one of the focal points for criminal life on the Lower East Side. The large hall was a favorite venue for underworld "rackets." Gangsters would organize, under the name of a fabricated social organization such as the Saranac Club or the Hemlock Club, a dance or ball. They would then force local merchants to buy tickets or advertisements in a souvenir booklet. They would have a nice party and make some money to boot. This practice is the origin of the word "racket," which first applied to the noise raised by these parties, then to the method of coerced ticket sales, then to strong-arm criminal activity in general, and then finally to any activity or job.

It was during such a party on December 2, 1911 that the neighborhood's most feared mobster, Big Jack Zelig (whose real name was either William Alberts or Harry Morris) shot and killed Italian gangster "Julie" Morrello, "whom the police," according to the *New York Times*, "call one of the most notorious gun and knife fighters on the east side."

Zelig, born in 1882, grew up on the mean streets of the Lower East Side and passed his youth as a pickpocket before graduating to the less skillful but more lucrative life of the shakedown artist, racketeer, and enforcer. Until about 1910, however, he was an obscure and unremarkable criminal. But one night, in a bar fight in Chinatown, he singlehandedly took on, beat up, and knocked out three of the neighborhood's most feared Italian gangsters in front of an astonished crowd of cutthroats and desperadoes. This feat catapulted him to local fame and made him a hero on the Lower East Side. He collected some particularly ruthless henchmen—including the gunmen later executed in the Becker-Rosenthal case (see p. 190)—and declared a vendetta against the presence of "foreign" (i.e. Italian) gangs on the East Side.

"Julie" Morrello was a gunman for Zelig's main rivals, the Jack Sirocco gang. When Morrello heard about the Stuyvesant Casino ball, hosted by his nemesis Zelig, he vowed to "shoot it up." This was a gangster virility ritual that involved standing in the middle of the ballroom floor, taking out a gun or two, and blazing away into the air. Zelig swore—and made sure that word got back to the Italian gunman—that if Morrello showed up at the ball armed, he would not leave alive.

Both gunmen kept their promises. Morrello, after thoughtfully paying his $1 admission at the door of the Casino, bounded up the stairs, only to run into Zelig at the top. The Jewish gunman immediately and remorselessly put four bullets into his adversary, who managed to stagger down the stairs, get out the door and collapse on the sidewalk where you now stand. Taken to the hospital, he died without revealing the identity of his assailant. Zelig was never tried.

The killing further increased Zelig's stature. Detective Shoenfeld reported that "from this day on he became the most feared man in New York." But even this tough gangster met his Waterloo, in a manner revealed later in the tour.

Step up to the southeast corner of East Ninth Street, now the site of the Veselka Restaurant.

6 In 1937 the second floor of this building, 144 Second Avenue, was occupied by an all-night cafe and gambling joint called the Boulevard Restaurant, or sometimes, after its owner, the Dutchman's. On April 10 of that year, at 3:20 AM, it was invaded by a motley and inexperienced gang of young robbers intent on grabbing what they thought would be a fat stash of gambling proceeds. The optimism of the greenhorn robbers was unwarranted: at the moment they chose to take the place, two plainclothes policemen, Detective Michael Foley and Detective John R. Gallagher, were inside, enjoying a coffee break with the Dutchman.

Leading the charge up the stairs was twenty-year-old Arthur "Hutch" Friedman, armed with a borrowed .32 pistol. Close on his heels were seventeen-year-old Dominick Guariglia (unarmed); Benjamin "Little Benny" Ertel (with a .38 that evidently did not work); and twenty-two-year-old Joseph Harvey O'Laughlin (with a .38 that did). Left behind on the sidewalk outside, with uncertain degrees of participation in the crime, were Philip "Sonny" Chaleff and Isidore "Little Chemey" Perlmutter.

As Guariglia barked, "This is a stick up! Everybody out!," he and Friedman began to herd patrons toward the kitchen in the back. O'Laughlin approached the Dutchman and his two friends: "All right, you bastards," he shouted, "in back with the rest!" Instead, the two lawmen went for their guns, and in a wild, quick flurry of shooting, Foley was fatally wounded. What started out almost as a lark had become a capital crime.

The case of these novice gangsters, dubbed "The East Side Boys" by the press because they all came from the Lower East Side neighborhood around East Broadway and Clinton Street, was briefly notorious. Guariglia, O'Laughlin, Friedman, Chaleff, and a fifth defendant (Isidore "Beansy" Zimmerman, who was not present at the incident but was accused of supplying one of the .38 pistols), were found guilty of murder in the first degree on April 14, 1938.

On January 26, 1939, Guariglia, O'Laughlin, and Friedman were executed at Sing Sing. Chaleff and Zimmerman's sentences were commuted to life imprisonment. Chaleff died in prison in 1954.

Two of the "East Side Boys" named in the indictment, Ertel and Perlmutter, went on the lam and were not tried with the others. Ertel was apprehended in Washington D.C. in 1938, and tried and executed in 1940 for his part in the robbery. Perlmutter died in 1956, never having been brought to justice.

Isidore Zimmerman's case is interesting. He was never accused of direct participation in the robbery, and all parties admitted he was nowhere near the restaurant that night. He was indicted, rather, for supplying one of the pistols, a charge he denied throughout his twenty-four years in prison. He was released in 1962 when it was proved that one of the witnesses against him in his original trial had lied. The State declined to retry him, and Zimmerman, after a very long absence, returned home.

Turn around and go back to St. Mark's Place. Turn right onto the block between Second and Third Avenues and walk on the south side of the street to the middle of the block. Look across the street at the All-Craft Center (a community organizations headquarters) at 21–25 St. Mark's Place.

7 This building is often remembered as the address of the Electric Circus, a popular rock club situated here during the street's glory days in the 1960s. But years before this was Arlington Hall, a neighborhood host to weddings, bar mitzvahs, balls, and other get-togethers that the local tenement dwellers hadn't room for at home.

On January 9, 1914, labor racketeer and thug Jack Sirocco and his gang rented the building for a ball. This move was something of a provocation. Here was an Italian gang brazenly strutting its stuff in Jewish gang territory. And this soiree came in the midst of a struggle between the Sirocco group and the ascendent gang in the neighborhood, Dopey Benny Fein and his boys.

Dopey Benny Fein was then at the height of his power. Almost single-handedly he had organized the nascent practice of labor racketeering and thuggery into a business. He brought order to what had previously been a scattered and occasional thing, setting up fee schedules, instituting written contracts, apportioning territory. He was, though, a man of principle: he broke heads only for the unions. Fein once refused $15,000 to work for a manufacturer: "My heart lay with the workers," he explained.

Sirocco's gang, in contrast, worked for the capitalists. The gangs had come head to head just two months before when they took opposing sides during a strike by the Handle and Umbrella Makers' Union. A battle on Broome Street had resulted in the killing of one of Fein's men, Maxie Greenwalt, by one of Sirocco's minions, Johnnie Dike. So while Sirocco planned his ball, Fein vowed revenge.

Early in the evening on January 9, before the party got rolling, nine men took up posts in the recessed doorways behind you. They were Isidore "Jew Murphy" Cohen, Abie "Little Abe" Beckerman, Angie "Augie the Wop" Del Gracio, Irving "Waxey Gordon" Wexler, Joe "Brownie" Brown, Julius "Little Yutch" Eisenberg, Morris "the Mock" Kaplan, Harry "Shorty" Gordon, and David "Battling Dave" Sanders. As the Sirocco boys started up the stairs to the entrance, the well-monickered gang opposite opened fire. A fusillade of pistol shots slammed against the hall as the Sirocco boys dived for cover and began shooting back. The Fein boys were not so handy with their pieces: not one of their targets was hit. An innocent bystander, elderly Frederick Strauss, was shot and killed in the random fire. It was two years before Irving Wexler and Isadore Cohen, alone among the gunmen, were put on trial, and, because of a lack of witnesses, both were acquitted. Wexler went on to become one of the city's most successful bootleggers.

Fein's power collapsed after this incident, and later that year, under pressure in an unrelated case, he began naming names to the district attorney. After that, it's said, he went straight.

Walk a little farther down the block, to 8 St. Mark's Place, once the site of a brownstone that housed the office of Madame Van Buskirk, one of the city's most famous and notorious abortionists in the 1860s and '70s.

8 Throughout most of the nineteenth century, common law and courts allowed abortions before "quickening," that is, the perception of fetal movement, which usually begins around the fourth month of pregnancy. Although New York passed several antiabortion laws during that time—the first in 1828—generally this common-law notion was either part of the enactment or conceded by the courts. Prosecutions were rare and convictions even more so. The attitude of most people was that before quickening, the termination of a pregnancy was of little consequence. The question of abortion was neither a prominent social issue nor a personal moral quandary.

Beginning in the 1840s, abortion, like many other aspects of American society, became increasingly commercialized. This trend was prompted by, and in turn encouraged, a huge increase in the rate of abortions. Termination of pregnancy, once a desperate move by poor, unmarried women to avoid public shame, crept into the married middle class as a means of family planning. Doctors began to specialize in abortions, do business relatively openly, advertise their cures for "female irregularities" and "menstrual obstructions" in the daily papers, and sell abortifacients by mail.

But in the years following the Civil War, a campaign spearheaded by the newly organized American Medical Association and plugged in the *New York Times* and several other newspapers (which began to pull their abortion advertising) resulted in a change in public and legal attitudes. Contributing to this shift was the sensationalized Alice Augusta Bowlsby case of 1871. Her decomposing body was found in a trunk checked at the Hudson River Railway Depot at West 30th Street and Tenth Avenue and traced to abortionist Jacob Rosenszweig, who did business as Dr. Ascher at 3 Amity Place (now West Third Street) and 687 Second Avenue. Tried for the death of his young patient, Rosenszweig was released on a technicality, an incident that caused outrage in the city and increased calls for tightening the criminal code. The very next year New York for the first time made abortion a felony. A modified bill was passed in 1881, and this law remained in force, virtually unchanged, until 1970, when abortion was in great measure legalized.

During the laissez-faire decades of the nineteenth century, the most famous abortionist in New York, indeed the country, was Madame Restell. She was so well known that the practice of abortion was sometimes referred to as "Restellism." Restell, whose real name was Ann Lohman (née Trow), came from England in 1831. Her practice, which she began sometime around 1835, flourished until the 1870s, despite several arrests (which did little but give her free publicity), public censure, and newspaper exposés. She started in a modest home at 146 Greenwich Street and ended up a millionaire with a mansion on the northeast corner of Fifth Avenue and 52nd

The unfortunate Alice Augusta Bowlsby.

Street (next door, ironically, to St. Patrick's Cathedral, which was completed the year of her death). At its apex in the 1870s, her empire included branch offices, traveling salesmen, and a mail order business for her "Female Monthly Pills." On April 1, 1878, facing charges spearheaded by reformer Anthony Comstock that promised to put her out of business, she committed suicide.

After Restell, the most famous doctor in the city for "female irregularities" was probably Madame Van Buskirk, who practiced here at 8 St. Mark's Place. Edward Crapsey, in *The Nether Side of New York*, published in 1872, mentions "Mme. Van Buskirk, whose real name is Gifford, noted as one of the boldest and worst of her tribe, and whose den in St. Mark's Place has long been known as one of the most infamous places in the metropolis."

Continue to the corner and look across the street at Cooper Union.

9 The southwest corner of St. Mark's Place and Third Avenue, next to Cooper Union, holds a great distinction in the city's criminal history. It is the site of the first recorded Mafia rubout in Manhattan.

On the evening of October 14, 1888, Antonio Flaccomio was stabbed on this corner by Carlo Quarteraro. The *New York Times* reported that "Inspector Byrnes said yesterday that the persons concerned in the tragedy are Sicilians, and hail from Palermo, the chief seaport of Sicily. The criminal classes of Sicily are banded together in a secret society known as 'The Mafia,' all the members of which are pledged to protect each other against the officers of the law. The members of this society are chiefly forgers, counterfeiters, and assassins. Murder with some of them is simply a pastime."

Flaccomio was dining at an Italian restaurant, La Trinacria, at 8 St. Mark's Place (one hopes after Madame Van Buskirk had vacated) with a friend, one Polazzi, and two brothers, Carlo and Vincenzo Quarteraro. Polazzi was on bad terms (to put it mildly) with the Mafia for cooperating with the police in breaking up a counterfeiting operation in the city, and the dinner was most likely a set-up by the Quarteraros. But when Polazzi, suspicious, excused himself to get a knife, the brothers turned on Flaccomio and accused him of befriending an informer. He left the restaurant, but not fast enough: Carlo Quarteraro caught up with him at the corner and plunged a knife into his heart.

Carlo fled the country, reportedly disguised as a priest. His brother Vincenzo was tried but the jury on his case deadlocked and he was set free.

NEW YORK CRIMINAL FIRSTS

First recorded murder—The killing of Gerrit Jansen by Jan Gysbertsen on May 15, 1638 (see p. 4).

First recorded case of arson—Lysbet Antonissen, slave of Martin Cregier, set fire to her owner's home on January 3, 1664. She was sentenced to be chained to a stake, strangled, and burned, but the sentence was suspended.

First prostitute—Grietse Reyniers, who arrived in New Amsterdam in 1633 (see p. 70).

First bank robbery—The robbery of the City Bank, near Wall and William Streets, by Edward Smith on March 20, 1831 (see p. 66).

First Prohibition conviction—Harry Deed, bartender at McCarthy's Cafe on Nassau near John Street was arrested on July 3, 1919. Though he claimed that he served whisky through inadvertence, he was fined $10.

First recorded bribe—In 1647, Tomas Willit, a seagoing trader, bribed Fiscal van Dyck, who was in charge of customs, with a beaver "in order that the fiscal would be content to let him sail unhindered." It's somehow not surprising to find that Willit later became New York's very first mayor.

First kidnapping—Although victim Charley Ross, the four-year-old whisked away on July 1, 1874 in the country's first kidnapping for ransom, was taken in Philadelphia, his abductors, William Mosher and Joseph Douglas, were New Yorkers. They confessed five months later as they lay mortally wounded after an attempted burglary, but the child, thought to have been brought to New York, was never found.

Jacob Rosenszweig, a.k.a. abortionist
Dr. Ascher.

Walk north for the short block above St. Mark's Place, take a right and
continue up Stuyvesant Street. (Incidentally while you're passing by, you
might be interested to know that 25, 27, 29 and 31 Stuyvesant Street, all
fine homes dating to the 1860s, were, in the early part of this century,
brothels.) Continue to St. Mark's-in-the-Bowery Church.

10 The old and bare churchyard at St. Mark's-in-the-Bowery provides an
appropriate setting for one of Manhattan's most sensational and ghoulish crimes. On the night of November 6, 1878, several unsqueamish
thieves managed to carry off merchant prince A. T. Stewart's decomposed body for ransoming. Not only a macabre crime, but also a brash
one, for the churchyard remains much as it was then, flat and high, exposed to view, surrounded by residences. Yet these bodynappers managed to dig into the vault, rummage about and break open Stewart's
casket, and exit with an uncooperative corpse over the very fence you
see here.

   Despite the fact that, as the initial police bulletin stated, "The de-
composition of the remains is so offensive that they cannot be concealed," the robbers got clean away.

   Alexander Turney Stewart was something of the John D. Rockefeller of dry goods—thin-lipped, tight-fisted, ruthless in his scramble
to the top. In 1848 he built the country's first department store, the
Marble Dry Goods Palace, at the northeast corner of Broadway and
Chambers Streets (a building that still stands). Its opulence and size

amazed New York shoppers of the time. Fifteen years later came the even more impressive Cast Iron Palace at Broadway between Ninth and Tenth Streets. It featured a huge domed skylight, a sweeping double staircase, six steam-powered elevators, close to twenty acres of floor space, and—in an unnerving precursor of muzak—an organ playing constantly during shopping hours. Dubbed "The Greatest Store in the World" it, along with sharp real estate investments, made Stewart the country's second-richest man, just a little shy of beaverman John Jacob Astor.

Though some thought him a brilliant businessman and a marketing genius, others found little to praise. "A. T. Stewart was one of the meanest men that ever lived," observed one contemporary after his death. "He squelched hundreds of smaller dealers without compunction and ground his employees into the very dust of humiliation and impecuniosity." A New York journalist of the day, Matthew Hale Smith, agreed: "His whole manner was hard and repulsive. He [had] sharp, cold, avaricious features; a clear, cold eye; a face furrowed with thought, care, and success; a voice harsh and unfriendly in its most mellow tones. He lived wholly by himself . . . he had probably not a bosom friend in the world." After the Civil War, President Grant tried to appoint Stewart Secretary of the Treasury, but the public outrage was so fierce Grant was forced to back down. Stewart died on April 10, 1876.

No surprise, then, that there was a secret snickering when A. T. Stewart was snatched from his grave. Police Chief Walling paraphrases one "semi-anarchist" newspaper as writing "there is a sort of grim justice in it, and the very irony of greed, that this cruel, avaricious, hard-hearted man, who oppressed his employees, ruined his creditors and drove his poorer competitors to bankruptcy should now have his flesh drop off and his bones rattled in a thieves' bag, while the millions he earned are enjoyed by others."

Only after Stewart was unearthed was it revealed that there had been an earlier attempt to grab the corpse. Just a month previous, on October 9, the Stewart slab had been moved, but, evidently, the vault not entered. Judge Harry Hilton, the merchant prince's lawyer and heir, responded quickly with stringent security measures. New locks were put on the gates, the slab was moved to a vacant spot some ten feet away from the actual vault entrance, and the spot where the stone once lay was sodded over. Supposedly, only three people knew the real location of the vault, two of them officials of the church, Sexton George W. Hamill and Assistant Sexton Frank Parker. A night watchman was hired to visit the churchyard every hour. Just three days before the successful snatch, he was dismissed.

Yet the thieves went straight to the unmarked vault without any indication that they probed in surrounding sod or touched the decoy tombstone. According to the *New York Times*, "the exact spot overlying the central slab had been so accurately determined, despite the entire lack of indicating marks, that a rectangular hole had been dug of only just sufficient dimensions to enable it alone to be raised. There was not an inch more than was necessary either way." The casket cover was unscrewed, a lead lining cut open, and the locks and hinges of the coffin itself broken. Along with the body, the thieves took a silver inscribed plate, several silver knobs and handles, and a swath of velvet from the lining. They left in trade a small coal shovel and a tin lantern.

The only other clue was a macabre one: a trail of viscous human desquamation in the west side of the churchyard. The thieves had evidently retired with their dripping corpse this way, exiting by the southwestern corner where a tree hung over the fence and provided access to a balcony on the building next door. The building, though not the balcony, still stands.

The police went into action immediately—and just as quickly got nowhere. They found where the shovel and lantern had been bought, and then the trail turned ice cold. There were many reports of suspicious men, shadowy gangs, overheard conspiracies, loitering carriages, furtive strangers. None of these led anywhere. And when a break did come in the case, it was not through any action of the police.

In January 1879, a lawyer named General Patrick H. Jones, once postmaster of the city, arrived at police headquarters with a letter he had purportedly received from one "Henry G. Romaine." Along with a ransom demand of $200,000, it related the following story:

> The remains were taken before twelve o'clock on the night of the 6th and not at three o'clock on the morning of the 7th of November [as the police suspected]. They were not taken away in a carriage, but in a grocer's wagon. They were not taken to any house near the grave-yard but to one near One Hundred and Sixtieth Street. They were then enclosed in a zinc-lined trunk and left on an early morning train. They went to Plattsburg and from there to the Dominion [Canada]. There they were buried. Except that the eyes have disappeared, the flesh is as firm and the features as natural as the day of internment, and can therefore be instantly identified.

That last sentence, at the very least, was patently untrue.

The writer provided a piece of paper in the shape of a swath of velvet cut from the coffin lining, and a small strip of the velvet itself. Judge Hilton refused the demands related by Jones. (The part played in this affair by the postmaster-lawyer, evidently in close contact with the thieves, is murky at best, but since Police Chief Walling did not raise a whisper, neither will we.) "We must never compound a felony," said Hilton primly. "It isn't, of course, the money, but the principle. If we were to pay these infamous scoundrels, what rich man's or woman's dead body would hereafter be safe?" Despite this stiff-necked posturing, Hilton eventually offered $25,000. Henry G. Romaine declined.

Not until the spring of 1881 were negotiations reopened, again through Jones, but this time with the widow Stewart. She agreed to a ransom of $100,000, but adroit last-minute negotiating brought the price down to a mere $20,000: the grave robbers were obviously anxious to rid themselves of their unpleasant contraband. As stipulated, a relative of Mrs. Stewart drove out to the untamed wilds of Westchester County during the night. On a lonely lane, he encountered a masked man and exchanged his bag of money for a bag of bones. His guarantee was a bit of velvet from the casket.

A. T. Stewart, or at least the skeleton purported to be him, was reburied in Garden City Cathedral, Long Island, the next night in a vault rigged with an alarm system.

Who nabbed Stewart's bones? Judge Hilton suspected Sexton Hamill or Assistant Sexton Parker of complicity. But Police Chief Walling, intimately involved with the investigation, unreservedly dismisses the two as suspects. Crime writer Jay Robert Nash mentions Traveling Mike Grady or George Leonidas Leslie, two well-known criminals of the period, as possible suspects. But Grady was a simple burglar and fence, and past his prime by twenty years. Leslie, inconveniently, had been murdered six months previous. Which leaves us, as the police of the time were left, with no suspects at all. The graverobbers remain unidentified to this day.

You can enter the east churchyard through the gate on the right of the church. Walk to the center of the yard and you'll see a large iron plate with a cross on it. This is the Winthrop vault, number 111. Closer to Second Avenue is a smaller red stone marker for the Bibby vault, number 113. Stand between them and you'll be right on top of vault number 112, where Stewart once reposed.

Exit the churchyard and continue up one block on Second Avenue to the corner of 12th Street.

11 Here, on the southwest corner of Second Avenue and 12th Street, is where Mafia chief Joe "the Boss" Masseria settled the score with upstart Umberto Valenti. On August 11, 1922, two days after his brush with death in the hat shop (see p. 206), Masseria sent a message to Valenti proposing a peace conference and intimating that he was tired of fighting and ready to talk business. They met at John's Restaurant, on 12th Street a few yards east of Second Avenue (still open for business). Their conversation seemed to have been amiable, for they sauntered out in a friendly manner toward Second Avenue. Upon reaching the corner, however, Masseria gave a secret signal, maybe a scratch of the nose or a straightening of the tie. In response, two of his boys appeared out of nowhere and began blazing away at the defenseless Valenti, who darted across the street toward a waiting taxicab at this corner. He wasn't quite as agile as Masseria had been, though: he just managed to open the car door before falling dead. Masseria was charged in the murder, but, unsurprisingly, no witnesses could be coaxed to come forward.

ALSO INFAMOUS

Famous gunslinger Harry Longabaugh, better known as the Sundance Kid, lived in a boardinghouse at 234 East 12th Street for a number of months in 1901. The Sundance Kid soon left with Butch Cassidy (Robert LeRoy Parker), for Bolivia, where they continued their criminal careers until their deaths in a shootout with the Bolivian army in 1907.

Walk another block north to 13th Street and an intersection doubly blessed, or cursed, with two famous deaths.

12 With a chestful of money, James Murray was afraid to shack up with his fellow sailors in John Johnson's boarding house downtown on Front Street, so the landlord graciously offered his own room on a March night in 1824. This courtesy allowed Johnson, either alone or with a boarder named Jerry, to crush Murray's head with the blunt side of a hatchet. Jerry escaped upstate (and was never found) while Johnson was left to drag the body into Cuyler's Alley, a small street now subsumed in the middle of the NYSE Stock Clearing Building downtown on Water Street. The body was discovered the same night and was quickly identified and traced back to Johnson, who confessed within days (see p. 21). His trial was a sensation, playing to packed crowds, and his execution, on April 2, 1824, on this spot, was reportedly witnessed by 50,000 people, a figure which, if accurate, means that over one-third of the entire city showed up to watch a landlord dangle.

Nearly a hundred years later, with the wide, empty fields replaced by cement and tenements, this intersection witnessed another execution, one without state sponsorship. On the evening of October 5, 1912, gang leader "Big Jack" Zelig, "the most feared man in New York," whom we met several blocks south at the Stuyvesant Casino (see p. 208), was rubbed out on a Second Avenue streetcar as it passed this intersection.

The events that led up to his murder began back in the Casino. On the evening of October 4, 1912, Zelig was attending another ball and drinking wine with some cronies. A low-level pimp, Philip "Red Phil" Davidson, approached Zelig and tried to elbow in at the table. This was a huge breach of underworld etiquette, as Zelig was the premier east side mobster at the time, and Davidson was, in gangster terms, a nobody. Oblivious or uncaring, Davidson insisted on buying rounds and laid out some money. Zelig reluctantly threw it into the kitty.

The next day Zelig was playing cards at Segal's Cafe (see p. 205) when Davidson entered and again began badgering the gangster. An altercation resulted and Zelig slapped Davidson, who left the cafe. He returned a few minutes later and again approached the boss. "Let's be friends," he said. Zelig, busy playing cards, replied laconically, "Why not?" The two shook hands. Davidson left the cafe.

A few hours later, Zelig boarded a streetcar heading uptown on Second Avenue. Stealthily, without being observed, Davidson got on a block or two later. He crept up to Zelig, placed a .38 revolver behind his left ear, and fired.

Captured shortly after, Davidson said that he killed Zelig because the boss had robbed him of $400. But Zelig had never met Davidson before the incident at the Stuyvesant Casino, and those who knew the pimp doubted he ever had $400 to steal. Perhaps the petty crook was merely sore over his treatment in the cafe. But the likeliest explanation lies in another case—the Becker-Rosenthal murder (see p. 190).

Members of Zelig's gang—Harry "Gyp the Blood" Horowitz, Louis "Lefty Louis" Rosenberg, and Jacob "Whitey Lewis" Seidenschner—had been involved in this notorious murder case, and Zelig was due to testify at the trial, set to begin October 7 (two days after he was killed). Davidson, it is safe to assume, had been sent to keep Zelig from testifying. Oddly, both the defense and the prosecution claimed the gang chief as a witness, so it wasn't clear who was doing a favor for whom. Davidson pleaded guilty to second-degree murder and served twelve years of a twenty-year sentence in Sing Sing.

Detective Shoenfeld, prim moralist though he was, could not help but mourn a man he obviously respected. Immediately after the killing, he wrote: "Jack Zelig is as dead as a door nail. Men before him—like Kid Twist, Monk Eastman and others—who had been leaders of so-called gangs—were as pygmies to a giant. With the passing of Zelig, one of the most 'nerviest,' strongest and best men of his kind left us."

Take a right and walk a block to the first tenement, 324 East 13th Street. This building was the next door neighbor, before the telephone company scraped out half the block, to 320, the site of the famous Dr. Meyer case. Imagine, for the sake of this tour, a twin tenement to the right.

13 In the winter of 1892, Henry Meyer, his wife, and two comrades in crime, Gustave Brandt and Charlie Muller, rented a ground floor apartment here to carry out one of the oddest insurance frauds ever perpetrated. Francis Wellman, prosecutor at the resulting murder trial, said, "No fiction writer would dare to invent so incredible a tale. When the case was given to me to try, I could not believe that even a stupid crook would trust an accomplice to help carry out a scheme so fantastic—but the proof was overwhelming."

Dr. Henry C. F. Meyer (his medical degree came from a homeopathic school) was an old hand at insurance scams, a craft he first practiced in 1888 in Chicago. At that time, Meyer convinced a gullible friend to take out an insurance policy naming the doctor as beneficiary. A few months later, on a sweltering summer day, he invited his friend to go rowing with him. Meyer took with him a couple of bottles of beer, one of which he had doctored with nitroglycerin (a vasodilator and heart stimulant). In the middle of a lake, Meyer handed his comrade a beer and then the oars. Before the sweating and red-faced rower had reached the shore, he collapsed of a heart attack, and Meyer quietly let his beer bottle slip under the water. The scheme worked so well that he tried it again, with the same success, the next summer. He then tried to cash a fraudulent policy on his father-in-law (who died of natural causes), but was caught and sent to Joliet prison.

Meyer met Gustave Brandt and Charlie Muller in Joliet. The doctor, completely unreformed, proposed to his friends a new insurance scheme, which they enthusiastically seconded. It was a decision that Brandt would not live to regret.

The plan called for the group to take out a life insurance policy under the name of Gustave Baum, an old cellmate of theirs that had wandered off west somewhere. Meyer's wife, masquerading as Mrs. Baum, would be named as beneficiary. One of the conspirators would then impersonate their cellmate and pretend to sicken. Meyer would call in a legitimate doctor to tend to the shill, a move that would dispel the doubts of any suspicious insurance company.

Here was the twist that Meyer maintained would make the plan foolproof: to hoodwink the doctor, Meyer would administer small but progressively larger doses of poison to the impersonator. The doctor would watch his patient deteriorate despite his best efforts. For the denouement, Meyer would substitute a corpse nabbed from Bellevue Hospital; the unsuspicious doctor, said Meyer, would never notice the difference in a dark sickroom. The conspirators would have a legitimate death certificate for the grieving widow to produce and the four would split the proceeds. And just who would impersonate Baum? All eyes turned to Brandt. Unbelievably, Brandt—a man who knew Meyer had already dispatched at least two others for cash—agreed. "I will become ill, to please Mrs. Meyer," he said. "Give me any medicine you please, but don't give me enough to kill me."

Because all of the plotters were well known in Chicago, they moved to New York and took up a faux domestic life here on 13th Street to carry out their plan. Every evening Brandt would take his dessert in bed with a sprinkling of antimony, and every day Dr. S. B. Minden, a local physician, would note his patient's declining condition amid continuing puzzlement. He thought his patient suffered from dysentery.

Perhaps Brandt really believed that Meyer would find an identical corpse to substitute at the last moment, but the ringleader never entertained the notion. Earlier he had told a friend that "Brandt is good for nothing but to drink whiskey, smoke cigarettes and read the papers. The sooner we get him out of the way, loaded down good and heavy with life insurance, the better for us." On March 29, 1892, he gave Brandt, too weak to rise, a dose of arsenic that finished him off. A later autopsy would show three grains of arsenic and 157 milligrams of metallic antimony in Brandt's body.

Dressed in black, Mrs. Meyer then made the rounds of her insurance companies. She collected $3,000 from her Washington Life agent, but the man at Mutual Life was a little more careful, or a bit more hard-hearted. Something about Mrs. Baum and her friend William Heuter (none other than Meyer) raised his suspicions. He ordered an investigation, and Meyer and crew promptly fled the city, leaving just minutes ahead of a Pinkerton detective. They were discovered a year later living in Detroit, plotting yet another insurance fraud, and were brought to New York for trial.

The Meyer case was almost as celebrated as the trials of fellow poisoners Carlyle Harris (see p. 184) and Dr. Robert Buchanan (see p. 133) and featured several of the same lawyers. On May 18, 1894, Meyer was convicted of murder in the second degree and was sentenced to life in Sing Sing prison. Three years later he went mad and was sent to Matteawan State Institution for the Criminally Insane, but eventually regained his sanity—in the legal sense anyway—and went back to Sing Sing. He was paroled around 1914 and disappeared. His wife was never tried. Muller saved himself by becoming the state's star witness.

Continue towards First Avenue and pause at 354 East 13th Street,
where, three-quarters of a century ago, the poor Varotta family once had
an apartment.

14 Of the many Black Hand threats, bombings, and killings that once
panicked New York (see p. 102), the kidnapping and murder of five-
year-old Giuseppe Varotta on May 21, 1921, was by far the most notorious. Little remembered today, the crime rocked the city at the
time. Michael Fiaschetti, then head of the NYPD's Mafia-fighting
Italian Squad, called it "the most famous case that ever came into the
office . . . ."

In the spring of 1921, word got around in the close-knit neighborhood that Salvatore Varotta had been awarded $10,000 in a lawsuit re-
sulting from an auto accident. The story was exaggerated—Varotta
had yet to receive any money—but the supposed piles of cash were
irresistible to some of the local toughs, and on May 21, 1921, they
kidnapped his young son Giuseppe. They sent the requisite Black
Hand note, full of crossed daggers and lurid skulls, demanding
$2,500 or "you will never see your boy again, dead or alive, for he
will be drowned and the rest of you all will be killed and the house
burned." The kidnappers must have soon realized they had kidnapped a cash-poor child. They wanted something for their troubles,
however, and over the next several weeks negotiated with Varotta,
gradually lowering their price to $500, still a fortune for the poor
family. In the meantime, Fiaschetti's Italian Squad had become involved. They put the Varotta apartment under surveillance (and noticed that the kidnappers were doing precisely the same thing), and
had a young Italian policewoman, under the guise of a relative, move
in with the family.

On June 2, a gang member came to the apartment to pick up the
loot (apparently the kidnappers assumed that Varotta would be too
frightened to call the police, or perhaps they were just not very
sharp) and was arrested on the scene. Five other gang members, loitering outside by the stoop (again, not very sharp) were arrested at
the same time. But there was no sign of little Giuseppe, and though
several of the suspects confessed to the abduction, they refused to
disclose the child's whereabouts.

The story hit the newspapers at this point with great emotion over
the plight of the kidnap victim and desperate pleas for his life. It was
too late—Giuseppe Varotta had been killed to prevent him from
identifying his captors. On June 11, the boy's body was found in a
small box that washed up on the shore of the Hudson River near
Piermont.

The leader of the gang (one can hardly call him the mastermind) was Antonio Marino, who lived directly across the street at 349 East 13th Street. Other gang members included James Ruggiero (Marino's son-in-law), John Melchionne, Roberto Raffaelle, Santo Casumano, and Giuseppe Palastro, most of whom lived in the neighborhood.

This block, in fact, was part of an Italian enclave in the predominantly Jewish east side that was well-known for its crime and desperate men. The *New York Times* called the area "the rendezvous of Black Hand bands," and listed, in a 1911 article, 16 Black Hand bombings within a three-block area in that year alone. Two years later detective Shoenfeld recorded "Italian blackhander" hangouts at 418 and 430 East 11th Street. The Varotta kidnappers killed their victim because he knew exactly who they were: his own neighbors.

Marino, Cusumano, and Raffaelle were convicted of murder in the first degree and sentenced to the electric chair. But because their confessions were beaten out of them, their sentences were later commuted to life imprisonment. Ruggiero claimed that he was coerced into participation by his father-in-law and was released for aiding the prosecution. Melchionne was brain damaged by the beatings he received and was sent to Matteawan State Institution for the Criminally Insane. The troubles of the Varotta family, however, did not end. They continued to receive death threats, and several attempts were made to kill them, evidently because they had testified against the defendants. The police department guarded their home for two years, but eventually the family had to be spirited out of the city and, in perhaps the first use of a witness protection program, given new identities.

ALSO INFAMOUS

Salvatore Lucania, who later adopted the nom de guerre Lucky Luciano and became perhaps the most famous Mafioso of them all, was brought from Italy around the age of ten and lived with his family at 265 East 10th Street. Little Lucky went to school at PS 19 at 344 East 14th Street, now the Emanuel-El Midtown YM-YWHA, which is right across the street from you.

Continue along the street to 428 East 13th Street, the middle of the block between First Avenue and Avenue A.

15 The saga of Maria Barberi was a brief and now forgotten cause célèbre, but it was prominent and popular enough in its day to keep Maria from being the first woman to die in the electric chair. She actually did a whole lot better than just that, for she emerged unscathed and unpunished for a murder that she readily admitted.

On April 26, 1895, Barberi killed her lover, Domenico Cataldo, in a saloon here at 428 East 13th Street, by slicing his throat with a straight razor. Cataldo, his head almost severed by Barberi's furious stroke, staggered the four hundred feet to the corner of Avenue A before expiring in the gutter. Barberi walked home. A month before, she had moved in with Cataldo upon a promise of marriage, but the cad seems to have had no intention of making her an honorable woman. That day, when he refused yet one more desperate plea from Barberi, spitting out, according to the popular press, "Bah! Pigs marry, I don't!" she drew the line, as it were, across his throat. She considered herself merely a wronged women avenging a betrayal. A street ballad of the day presented her case:

'Tis not for me to speak aloud
On lofty themes. I tell
As one among the lowly crowd
How young Maria fell.

Swift as a flash a glittering blade
Across his throat she drew,
"By you," she shrieked, "I've been betrayed:
This vengeance is my due!"

Behold her now, a wounded dove:
A native of a clime
Where hearts are melted soon with love
And maddened soon to crime.

A jury, however, natives of another clime, convicted her of first-degree murder.

By the time of her sentencing, her case and cause had been adopted by a clamorous section of the public and had become a national issue. She managed to garner the support of progressives, who felt that Barberi was the victim of an unfair social and legal situation, and conservatives, who thought it unseemly to strap a lady into the electric chair. Letters and telegrams came pouring in from across the country and around the globe, demanding justice for the wounded dove. She managed to win a new trial the next year, and went back into the courtroom armed with a defense based on insanity, or "psychical epilepsy" as it was then dubbed. After a month-long trial, she was found insane, and then, strangely, released. She promptly disappeared from history.

Continue to the corner of Avenue A, turn right and walk down two blocks. Just east of the corner is 507 East 11th Street, notorious as a major drug outlet in the 1980s.

16 Drug trafficking is not a recent phenomenon in this neighborhood. Just after the turn of the century there was an extensive drug trade in cocaine, heroin, morphine, and opium. Detective Shoenfeld reported that at least $100,000 (in 1917 dollars) of cocaine was imported by Jewish dealers monthly through Canada. In addition, cocaine was imported by Italian dealers through Italy and Canada, and by others from the West Indies and South America. Prominent local dealers at that time included Dinny Fox and Bennie Silver, Little Archie and Big Nose Benno, the Manheimer Combination, Hymie Fishel, Joe Asch, and Waxey Gordon, who later became nationally known as a bootlegger. Just before World War I, there were at least thirty drug outlets in this neighborhood.

Shoenfeld described a typical score in 1914 at Dreyfus's Drug Store on the northwest corner of Second Avenue and 14th Street:

> Walk into a telephone booth in the drug store and stand there for about two minutes, take a half-dollar and tap on the window of the telephone booth with it a few times; remain there and the druggist or one of the clerks will come to the booth and hand you a package or box containing cocaine for which [you] should hand over the 50c piece. The time to do this is between 11 and 12 P.M.

World War II cut off the supplies of opium from Asia and interrupted European distribution routes. Drug use plummeted for the following two decades.

It wasn't until the 1960s, when the counterculture melded with the consumer culture, that drug dealing once again boomed, outstripping the levels of use seen earlier in the century. By the late '70s, this neighborhood hosted the largest retail heroin market in the world (see p. 231) and, outside of Harlem, the largest junkie population in the city. In the early '80s, police pressure squeezed out much of the street-level heroin dealing, but the introduction of crack around 1986 resulted in a renaissance of street dealing.

The building you're now standing near provides an illustration of the current nature of the drug trade. From the early 1980s to 1988, it was the headquarters and retail outlet for the huge cocaine empire of Alejandro "The Man" Lopez. Customers would line up on the sidewalk outside in a queue that ran from here to Avenue A and slowly make their way inside to buy "Rock Solid" or "Pony Pak" brands of cocaine from a barred window inside. (No more coy antics in a phone booth, as in 1914.) Lopez's operation racked up some $4 million a year in sales. This building was called "The Rock" and featured solid-steel doors, a secret escape hatch, and even a nightclub for Lopez's employees and friends. "The Rock" was well-known and its employees were feared throughout the neighborhood.

Lopez's empire was broken in 1988 and he was sentenced to 33⅓ years. Things calmed down at 507, but new retailers and outlets have arisen nearby. The drug trade is too profitable to lie still.

Continue east on 11th Street to the southeast corner of 11th and Avenue B.

17 At a quarter to 11:00 on the night of January 27, 1972, two rookie patrolmen, Gregory Foster and Rocco Laurie, were on their beat, poised on this corner of 11th Street and Avenue B. As they stood, perhaps talking, perhaps only pausing silently for a moment, three, or maybe four, men came toward them across the intersection, parted to pass, then suddenly spun around and unleashed a thundering volley of shots into the backs of the two cops. As the pair went down, the men stood over them and fired again and again— Laurie took six slugs, Foster eight. One of the gunmen fled north up Avenue B, the others jumped into a getaway car and sped away. Hours later the car was found idling by the L subway station at 14th Street and First Avenue. Empty shells were found in the station itself, indicating that the killers had fled, courtesy of the MTA, into Brooklyn. Foster died instantly, Laurie on the operating table early the next day.

Two cops mercilessly assassinated was shocking enough, but Foster and Laurie were only the latest victims of a nearly yearlong vendetta against the NYPD. On May 19, 1971, patrolmen Nicholas Binetti and Thomas Curry flagged down a car at Riverside Drive and 106th Street for a minor traffic violation. Suddenly, their patrol car was riddled by a burst of machine-gun fire from the car. Though gravely wounded, neither died. Two days later patrolmen Waverly Jones and Joseph Piagentini, walking out of a project called the Colonial Park Houses at 159–20 Harlem River Drive in Inwood, were ambushed. This pair was not so lucky—the attack was fatal for both.

The UPI received a communiqué after the Foster and Laurie shooting:

> This is from the George Jackson Squad of the Black Liberation Army about the pigs wiped out in lower Manhattan last night. No longer will black people tolerate Attica and oppression and exploitation and rape of our black community.
> This is the start of our spring offensive. There is more to come.
> We remember Attica.
>
> The George Jackson Squad of the BLA

The Black Liberation Army had arisen in 1969 from the ashes of a Black Panther Party decimated by harassment, arrests, and schisms (see p. 140). Unlike the Panthers, who were given to grand public gestures and self-promotion, the BLA was an underground and extremely secretive group of revolutionary black nationalists. They considered the Panthers too moderate, even sell-outs. The BLA viewed black ghettoes as sovereign territory, the police as invaders, and themselves as the armed resistance. To this group, Foster (black) and Laurie (white) were but foot soldiers of an enemy army.

From the investigations of the Binetti-Curry and Jones-Piagentini murders the police had a sheaf-full of suspected BLA members, and eyewitnesses in the vicinity of 11th and B picked out several mugshots. Within a week the police knew who they were looking for.

They found them, by accident, in St. Louis. A shootout after a routine stop for a traffic violation led to the arrest of Henry Brown and the death of Ronald Carter, shot accidently by Brown in the confusion. In their car the cops found an arsenal of assorted handguns, rifles, ammunition, and, most important, Laurie's .38 caliber Smith & Wesson. Shortly after, a U-Haul trailer was found filled with household goods, mattresses, and political literature. It had been moving day for the BLA. Investigators found that the trailer had been rented by JoAnne Chesimard and Andrew Jackson, two others wanted for questioning in the case. The other main suspects were Ronald Anderson and Herman Bell.

Henry Brown was eventually acquitted of the Foster-Laurie killings but was hauled back to St. Louis to begin a twenty-five-year sentence in another case. Andrew Jackson was arrested in April 1973 in Brooklyn. Herman Bell was arrested in New Orleans in October of that year. JoAnne Chesimard, who had changed her name to Assata Shakur, was captured in 1973 in a shootout on the New Jersey Turnpike. In 1979, she escaped from prison (see p. 139) and now lives in Cuba.

Walk two doors down to 169 Avenue B.

18 There was a large and dynamic hippie community in the mid-1960s in the East Village. It centered around Tompkins Square Park and the surrounding blocks and supported, along with a number of cafes, clubs, hangouts, and head shops, its own celebrities and stars. James "Groovy" Hutchinson and best friend Ronald "Galahad" Johnson were probably the best-known hippies this side of San Francisco's Haight-Ashbury. Their East Village crash pad for strays, runaways, and curiosity-seekers was a popular spot and had received a great deal of attention from the media, then hot on the trail of the shocking new youth phenomenon. Hutchinson was celebrated in the press as "his generation's young rebel" and "an urban Huck Finn."

Hutchinson grew up in a working-class family in Central Falls, Rhode Island. He was a gang member and petty thief as a youngster, and his instinctive antiestablishment orientation and clownishness made him a natural—almost quintessential—hippie.

Linda Fitzpatrick represented another kind of quintessential hippie: an upper-middle class child who dropped out to live free and natural. In her case, however, that journey hid a darker side. She was an alienated and unhappy young woman who fell quickly into the drug scene and went from marijuana to LSD to shooting methadrine in a matter of months.

She dropped out of prep school in September 1967 to go to New York, telling her parents that she was working steadily and living with her friend Paula Bush at the respectable Village Plaza Hotel. Actually, she was panhandling and selling pot while living with her friend Paul Bush at the decrepit and flea-ridden Village Plaza Hotel. Soon she moved out and drifted among friends, lovers, and crash pads in the East Village.

Throughout Fitzpatrick's metamorphosis, her parents remained painfully ignorant, not only of her whereabouts, but of her character as well. They continued to think of her as the obedient and precious child who liked to shop at Ann Taylor and ride horses.

She was last seen on October 7, 1967, lying with Hutchinson on a sleeping bag spread out on the sidewalk in front of the Psychedelicatessen at 164 Avenue A, strung out on speed, quite incapable of shopping or riding.

Early the next morning, the bodies of Hutchinson and Fitzpatrick were found bludgeoned to death in the boiler room of this building. Word had it that they were enticed to the basement in hopes of purchasing LSD and then had their heads beaten in with bricks.

The Groovy Murders, as the killings were called by the press, popularized the term "generation gap" and shocked American parents who, like the Fitzpatricks, found that their sons and their daughters were beyond their command. For the hippies of the East Village, it was a reminder that, despite their beatific intentions, they could not avoid the brutality of an unhip world.

Two years after the killings, Thomas Dennis, a twenty-seven-year-old drifter, and Donald Ramsey, a twenty-eight-year-old ex-convict, pleaded guilty to the Groovy Murders. The motive and circumstances remain unclear.

Continue down Avenue B to Tompkins Square Park and enter the park through the entrance opposite East Ninth Street. Walk to the pavilion on your right, where you'll see a small memorial tablet to the victims of the *General Slocum* tragedy.

19 This very humble monument is one of the few reminders of one of the city's worst catastrophes, the sinking of the *General Slocum* excursion ship in the East River in the summer of 1904.

Since 1887, St. Mark's Lutheran Church on Sixth Street (the building is still extant, and now houses a synagogue) had hosted a picnic excursion to Long Island. The affairs had always proved quite popular, and the eighteenth version, set for June 15, 1904, was no exception. Over 1,300 expectant picnickers, mostly women and children (for the trip was on a working Wednesday), marched down to the Third Street pier and crowded into the *General Slocum*, a three-decker sidewheeler owned by the Knickerbocker Steamboat Company.

The excursion boat left the pier at 9:40 A.M., first heading south, and then coming about just past the Williamsburg Bridge. At some point in the following ten or fifteen minutes, as the boat steamed up the East River, passed midtown and Roosevelt (then Blackwell's) Island, and entered the treacherous waters of Hell Gate, a fire sparked to life. It probably started in a packing barrel full of hay that had been stored, illegally, in the forward cabin. The fire smoldered for a few minutes, and then, as the *General Slocum* drew even with the Bronx, it exploded into flames. A stairwell created a flue that sucked the fire into the deck above, where it rolled forth like a wave.

The safety equipment on the 13-year-old *General Slocum* was inadequate and antique, the crew unprepared and undrilled for emergencies. Frightened crewmembers grabbed for the old ship's canvas firehoses; rotted, they burst when the water was turned on. Panicked passengers grabbed for life preservers; dilapidated, they crumbled into cork dust.

It took only about fifteen minutes for the ship to incinerate. Hundreds of passengers died in the flames. Hundreds more were drowned when they jumped or were thrown into the strong currents of the East River. The best estimates put the number of dead at 1,021.

The captain of the ship, William Van Schaick, was found guilty of negligence and sentenced to ten years in Sing Sing, though he was pardoned after three and a half. No one else—including the president and directors of the Knickerbocker Steamship Company and the city official who inspected and passed the ship's safety arrangement—was ever punished.

Exit the park the same way you entered and continue down Avenue B until you reach the intersection with Second Street.

20 During the late 1970s and early '80s, this intersection probably saw more heroin retailing than any other spot on earth. The scene at the

CRIMES OF TOMPKINS SQUARE PARK

Daniel Tompkins voter fraud, 1801—The park's namesake, New York Governor from 1807 to 1817 and Vice President under James Monroe, Tompkins engineered a voter fraud in the city council election of 1801. To get around restrictive property qualifications, he helped furnish money for thirty-nine penniless mechanics to purchase a lot and thus gain the vote.

   Tompkins Square Massacre, 1874—Amidst a long winter depression, a public meeting was called in the park for January 13, 1874, to lobby for public works projects. The city government saw red, and sent mounted police into the crowd of 10,000 with nightsticks swinging, driving men, women, and children into the streets and injuring scores.

   Gangster rendezvous, 1913—In his meticulous notes, detective Abe Shoenfeld noted at this time that the park was "a hangout for petty strong-arm men and petty thieves."

   Memorial Day incident, 1967—A group of hippies and local residents were singing folk songs and strumming guitars at a volume loud enough to bring the police. A battle ensued when the songsters resisted and thirty-eight were arrested for disorderly conduct.

   Police Riot, 1988—An August 6 demonstration by local activists over use of the park turned violent when the police—some of whom taped over their badge numbers—rioted and rampaged through the streets and shops, indiscriminately beating protesters and bystanders. Forty-four civilians were hurt. No police officers were ever charged or disciplined.

time was unworldly, a Casbah gone mad: hundreds of bedraggled addicts milled around the sidewalks and streets, an eerie murmuring filled the air, sellers called out their wares—"China White!" "Mr. T!" "Black Sunday!" "Poison Rubber!"—and steerers kept the beholden, cattlelike junkies in lines with the smack of a stick.

   This was a full-service center. Works—used needles, used syringes, used cotton, a dirty spoon—could be rented. Space could be had in a nearby shooting gallery, which could be a vacant apartment, unoccupied basement, busted storefront, or unusable stairwell in any of the abandoned buildings that often outnumbered the occupied structures on the surrounding blocks. The more affluent lined up in their cars, creating traffic jams and gridlock on the weekend nights, and made transactions from the comfort of their front seat.

   On January 17, 1984, the NYPD initiated Operation Pressure Point, a clampdown that sent over two hundred cops into the Lower East Side and East Village. Operation Pressure Point called for massive sweeps followed by intensive foot patrols and the stationing of cops on almost every corner. In three months over three thousand arrests had been made, and though most were for minor violations, the police claimed they had disrupted business and sent the dealers scurrying. Others said they had merely moved inside or downtown or over the Williamsburg Bridge to Brooklyn. Either way, the boom times at Avenue B and Second Street were over.

MUG SHOTS

DANIEL RAKOWITZ
Deranged Killer

Daniel Rakowitz was a well-known character in the neighborhood around Tompkins Square Park in the late 1980s. Part of a rootless young crowd that squatted in the park, he earned a reputation as an oddball among even this seriously iconoclastic group. He was often seen wandering about with a chicken on his shoulder, mumbling about the devil and police control. To those who would listen he announced that he was Jesus and would soon take over the country and legalize marijuana.

Bemusement turned to horror, however, when it was discovered that, on August 19, 1989, Rakowitz had murdered his roommate, Monika Beerle, a Swiss dancer and student, and, over the next several weeks, dissected and boiled her remains in the kitchen of their apartment at 700 East Ninth Street. A friend of his actually walked in while Beerle's head was in a pot on the stove, but did not notify the police. "I didn't want to hurt him anymore," she explained. Rakowitz put Beerle's skull and bones in a plastic pail that he deposited in a locker at the Port Authority bus station.

Rakowitz then bragged about the killing to the crowd of regulars in the park, but he was known to be so demented that nobody took him seriously. Some, however, grew a little queasy when they recalled the soup that he had not long before brought into the park and ladled out to the homeless. (It is unknown if Rakowitz actually turned his victim into stew.) But the police eventually got word of rumors of the homicide, picked him up, and received a tangled, bizarre confession filled with talk of satanism, animal sacrifice, and the new religion that Rakowitz had started. In a later interview he said, "I'm the New Lord, and I will take leadership of the satanic cultists to make sure they do everything that has to be done to destroy all those people who do disagree with my church . . . . And I'm going to be the youngest person elected to the U.S. presidency."

Born in 1960 in the little town of Rockport, Texas, Rakowitz evidently showed signs of mental illness quite early, and was given psychiatric care and medication even as a pre-teen. He came to New York some time around 1985 and quickly established his reputation.

He was found not guilty by reason of insanity on February 22, 1991 and shipped off to a state hospital for the criminally insane.

Monika Beerle, who was studying at the Martha Graham School of Contemporary Dance, had moved in with Rakowitz only out of a desperate need for an apartment. She had lived with him for only sixteen days.

Walk toward the middle of the block between Avenues A and B and pause outside 171 East 2nd Street.

21 When Patrolmen Dudley Reid and Robert E. McFeeley arrested Robert Friede—on February 7, 1966, as his car idled just a little to the east of this address—they figured they had picked up the usual nodding junkie. He displayed the usual pinpoint eyes and the usual needle marks. But their prisoner was very uncommon in at least one respect: Friede was a member of the ultra-wealthy Annenberg family. His grandfather was Moe Annenberg, founder of a huge media empire that included *TV Guide*, the *Daily Racing Form*, the *Philadelphia Inquirer*, *Seventeen* magazine, and several radio and television stations. The Annenberg fortune was once one of the largest in the United States. Money failed to insulate the family, however, and Annenberg's grandson was a heroin addict.

The bust was unusual in another way as well: checking the trunk of Friede's car, the policemen made a macabre discovery. Tucked under a blanket was the body of a young woman. The corpse turned out to be Friede's nineteen-year-old girlfriend, Celeste Crenshaw, also from an upper-crust background. By that afternoon, the newspapers were right on top of the story, with headlines such as "Society Girl's Body Found in Heir's Car on East Side" and "The Frozen Body of Girl Student in Car of Annenberg Heir."

Friede and Crenshaw were pioneers in the incipient underground drug scene that in a few years would burst out of the slums and into the colleges and high schools of America. The Friede-Crenshaw case received a great deal of publicity not only for its rather grotesque details, but also because it showed that hard drugs and their fatal effects had seeped into the staid white upper class.

Two weeks before his arrest, on January 24, 1966, Friede had been partying with Crenshaw in his apartment on 36 East 69th Street. He gave Crenshaw an injection of heroin and she promptly collapsed from an overdose. Friede attempted to revive her with a shot of amphetamine, but, high himself, he soon fell asleep. When he woke the next morning, his girlfriend was dead.

Paralyzed with fear, Friede kept the body for thirteen days, sustaining himself the entire time on a steady diet of heroin. For the first week he kept the corpse in his apartment with the air conditioner turned up. Then he rented a car and moved Crenshaw into the trunk. For nearly another week, the car was parked on the street outside his apartment. Finally, Friede decided to dump the body upstate. He had been on East Second Street to pick up a couple of friends who had promised to help him.

The young heir pleaded guilty to second degree manslaughter and was sentenced to two and a half to five years (technically, the sentence was for violation of parole; he drew a suspended sentence for the manslaughter charge).

Continue on Second Street a block and a half to 67 East Second Street.

22 One of the most incendiary protest campaigns against the Vietnam War had its source in a tenement apartment here, the secret arsenal and bomb factory of Sam Melville, leader of a group of activists and revolutionaries that also included Jane Alpert. Starting with the detonation, on July 26, 1969, of two dynamite bombs on a pier on the Hudson, the group's campaign eventually included eight Manhattan targets and several in other cities. Not one of their many bombs caused a fatality.

The young white revolutionaries, fueled by the increasing stridency of the antiwar and radical movement of the time, and their own conviction that revolution was just around the corner, set to work in a tireless fashion. The U.S. Induction Center on Whitehall Street was taken out, and the group released a flamboyant communiqué—"This action was taken in support of the NLF, legalized marijuana, love, Cuba, legalized abortion, and all the American revolutionaries and GIs who are winning the war against the Pentagon. Nixon, surrender now!"

The group also hit the Marine Midland Bank on Broadway (evidently on a whim of Melville's, who was not a stable character, even for a bomber; justification for the act was concocted after the fact), the Criminal Courts Building at 100 Centre Street, and targets in Minneapolis, Milwaukee, and Chicago (although this last bomb failed to go off).

Then, the group's *pièce de resistance.* On the night of November 11, 1969, bombs went off nearly simultaneously on the nineteenth floor of the General Motors Building, the twentieth floor of the RCA building, and the sixteenth floor of Chase Manhattan Bank. This stupendous run caused panic throughout the city and precipitated more than two hundred bomb threats, but failed to produce a spontaneous uprising of the masses.

The very next evening, November 12, Sam Melville slung a knapsack of bombs over his shoulder and headed out from this building with accomplice George Demmerle. His intention was to place explosives in the Army trucks parked outside the National Guard Armory at Lexington Avenue and 26th Street. The trucks would be driven inside at night and the bombs would be perfectly placed for maximum damage to the state's property. However, George Demmerle turned out to be an FBI informer. Melville's intentions were known all along—he was arrested with his ticking bombs alongside the Armory.

Melville pleaded guilty to Federal bomb conspiracy and state arson charges, and was sentenced to eighteen years. In September 1971, he was killed in the Attica Prison uprising. Jane Alpert pleaded guilty to a lesser charge of conspiracy to destroy government property. Before sentencing, she went underground, reemerging on November 14, 1974, and eventually serving two years in prison. George Demmerle pocketed a $25,000 reward from Marine Midland Bank and disappeared.

Walk over to East Third Street. Seventy-seven East Third Street is the headquarters of the Manhattan chapter of the Hell's Angels Motorcycle Club. This is a functioning clubhouse: be discreet.

23 The notorious Hell's Angels Motorcycle Club was founded on March 17, 1948 in San Bernadino, California. The Manhattan chapter was chartered on December 5, 1969 by Sandy Frazier Alexander. An ex-marine, he moved to New York in 1967 and, looking for excitement, joined the Aliens Motorcycle Club. He quickly decided they weren't tough enough and decided to establish a squad of the growing and popular Hell's Angels in Manhattan. Soon, Alexander's power and reputation rivaled that of the most famous Angel in the country, Sonny Barger of Oakland, California.

A reputation as rebellious free spirits and hard-driving individualists has long clung to the Angels. They have been romanticized in movies such as *The Wild Ones* and *Easy Rider*, and adopted by celebrity counterculturists such as Ken Kesey, Jack Nicholson, Hunter Thompson, the Grateful Dead, and the Rolling Stones. More antisocial than antiestablishment, the Angels are in fact a violent, racist gang of brutal misfits.

Originally little more than hell-raising thugs, the Angels transformed themselves in the 1970s into a well-oiled criminal organization specializing in the manufacture and sale of amphetamines.

A massive FBI raid here on May 2, 1985 resulted in scores of arrests on drug charges and splintered the chapter. Alexander was sentenced to sixteen years in prison. In a later trial, three Angels, including charter member William "Wild Bill" Medeiros, testified for the government, revealing that the gang imported massive quantities of amphetamines from Oakland and Montreal for resale and had murdered at least two members suspected of informing. President Brendan Manning, Alexander's successor, was sentenced to eight years in jail for his involvement.

A mural and a bronze plaque across the street from headquarters memorializes Vincent "Big Vinnie" Girolamo. He distinguished himself in Angel annals on September 21, 1977, when he threw thirty-two-year-old Mary Anne Campbell to her death from the clubhouse roof as other members cheered him on. He died in 1979 from a ruptured spleen suffered during a fight with a fellow Angel in Oakland, California.

Nearest subway: Second Avenue F
Nearest bus line: M 15; M 21

7

Murray Hill, Midtown, and the Upper East Side

A Criminal Sketch of Midtown East _____

In the early seventeenth century, while a desperate band of Dutch adventurers crowded into the toe of Manhattan Island and created an unruly little town, this area remained a peaceable expanse of green forest and verdant brush. Land was bought and sold and a handful of homesteads were established, but there was no systematic settlement here for another two hundred years. But though undeveloped, it was hardly Elysian: The third recorded murder in Manhattan's history (four years after the first) took place here. As related in an early account, the killing of Claes Rademaker in March 1642 has the character of a Greek tragedy:

He lived a short league from the fort by the Densel-bay [Turtle Bay], where he had built a small house, and had set up the trade of wheelwright [Rademaker means wheelwright; he was also known as Claes Swits]. It was on the Wickquasgeck road over which the Indians passed daily. It happened that a savage came to this Claes Rademaker for the purpose of trading beavers with him for duffels cloth, which goods were in a chest. This chest he had locked up, and had stooped down in order to take his goods out, when this murderer, the savage, seeing that the man had his head bent over into the chest, and observing an axe standing behind him, seized the axe, and struck Claes Rademaker on the neck therewith, so that he fell down dead by the chest. The murderer then stole all the goods and ran off. The Commander sent to them and made inquiry in Wickquasgeck why this Dutchman had been so shamefully murdered. The murderer answered that, while the fort [Fort Amsterdam, put up in 1628 near the Battery] was being built, he came with his uncle and another savage to

Midtown East

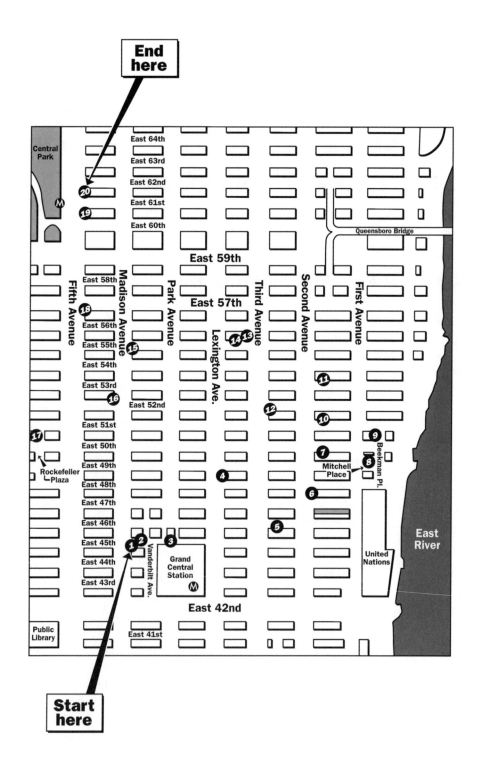

the freshwater, bringing beavers, in order to trade with the Dutchmen, that some Swannekes (as they call the Netherlanders) came there, took away from his uncle his beavers, and then killed him. He was then a small boy, and resolved that, when he should grow up, he would revenge that deed upon the Dutch, and since then he had seen no better chance to do so than with this Claes Rademaker.

The colonists made attempts to capture the culprit, but without success.

Then as now, a murder was hardly enough to deter the intrepid New Yorker, and several large country estates arose here during the seventeenth and eighteenth centuries. One of them, owned by James Beekman, became a landmark of espionage during the War of Independence. Nathan Hale, revolutionary spy and hero, was tried in the greenhouse of the Beekman estate and sentenced to death by the British. The exact location of his execution is unknown, but was probably by the Dove Tavern at Third Avenue and 66th Street. And Major John Andre, the redcoat spy, stopped at the Beekman house for a last briefing on September 18, 1780, before continuing on his way to a rendezvous with Benedict Arnold, who planned to deliver West Point to the British. Andre was captured near Tarrytown and hanged at Tappan, New York on October 2, 1780. With the United Nations now nearby, the neighborhood is again a locus for espionage.

General lawlessness and bad behavior, however, took another fifty years to take root. In the second quarter of the nineteenth century, a squatter's community known as Dutch Hill developed around East 42nd Street and Second Avenue where hard-bitten, hard-drinking residents eked out an existence picking rags and garbage. "On 'Dutch Hill,'" stated *The Dangerous Classes of New York*, published in 1872, "one can hardly enter a shanty where is a sober family. The women all drink; the men work, and then carouse." The most famous citizen of the Hill was John "Genteel Jamie" Corcoran (the nickname was ironic), who moved onto land on 40th Street about 1850 and eventually became the patriarch of a notorious criminal clan. From his home, "Corcoran's Roost," located at what is now 25 Tudor City Place, his extended family ventured forth to thieve and plunder. The height served them well in their frequent battles with the police, enabling them to heave rocks and bricks, and undoubtedly and epithet or two, upon their nemeses.

Urban development came shortly after the Civil War, and much of the area became a relatively affluent neighborhood of brownstones. But the construction of the Third Avenue elevated subway in 1878 and the Second Avenue elevated in 1880 brought a decline. Residents who could afford to moved away from the shadowed, noisy streets, and pawn shops and low bars proliferated. The blocks by the East River filled up with factories, coal pens, stables, and slaughterhouses.

The untamed heights of Dutch Hill.

The brownstones were converted into rooming houses. An account of the 1880s calls the neighborhood "mixed and troublesome."

This characterization remained accurate for another fifty years. The WPA guide to New York, published in 1939, takes note of the district's "squalid tenements." The many rooming houses supported a transient population that included some very unsavory characters: In an interesting coincidence, in November 1934, multiple murderer Robert Irwin (see p. 255) was living at a boardinghouse at 316 East 50th Street at the same time that serial killer Albert Fish (see p. 261) was rooming around the corner at 200 East 52nd Street.

Criminal gangs that stalked the district a hundred or so years ago included the Bridge Twisters, the Tunnel Gang, and the Terry Reilleys. Later on, in the 1920s, the Four Fierce Flanagans made their appearance. Police Captain Cornelius Willemse called them " . . . the toughest, bravest outlaws I ever had the misfortune to meet." Tom, Joey, Frank, and the Harp prowled this neighborhood as robbers, racketeers, and beer runners until 1930, when Joey and Tom were killed and Frank and the Harp were put away.

The fortunes of the neighborhood changed once again after World War II, in large part due to the dismantling of the els (the Second Avenue el came down in 1942 and the Third Avenue el in 1956). The emergence of the east side as Manhattan's most affluent neighborhood dramatically changed the flavor of crime here. Celebrity murders replaced gang rubouts, embezzlement took over for armed robbery, big-ticket burglaries edged out retail stick-ups.

Today, beneath the veneer of affluence, there is a buzzing hive of lawlessness. Sophisticated financial scams and frauds are quietly carried out in the thicket of office buildings along the avenues. Very expensive and very business-like prostitutes discreetly do business in row houses and apartment buildings. The neighborhood's many luxury hotels provide a living for hundreds of professional thieves (the NYPD has a special squad just for hotel robberies). There may be fewer criminal incidents here than in many other precincts of the city, but when they do occur, they tend to be impressive, as the following tour proves.

Stalking Midtown East

Nearest subway: 42nd Street - Grand Central 4 5 6 7 S
Nearest bus lines: M 1; M 2; M 3; M 4; M 42; M 98,
M 101; M 102; M 104; X 25; Q 32

Our tour begins with one of the city's most famous criminal incidents, the bestselling, Academy Award–winning French Connection heroin bust. One of the major locations in this intercontinental escapade was the Hotel Roosevelt, here on the corner of Madison Avenue and 45th Street.

① Near midnight on January 11, 1962, the four criminal principals in the French Connection drug pipeline met under the 45th street awning of the Hotel Roosevelt. They talked quietly in the dark for about ten minutes, hashing out the details for delivery of a huge shipment of heroin from the labs of Marseilles to the streets of New York. The cabal represented an international effort. From France: the elderly, aristocratic Jean Jehan; Corsican gangster Francois Scaglia; and J. Mouren, a French drug smuggler. The American end of the connection was held up, not very competently, by Pasquale "Patsy" Fuca, a young mobster with connections to the Lucchese Mafia family. The conference concluded, they walked to Madison, piled into Fuca's blue Buick compact, and slipped unhindered into the night.

But not unnoticed. Two cops—Sonny Grosso and Eddie Egan—were tucked away down the block in an unmarked car. Several months earlier the partners, later to be propelled to cop stardom for their roles in the case, had stumbled upon the connection by accident. They spotted Fuca one night in early October 1961 in the Copacabana nightclub hanging out with wiseguys and flashing fistfuls of cash. Out of curiosity the cops tailed him home to Brooklyn. When they found out that this big spender owned nothing grander than a luncheonette, they figured they were onto something. When they found out that his uncle, Angelo Tuminaro, was a well-known drug wholesaler from the Lucchese Mafia family, they knew it. They kicked into motion a huge investigation that would eventually involve dozens of NYPD cops and FBI agents to shadow suspects, listen to wiretaps, and try to guess who was who and what the hell was going on.

The conspirators met at the Roosevelt at least three times during the following week to hash out the details of the huge deal. It was Fuca's first big score, the Brooklyn boy's first brush with international drug runners. He was nervous and anxious not to show it. Perhaps that's why he never noticed that for the preceding three months he had been almost continually tailed.

On January 16, with the deal concluded, the heroin was transferred. The bulk of the shipment—nearly 110 pounds of high quality heroin—lay ingeniously concealed in the frame of a car parked in the garage of the Waldorf-Astoria. The Europeans had found an equally ingenious way of bringing the car into the United States. They wrangled the help of a very popular, but apparently not very bright, French television star, Jacques Angelvin, who hosted a hit show on Paris nightlife and show business. When Angelvin decided to visit the United States, his friend Scaglia suggested that he ship a car with him on the ocean trip over, a particular car, and earn some extra money on the side. Angelvin, well aware of what would be packed into the chassis, agreed.

Under instructions from Scaglia and Jehan, Angelvin drove his car to a parking garage at 45 East End Avenue and returned in a cab to the Waldorf. Later that night, Fuca picked up the car and drove it to a body shop in the Bronx, where, with his brother Tony and the Frenchman Mouren, he labored for three hours to remove from the frame of the car, what was, at the time, one of the largest single shipments of heroin ever to enter the United States.

Fuca's moment of triumph was not long. The cops moved in two days later. Fuca was arrested in his father's home in Brooklyn, where the police found twenty-four pounds of heroin concealed in the basement. Another 88 pounds were found in his brother Tony's basement in the Bronx. The Fuca brothers drew seven-and-a-half to fifteen years each. Scaglia was sentenced to a maximum of twenty-two years; Angelvin to three to six years. But the police missed some of their quarry. Jehan slipped away, possibly with as much as $500,000. Mouren too, escaped back to France.

The French Connection, up to that time the largest narcotics seizure ever made by a municipal police force, became famous with a popular book and a hugely successful movie. But victory turned to mortification when it was discovered, ten years later, that all of the confiscated French Connection heroin had been stolen from the NYPD.

In fact, beginning around 1969, almost four hundred pounds of heroin and cocaine (with a value of around $70 million) had been stolen from the Office of the New York City Police Property Clerk, a huge warehouse where impounded evidence is stored for trial. It was the most humiliating incident in the history of the department.

Despite several investigations, no one was ever brought to trial or even formally accused of the thefts. But the mastermind was probably Vincent Papa, one of the city's major narcotics traffickers in the early '70s. And he likely had help from members of the police department's Special Investigating Unit, an elite squad formed after the success of the French Connection investigation to nab major drug dealers. The unsupervised, freewheeling group, however, went from investigating to consorting to cooperating with the dealers they were supposed to bring to justice, soon becoming, as one observer wrote, "the most corrupt law enforcement unit in American history." They were later disbanded in disgrace. Papa was murdered in Atlanta Penitentiary, where he was serving time on an unrelated charge, in July 1977.

Remain where you are for the next incident.

2 The Roosevelt was built in 1924 on a site previously occupied by the Knickerbocker Athletic Club, which was founded in 1896 during the sports craze of the late nineteenth century as a health club for the city's elite. The Knickerbocker was the principal setting for what one crime writer has called "the greatest murder mystery that New York ever has known." Poe might have called it "Murder at the Gymnastique Alliance." Arthur Conan Doyle might have named it "The Case of the Knockedout Knickerbocker." We know it, however, as *The State v. Roland Burnham Molineux.*

On Christmas Eve 1898, Harry S. Cornish, athletic director at the Knickerbocker Athletic Club, found an anonymous gift in his office. Wrapped in tissue was a small blue bottle of Bromo-seltzer and a fancy little silver sheath—actually intended for toothpicks or matches—to make the bottle appropriate for a bureau or vanity. It seemed a waggish gift, a sly little poke at the holiday drinking in which Cornish would presumably overindulge. He took the bottle home and, when his aunt, Katherine Adams, complained of a headache, he prepared a fizzing glass of Bromo for her. She drank the potion and immediately collapsed on the floor. Within minutes she was dead, a victim of cyanide of mercury poisoning.

Shocking enough, of course, but the plot thickens. A month and a half earlier, the Knickerbocker Athletic Club had experienced an-

The Knickerbocker (formerly the Manhattan) Athletic Club, where murder was exercised.

other death among its membership. On November 10, 1898, Henry C. Barnet, a stock and commodities broker just thirty-two years old, died in his room at the club. Although he told the attending physician that it was "that damned Kutnow powders [a popular patent medicine] that had caused the trouble," the doctor diagnosed a bad case of diptheria and Barnet was quietly laid away.

With thrilling ratiocination, the police realized the two deaths were related. A small tin box of Kutnow's Powder, which Barnet said he had received unsolicited in the mail, was analyzed and found to be full of cyanide of mercury. Barnet himself was exhumed and found, too, to be full of cyanide of mercury.

Police attention was initially focused on Cornish. He was divorced, a sign at the time of a suspect character. Living in his household was Katherine Adams' daughter, Florence Rodgers, also suspiciously divorced. The police considered a love affair between the two and a plot to get rid of an obstructive mother, but dropped that theory when it failed to fit the facts—Cornish and Rodgers were not lovers. The authorities then turned to John Adams (no relation to victim Katherine Adams), secretary to Harry Ballantine, founder of the Knickerbocker. Adams was something worse than a divorcé, for he had never married at all. The newspapers noted that he lived with a young man in a residence said to house homosexuals. And, they added ominously, his room was decorated in the style of Oscar Wilde. But again, investigators could make no case.

The police then came to settle upon Roland Burnham Molineux, an upstanding, indeed foppish, member of a prominent society family. Molineux *père* was a Civil War hero. His son Roland managed a paint factory in Newark, New Jersey, and was, until the winter of 1897, a member of the Knickerbocker Athletic Club. He was one of their star performers, in fact: the reigning amateur horizontal-bar champion of the country, and just the kind of vigorous, class-conscious gentleman-athlete that the club cherished. Molineux had once roomed at the club next door to Henry C. Barnet. He had resigned his membership in a feud with the athletic director, Harry Cornish. A little more detective work, and Molineux was arrested.

The police had no confession and no smoking gun. But the prosecution at Molineux's first trial, which opened on November 14, 1899, threw out a net woven from the following circumstantial evidence:

1. The writing on the Christmas present sent to Cornish was judged by several handwriting experts to be that of Molineux's in a disguised hand;

2. Other letters surfaced, signed with the names of Barnet and Cornish, that used disguised handwriting again judged to be Molineux's. These were orders for patent medicines, including one sent to the Kutnow Brothers company for their popular powders.

3. A distinctive blue stationery, adorned at the top with a design of three interlocking crescents, was used for several of these orders, and letters were found on the same stationery in Molineux's own (undisguised) hand;

4. One of these letters, on the same distinctive blue paper and written in a disguised hand, was sent to a previous employer of a Knickerbocker Athletic Club worker for a reference check. Molineux and Cornish were said to be the only ones who knew of this previous employer.

5. The return addresses on the fake Barnet and Cornish letters were two private mail box services. The proprietor of one service identified Molineux as a customer who had rented a box in the name of Barnet. It was shown that Molineux was familiar with the address of the other because he once requested a subscription, under his own name, to a magazine that the proprietor published as a sideline from the same building.

6. The Cornish Christmas package was mailed from the general post office in New York, then located at the foot of City Hall Park, which was on Molineux's way to work. The silver holder included with the package was bought at a shop in New Jersey several blocks from his place of employment.

7. Molineux's job at a paint factory gave him access to Prussian blue dye, which can be used to make cyanide of mercury.

And finally, the motives: Barnet was a rival for the affections of Blanche Chesebrough (whom Molineux would marry just nineteen days after Barnet's death). And Molineux had carried on a long feud at the Knickerbocker with Cornish, the athletic director, whom gentlemanly Molineux considered vulgar, unprofessional, and self-aggrandizing. The year before, Molineux had gone to the board of directors with an ultimatum: either Cornish goes or he leaves. The board wished him well.

All of this was enough to convince the jury. It has also convinced history, for every discussion of this famous case assumes Molineux's guilt. But it failed, ultimately, to convince the legal system. All of the testimony and evidence concerning Barnet—his relationship with the defendant, the manner of his death, and the use of his name in letters—was disallowed because Molineux was indicted only for the death of Adams. His conviction was reversed upon appeal.

After his exoneration, Molineux enjoyed a brief literary career with a book and a play drawn from his prison experiences. In a bizarre stunt, he was hired by the *New York Herald* as a reporter for the famous Thaw murder trial (see p. 163). In 1913, he went insane from the effects of syphilitic infection and was committed to the Kings Park State Hospital for the Insane. He died there on November 2, 1917.

HOMES OF THE RICH AND SCURRILOUS

John Jacob Astor—223 Broadway. Fur dealer and slumlord Astor, a man of insatiable greed, schemed and cheated his way to become the richest man of his day. He died, roundly hated, on March 29, 1848.

Roy Cohn—39 East 68th Street (law office). Counsel for Senator Joseph McCarthy's communist witchhunt, disbarred lawyer, gay-basher (though himself a homosexual), tax evader, thief.

Jay Gould—northeast corner of Fifth Avenue and 47th Street.
Perhaps the most venal of the nineteenth century's robber barons,
Jay Gould built a fortune by illegal and unethical deals and scams. In
1869, Gould (his nickname was "The Mephistopheles of Wall
Street"), attempted to corner the entire U. S. gold supply. His
attempt failed, but not before causing a major panic on Wall Street.

**Harry and Leona Helmsley—Park Lane Hotel, 36 Central
Park South.** Tales of the greed and meanness of these real estate
billionaires filled the media after their indictment for income tax
evasion and fraud in 1988. "Only the little people pay taxes," Leona
said, earning the eternal enmity of New Yorkers. Harry was too ill to
be tried; Leona was found guilty on thirty-three counts.

Ivar Krueger—791 Park Avenue. Although he was an astute
businessman who had gained a fortune through control of the
Swedish Match Trust (hence his nickname, "The Match King"),
Krueger's avarice drove him to enlarge his fortune with forged stocks,
faked assets, and fraudulent deals. When he was found out, he
committed suicide on March 12, 1932.

Richard Nixon—142 E. 65th Street. Facing impeachment by
Congress for obstructing justice in the investigation of the Watergate
burglary, the thirty-seventh president of the United States resigned
from office on August 8, 1974. He moved to New York after the
untimely end of his presidential term.

Claus Von Bulow—960 Fifth Avenue. In two highly publicized trials
of the 1980s, Von Bulow, a well-to-do social climber born as Claus Borberg
(he changed his name to Von Bulow in middle-age), was first convicted, and
then exonerated, of the attempted murder of his wealthy wife.

Walk east on 45th Street, underneath the Park Avenue Rampway, and
pause in front of 230 Park Avenue, the Helmsley Building. In 1931, this
was known as the New York Central Building.

3 In the long chronicle of Mob killings, the assassination of Salvatore
Maranzano has achieved a kind of legendary status. Not only was the
killing a surprising hit on the most powerful Mob boss in the country, but it also supposedly inaugurated a huge nationwide gang purge
that eliminated the last of the "Mustache Petes"—the Old World,
old-style crime bosses—and opened the way for the rise of younger,
Americanized gangsters such as Lucky Luciano and Vito Genovese.
This purge has been poetically dubbed "The Night of the Sicilian
Vespers."

Salvatore Maranzano came to the United States in 1925, already a
seasoned Mafia member from Castellammare del Golfo in Sicily. He
stepped quickly into a major role in the organization on this side of
the Atlantic, indulging in bootlegging, gambling operations, and the

very lucrative business of smuggling aliens into the country. He was said to be a well-educated man who spoke Latin (learned in a seminary) and collected books on Julius Caesar, whom he considered a role model. By 1930, he felt powerful enough to challenge the leadership of Joe "the Boss" Masseria (see p. 206), then the most powerful Italian gangster in the city.

That struggle ended on April 15, 1931, with the assassination of Masseria at Gerardo Scarpato's restaurant, the Nuova Villa Tammaro, in Coney Island. Lucky Luciano, Masseria's trusted lieutenant, invited his boss to their favorite Italian eatery by the sea. Unbeknownst to Masseria, his aide, at the bidding of Maranzano, had arranged a double cross. While the two played pinochle after dinner, a car idled outside packed with a gang of ruthless hitmen: some accounts say the car contained the all-star cast of Vito Genovese, Joe Adonis, Albert Anastasia, and Bugsy Siegel. Other records mention Genovese and the relatively unknown Frank Livorsi and Joseph "Joe Stretch" Stracci. At some point during the card game, Luciano excused himself to go to the bathroom in the back and the four men entered from the front, blazing away with revolvers. Masseria was hit six times and killed instantly.

Maranzano moved fast to secure his position. He called together a huge meeting of Mafiosi in a social hall, declared himself *Capo di tutti Capi*, boss of bosses, and supposedly created the five-family structure that the New York Mafia retains to this day. But his domination was short-lived. Five months later, in a well-planned and perfectly executed operation, the would-be Caesar was dethroned.

On September 10, 1931, Maranzano was visited by a party of five uniformed men at his office on the ninth floor of the New York Central Building. They flashed badges and asked him to step into his private office alone. Maranzano was expecting a police raid; in fact, in expectation of just such a visit from the feds, he had recently told his minions not to bring guns into the building. So Maranzano courteously led the men into his office as his bodyguards stood aside. Only after entering the room did the boss realize his mistake. While several of the visitors pulled out guns and held Maranzano's bodyguards at bay, others followed Maranzano into his office and drew knives. The boss of bosses was quickly dispatched.

The killing was planned by the tireless team of Lucky Luciano and Vito Genovese. Not only did these two feel that Maranzano was becoming too powerful and too greedy, but they had also heard that the boss was fearful of their growing strength and had hired a well-known hitman from outside the Mafia, Vincent "Mad Dog" Coll, to whack the ambitious pair. Luciano and Genovese decided to strike first.

The assassination of the dominant figure in the Italian underworld of the time supposedly kicked off a massive, coordinated offensive in which up to forty—in some accounts up to ninety—of Maranzano's allies were killed. Crack teams of trained killers are said to have fanned out across the country and successfully dispatched their quarry within a day or two of Maranzano's death. "It was a remarkable example of planning and accomplishment," as the authors of *Murder, Inc.* put it, "that this mass extermination of Mafia executives across the country has never, as far as [we] have been able to learn, been linked, one with another."

Never been linked because the story is untrue. Accounts of this amazing operation are invariably undocumented, the victims unidentified, their killers nameless and their replacements unknown. "The Night of the Sicilian Vespers" has more in common with such venerable gangland myths as garlic-coated bullets and false-bottomed caskets than it does with the truth. Luciano and Genovese were able to grab the reigns of Mafia power without such slaughter.

Walk another block in the same direction to Lexington Avenue, turn left, and then continue up to East 48th Street. On the east side of the block between 48th and 49th Streets sits the New York Marriott East Side. Pause at the southwest corner of Lexington Avenue and East 48th Street.

4 There was something almost inevitable about Meir Kahane's untimely end. His whole life had been devoted to such blind hate and violent extremism that it was unsurprising when he was felled by an assassin's bullet. He had once said, referring to Palestinian terrorism, that "those terrorists who live by the sword should be ready to perhaps face the same fate . . . ." The words form his own epitaph.

Kahane came to public attention in the late '60s as the founder of the militant Jewish Defense League. He moved to Israel in the early 1970s and formed Kach, an ultra-right-wing political party that advocated expelling Arabs from Israel. Kahane won a seat in the Knesset, Israel's parliament, but he was later thrown out for his racist views. His charisma and unflinching militancy, however, made him disappointingly popular, and he continued a public career both in Israel and the United States.

On November 5, 1990, Kahane gave a speech for a Zionist group in the Marriott. He had just finished and was sitting at a table near the dais when, without a word, a young man approached him in the crowded room, leveled a .357 revolver at his head at point-blank range, and fired twice. Kahane went down and died almost immediately. In the ensuing pandemonium, the gunman fled the room, in the process shooting and wounding Irving Franklin, a bystander he encountered by the exit.

The gunman burst through the revolving front doors and, waving his pistol, commandeered a taxi. The cab made it about a block and a half (driving past where you are now standing), but, city traffic being what it is, the driver could not get through, even with the incentive of a gun to his head. The assassin jumped out of the cab by the post office, only to encounter Carlos Acosta, a postal service officer carrying his regulation post-office-issued revolver. The young man declined Acosta's request to freeze, leading to a shoootout on Lexington Avenue. Acosta received a slight wound to his right shoulder; his foe took a bullet to the chin and was subdued.

The gunman was an Egyptian, El Sayyid A. Nosair. He had gained entry to Kahane's speech because security guards assumed he was a Sephardic Jew. The government assumed the trial would be an open-and-shut case: the room was full of people, witnesses had seen Nosair flee, he was apprehended with a gun in his hand and ammunition in his pocket. The FBI, searching Nosair's apartment in Jersey City, New Jersey, had found evidence linking him to militant Islamic terrorist groups, but the prosecution, believing its case overwhelming, preferred to play it straight and not confuse the jury with vague talk of shadowy groups and conspiracies.

Defense lawyer William Kunstler, however, took the opposite tack. He hinted at murderous schisms and dark jealousies within the Kahane camp. He hammered on unusual procedures by emergency medical personnel and the coroner. He pounced on inconsistencies in eyewitness testimony.

It worked: the verdict showed that the jury was thoroughly confused. They found that Nosair possessed the gun that killed Kahane and wounded Franklin and Acosta, found him guilty of assault on the two injured men, but acquitted him of murdering Kahane. This odd and illogical verdict was reached despite the testimony of ballistics experts that the bullets recovered from the three men were all fired from the same gun. Even the jubilant William Kunstler, called the verdict "strange, irrational, [and] inconsistent." Nosair was sentenced to 7½ to 22 years.

The case took yet another bizarre turn in January, 1995, when Nosair was put on trial, along with eleven others, accused of plotting to bomb several sites in New York City as part of a *jihad*, or religious war. Nosair, although he was in prison at the time, was said to have been part of a loose group guided by Sheik Omar Abdel Rahman that, in the name of a virulent and violent interpretation of Islam, not only planned to bomb the United Nations and the Lincoln and Holland Tunnels, but were also behind the World Trade Center bombing on February 26, 1993 (see p. 10). The assassination of Kahane was now said by prosecutors to be part of the group's battle plan. On October 1, 1995, the defendants, including Nosair, were convicted on 48 of the 50 charges.

Proceed a block to Third Avenue and then turn right. Walk to 46th Street and turn left. Just east of Third Avenue is Spark's Steak House.

5 The Paul Castellano killing—carried out on December 16, 1985, in front of this restaurant—was, in many respects, the quintessential Mafia hit. It was dramatic, brazen, and perfectly planned. It came off without a hitch. No one else was hurt. The rubout showed such style and spunk, in fact, that it cheered, rather than disturbed, the city. It seemed to prove that New York, though suffering hard times, still had the classiest mobsters in the country.

Castellano was not considered a great loss, Mafiawise. Head of the powerful Gambino family, he was a careful and colorless boss, more technocrat than tough guy. Personally opposed to drug dealing and aware of the destabilizing effect it had on the organization, he banned his family from the lucrative field. This edict brought him into conflict with John Gotti, a scrappy and fast-rising Mafioso from Queens whose crew was deeply involved in the narcotics trade. When Castellano called him on the carpet, Gotti decided that it was time the boss retired.

In the beginning of December 1985, the Gotti crew were tipped off that Castellano would be hosting a lunchtime meeting at Spark's Steak House on December 16. Although Castellano would be arriving in broad daylight during the lunch rush in teeming midtown Manhattan, Gotti decided the circumstances were ideal.

Gotti threw a tremendous wall of firepower around Spark's that day. Four hitmen—who had been told who their target was only minutes before—took positions directly outside the entrance to the restaurant. They were Eddie Lino, "Fat" Sally Scala, Vincent Artuso and John "Carneg" Carneglia, all appropriately dressed in white trenchcoats. Another group of backup shooters—Joe Watts, "Fat" Angelo Ruggiero, and Iggy Alogna—were congregated by Second Avenue. Anthony "Tony Roach" Rampino, another backup, was directly across the street. Gotti and his underboss, Salvatore "Sammy the Bull" Gravano, waited in a car at the northwest corner of Third Avenue and 46th Street. Castellano was completely hemmed in.

These trained killers watched intently as their target, traveling in a black Lincoln driven by trusted aide Tommy Bilotti, turned right from Third Avenue and drew up to Spark's front door. The moment the boss and his driver stepped out of their car, the four hitmen rushed forward and in a moment—almost faster than it takes to tell—emptied their pistols into Castellano and Bilotti. Quick but accurate: the pair were killed instantly. The gunmen trotted to Second Avenue, jumped into waiting cars, and sped off. Moments later, Gravano and Gotti cruised by to inspect the work. Their ex-boss lay on the sidewalk with his head propped up on the car seat. Bilotti was sprawled in the street by the other side of the car. Said Gravano later, "It went pretty smooth." Gotti's gamble paid off, and he became boss of the Gambino family later that year.

Though it was long rumored that Gotti was behind the hit, the details of the operation were unknown until his underboss and best friend Gravano turned informer during Gotti's 1992 trial. Gotti was convicted on thirteen counts, among them the murder of Castellano.

MUG SHOTS

ARNOLD ROTHSTEIN
Mr. Big

Gambler, bookie, and crime boss Arnold Rothstein will forever be known as the grinch that fixed the 1919 World Series. He has been hated as a man who would subvert the hoariest of American traditions and feared as a man who had the power and audacity to try it. All his life, however, Rothstein denied the charge, and he was probably telling the truth.

Rothstein was born into a middle-class Jewish household in 1882, but, a rebel child, he found the action of the streets more alluring than the comforts of home. He left home at the age of seventeen. While hanging out in the clubs and poolrooms of midtown, Rothstein became an expert card player and pool shooter. As his winnings grew, he began to lend money to other gamblers, then to stake card games of his own, and then to book bets at the racetrack at Saratoga.

As important to his success as his gambling skills was his relationship with the powerful political kingpin "Big Tim" Sullivan. Sullivan was an old-style politician, the type who handed out turkeys on Thanksgiving, arranged city jobs for loose nephews, and marshalled tremendous power from a neighborhood base. Rothstein became a protégé of the ward boss, who gave the gambler protection and pull. In 1909, with his patron's help, he opened a plush gambling house on West 46th Street, his first permanent establishment. It flourished and led to several more, including some in Saratoga, over the next decade.

By 1916 Rothstein was a rich man with interests in several gambling houses and race tracks, and a large (probably the country's largest) bookmaking operation. He was the mastermind behind several large bucketshop operations (fraudulent stock brokerages) and Wall Street bond thefts. Later he became involved in labor racketeering, bootlegging, and narcotics smuggling. His power and reputation earned him such awe-inspiring nicknames as Mr. Big, The Brain, the Big Bankroll, and, simply, A. R.

The World Series incident took place in 1919, at the height of his reign as underworld banker and broker. The fix got started when several Chicago White Sox players, disgusted at their meager salaries (as little as $2,500), approached some gamblers and offered to throw the series for $100,000. The gamblers were interested, but figured there was only one source for that much cash: the Big Bankroll. When approached, Rothstein was indeed intrigued with the proposition. He kicked in $10,000 to find out what was happening, but after mulling things over, turned down the deal. He decided the gamblers involved were bunglers, that word of the conspiracy would eventually leak out, and that, somehow, it was too much of a good thing. Others were found to complete the deal. Despite his small role in the grand drama and his constant denials, however, the notion that Rothstein fixed the World Series remains, unerasable, in the popular mind.

Rothstein's death is one of the great Manhattan murder mysteries. He was discovered on the night of November 4, 1928 in the service stairway of the Park Central Hotel (now the New York Sheraton) with a bullet wound. When asked who shot him, he said, in perfect gangland style, "I won't talk about it. I'll take care of it myself." He never had the chance: his wound was fatal and Rothstein died two days later. The *New York Daily News* called it "the most sensational Broadway murder since the killing of Herman Rosenthal in 1912." Gambler George McManus, to whom Rothstein owed money from a high-stakes poker game, was tried and acquitted for the killing in a trial characterized by shoddy police work and a political cover-up. It's probable though, that, enraged when Rothstein failed to pay his debts, McManus did indeed pull the trigger on Mr. Big.

Continue past the restaurant to Second Avenue and cross over to the east side. Turn left and walk to the block between 47th and 48th Streets. The Embassy House apartment building now stands on the site once occupied by St. Boniface's Catholic Church, a setting for the Hans Schmidt murder case, a striking incident that once filled the front pages and is now forgotten.

❻ On September 3, 1913, a package was pulled out of the Hudson River near Woodcliff, New Jersey that contained the upper half of a soggy female corpse. Identification was made problematic by the want of a head. When the grisly find was publicized, Peter Sternemann gravely came forward and told police that he thought it was his daughter. The authorities were relieved to wrap things up so quickly until daughter Sternemann was found alive. A macabre parade followed. Casper Jianin thought it was his wife. She was discovered in

Havana. Mary Spillane announced that it was her sister. Relatives believed it was Ida M. Bowles. Francis Day identified the body as her sister Antoinette.

There was no one, evidently, looking out for Anna Aumuller, for the police had to discover for themselves that she was the victim. With some very respectable detective work, the police traced the pillowcase that enclosed the corpse through a sales receipt to an apartment at 68 Bradhurst Avenue. Aumuller had lived there with an unusual roommate: the Reverend Father Hans Schmidt, an assistant at St. Boniface's Church. When confronted by detectives, Schmidt confessed in great detail to the murder and dismemberment of Anna Aumuller, who worked as a maid in the rectory. "I was directed to kill Anna Aumuller by Saint Elizabeth. Saint Elizabeth is my patron, and she directed me to make the sacrifice of the girl I loved; the sacrifice to be consummated in blood, as was the sacrifice of Abraham," he lucidly explained. It seemed that Schmidt would be spared a capital trial and instead be shipped off for a lengthy stay in a mental hospital.

But when police went to another apartment that he rented, they were startled to find it full of counterfeiting equipment. And when they ran routine background checks, they found that Schmidt had a criminal record and a history of posing as a clergyman. The crazy priest suddenly looked a lot more sane.

Schmidt's roommate at the second apartment, Ernest A. Muret, was arrested. Muret had been working as a dentist, but, just as Schmidt was not a man of the cloth, neither was Muret a medical man. They were, in fact, partners in crime, and, in this case, a particularly gruesome one.

Schmidt eventually dropped the priest routine and revealed the strange truth. Aumuller, who had no idea that Schmidt was anything other than a godly man, fell in love with the priest. Schmidt concocted a wedding ceremony (at which he officiated!) and they became lovers. Aumuller was killed by Muret—who had no medical training—during a failed abortion. Schmidt dismembered the body and deposited it, piece by piece, in the Hudson River. He decided to feign insanity in an attempt to save himself and his partner.

Muret was never tried for the Aumuller killing, but was sentenced to 7½ years for counterfeiting. Schmidt was found guilty of first- degree murder and executed in Sing Sing on February 18, 1916.

Keep walking up Second Avenue to 50th Street, turn right and stop at 320 East 50th Street. This apartment building replaces a brownstone at 316 where the Robert Irwin murders took place on March 28, 1937.

7 Even before Robert Irwin was splashed across the front pages as "The Mad Sculptor" for a gruesome triple killing here at 316 East 50th Street, he was a minor celebrity in the psychoanalytical community. In the early '30s, he was a patient of Dr. Fredric Wertham, a prominent psychiatrist of the time now famous for his book *Seduction of the Innocent*, a 1950s diatribe against the evils of comic books. Wertham met Irwin in 1932 in Bellevue Hospital, where Irwin was recovering from an attempt to emasculate himself. He developed a close relationship with the young man, and treated him off and on for several years. In 1933 Wertham used him as an example of a patient suffering from "catathymic crisis" in a presentation in front of a large audience of psychiatrists. He explained that Irwin exhibited a ". . . pattern of violence which appeared to the patient at critical stages of the disease as 'the only way out.'" He later included Irwin in an article in *Archives of Neurology and Psychiatry*. He wrote that "This man is not cured. He will break out again either in some act of violence against himself or others." By the time the article appeared, in April 1937, the doctor's prognosis had proven tragically correct.

Robert Irwin was born into a poverty-stricken and religiously obsessed household in California. His mother burdened him with the name Fenelon Arroyo Seco, which he changed as a teenager to Robert. His father was an itinerant preacher who deserted the family when Irwin was a toddler. He showed talent as a painter and sculptor at a very young age, but at the same time showed signs of mental illness. He left home at eighteen. Hampered by a lack of money and frequent (voluntary) stays in mental hospitals, his artistic career never quite got off the ground.

In 1934, Irwin had taken a room in the boardinghouse of Mary Gedeon and fallen in love with the landlady's daughter Ethel. After a few months she tired of him and he moved out, but over the years, as he checked in and out of mental hospitals, he continued an obsession with her. On March 28, 1937, Easter Sunday, he was again in New York, unable to find work, without money and alone. As Wertham had warned, Irwin could think of only "one way out": he decided to kill Ethel Gedeon. That evening he came here to the Gedeon apartment to claim his victim. But Ethel had married and moved out. So instead Irwin, without much disappointment, strangled her mother. He remained in the apartment for several hours until Ethel's sister, Veronica Gedeon, returned home, and then strangled her. A boarder, Frank Byrnes, was asleep in his room during this rampage (he was deaf and presumably unaware of the homicides) and Irwin thought to eliminate him as a witness. He walked into Byrnes's room and drove an icepick several times into his head. Irwin strolled back to his boardinghouse two blocks away, where he dawdled for another week before leaving town. It took about this long for the police to land on him as a suspect after tracing a suede glove he had left behind at the murder scene.

Three months later, in the midst of a nationwide manhunt, Irwin traipsed into the offices of the *Chicago Herald and Examiner* and revealed his identity. He sold a confession to them for $5,000—which he used as a retainer to hire top lawyer Samuel Leibowitz—and then gave himself up to the police.

Leibowitz claimed that his client was "crazy as a bedbug." The prosecution said he was sane, and that his killing of Byrnes as a potential witness proved it. Eventually, to save his client from the electric chair, Leibowitz compromised with prosecutors and agreed to plead Irwin guilty to second-degree murder. (The plea presupposed that Irwin was sane, but Leibowitz ignored that.) The deal ensured that Irwin would live but remain permanently behind bars. He was given a 139-year sentence and wound up in Dannemora State Hospital for the criminally insane. He died in 1974.

Continue to First Avenue and take a right and then, at 49th Street, a left. This puts you in the very exclusive, but surprisingly gory, neighborhood of Beekman Hill. At least two front-page murders have taken place in these upscale environs. Our first stop is Beekman Tower at 3 Mitchell Place.

⑧ There was never a doubt that Vera Stretz shot and killed her lover Dr. Fritz Gephardt on the twentieth floor of Beekman Tower on November 25, 1935. She freely admitted it when asked shortly thereafter by a policeman, who found her sitting in a stairwell of the building. "But," she added enigmatically, "please don't ask me why." Until her trial several months later she said nothing, and appeared so calm that she was dubbed "The Ice Queen" in the newspapers, which covered the case with enthusiasm.

That characterization was shattered the moment she took the stand during a brilliant defense orchestrated by the famous lawyer Samuel Liebowitz. She gave her version of the killing amid copious tears and frequent breakdowns.

She told the courtroom that she had met Gephardt in December, 1934. Gephardt, a German whose trading company was headquartered in New York, was an energetic businessman as well as an early and eager Nazi and a close friend of Hermann Goering. After a short, intense romance, during which Stretz moved into Beekman Tower to be near Gephardt, she broke off the romance when he refused to marry. One night, shortly after, he called her to his room on a pretext and raped her. He then demanded that she perform fellatio on him, an act that she (and evidently many of the jury) considered to be outright perversion. She grabbed a gun she knew to be in his dresser drawer and shot him four times.

Leibowitz threw in references to Nietzsche and Nazism to explain Gephardt's depravity. But really it was the sight and sounds of Stretz's sobbing that convinced the jury that she was not lying about the events of that night. Her initial reluctance to explain her deed to the police was explained as embarrassment to mention the act her lover demanded. "I was so ashamed I would die rather than tell the police what had happened; ashamed of what had happened between Fritz and me." She was acquitted of all counts.

Walk along Mitchell Place to the end of the block and turn left. Walk to 20 Beekman Place, which has replaced several brownstones, among them 22 Beekman Place, the location of the Titterton murder.

9 On the afternoon of April 10, 1936, two upholsterers arrived at the fourth-floor apartment of 22 Beekman Place to deliver a couch. They found the door ajar and, after knocking gingerly, entered the apartment. There would be no delivery: their customer, Nancy Evans Titterton, a writer and book reviewer, lay dead in the bathtub. She had been strangled with her own blouse, which remained knotted around her neck. Clothing strewn about in the bedroom indicated that she had been attacked there and then dragged to the bathroom.

The police conducted a thorough investigation. They examined clothing and other articles found in the apartment. They dusted for prints, conducted chemical tests on fabrics, questioned painters and others who had been in the neighborhood, looked at the backyard and fire escapes. The twin bed was even taken apart. Nothing.

Then, as in a Sherlock Holmes puzzler, a seemingly inconsequential clue provided the break. The police had found a thirteen-inch piece of string under the body and had sent it to the police lab along with many other items. Word came back: the strand was upholsterer's twine.

Immediately, investigators turned their attention to the furniture deliverers who had discovered the body. They soon found out that one of them, John Fiorenza, had a criminal record. In addition, the young man had been to the Titterton apartment several days before the killing to pick up a love seat for repair. On the day of Titterton's death, he had arrived late to work. Confronted with this detective work, Fiorenza confessed: he had assaulted and murdered Titterton that morning and then reported to work. He knew beforehand the

grisly scene that he and his coworker would encounter that afternoon. Fiorenza was executed in the electric chair on January 21,
1937.

ALSO INFAMOUS

The country's most famous spy, Revolutionary War hero Nathan
Hale, was captured in Brooklyn while on a mission to gather
information about enemy fortifications in and around the city, then
under British control. He was tried in the greenhouse of the
Beekman estate at First Avenue and East 51st Street. A plaque on the
building on the northwest corner commemorates the incident. Hale
was hanged nearby on September 22, 1776, though the exact
location of his execution is unknown.

Continue to the end of Beekman Place and take a left on East 51st
Street. Walk a block and a half to 313 East 51st Street.

10 The Lonergan-Burton case was a classic: a cast of the rich and beautiful, a setting of swank nightclubs, and a plot wrapped around an inheritance, infidelity, and sex of several varieties.

On October 24, 1943, Patricia Lonergan (neé Burton) was found
bludgeoned to death here in this row house. She lay naked on a
bloodstained bed, her battered head propped against the headboard.
Two brass and onyx candlesticks, bent and broken, lay discarded on
the floor. She had not only been beaten about the head but, an autopsy revealed, strangled as well.

Lonergan, twenty-one years old, was the heiress of a multimillion
dollar fortune, and she lived in an appropriate manner. During the
hardships of the war years, while others counted ration stamps, she
partied at the Stork Club, El Morocco, the 21 Club, and other
swanky dens.

In 1939 she met Wayne Lonergan, a poor but suave Canadian.
Although not born to the upper set, he mingled easily with them
and aspired to their ways and means. By dating Patricia, he received entree to the haunts of the affluent and a shot at the $7
million she stood to inherit upon the death of her aged grand-
mother. In 1941, while romancing on the West Coast, they were
married in a quickie ceremony in Las Vegas. Life seemed to be
good for the Canadian adventurer. But the relationship quickly
soured to the point where Wayne decided that the rigors of war
were preferable to those of married life, and he enlisted in the

Royal Canadian Air Force to get away for a spell. He returned to his native country in September 1943. By that time Patricia had acquired several men to squire her during her forays on the town. On Saturday, October 24, she had been out with one of these regulars, Mario Gabellini. After a long night at the Stork Club, he brought her home at about 6 AM Sunday morning. She was found dead later that day. Initial suspicions focused on Gabellini, and he was taken into custody.

In the meantime, the victim's husband was traced to Montreal. It was known that he had been in New York on a weekend pass. It was discovered that his Canadian Air Force uniform was missing. When cops found scratches on his chin and face, Gabellini was dropped, Lonergan was grabbed and New York detectives were dispatched to bring him back to the city. The high-society murder had from its discovery attracted massive media attention, and when Lonergan was flown into New York he was mobbed with reporters and cameramen.

Lonergan explained away the incriminating evidence with, for that time, an outrageous alibi: that Sunday morning, after his own night on the town with a young actress (the two estranged Lonergans had almost run into each other at the Stork Club), he had dropped off his date and, he claimed, almost immediately picked up a soldier named Murray Worcester. Lonergan said he took him back to a friend's apartment where they had sex. They got into a fight several hours later, however, and the soldier had scratched Lonergan's face and then fled, stealing his uniform. The tale matched rumors that had longed circulated among nightclubbers that Lonergan was gay or bisexual. Two years before he had, in fact, told the U.S. draft board that he was homosexual and had been classed 4-F and rejected for service. For many people his account had the ring of truth merely because they thought it more damning to confess to a homosexual act than to murder. As one of the Canadian detectives who first heard this story remarked, "A guilty man, I would imagine, would not have offered us an alibi as degrading as this one."

After his story hit the papers, a former army private stormed into the district attorney's office. His name was Murray Worcester. He knew nothing of Wayne Lonergan, had not been in New York at the time, and had no idea how the suspect came by his name. A detective brought the two men face to face.

"Do you recognize this man?" Lonergan was asked. He shook his head.

"Well, this is your old friend," said the detective.

"I never saw this man before this minute."

"We know that Wayne," replied the detective. "This is Maurice Worcester."

Caught off guard, Lonergan blanched. He soon broke down and confessed.

He had come by the apartment here at 9:00 that morning. His wife had been sleeping, but she got up, unclothed, to let him in the bedroom. They immediately began to argue. He accused her of being the "belle of the El Morocco" and "behaving like a drunken sailor." As the argument heated up, she told him to get out. Suddenly enraged, he picked up a candlestick and broke it over her head. She screamed but, perhaps stunned, did not move. He grabbed the other candlestick, hit her again, and then took her by the throat and strangled her. "I stood there and I realized she wasn't moving," he said. "I stepped back and I was horrified at this mess of blood all over the place."

Lonergan hurriedly walked back to the apartment he was staying at on 79th Street. He threw the bloodied uniform in a duffel bag, took a walk to the East River, and tossed the incriminating laundry into the water. He coolly kept a lunch date at the Plaza and then, late in the afternoon, boarded a plane back to Toronto.

The trial was a major media event. The *New York Times* later stated that " . . . Mr. Lonergan's fight to escape the electric chair had drawn the largest press delegation in a New York courtroom since the trial in 1927 of Ruth Snyder and Henry Judd Gray for the murder of Mrs. Snyder's husband." (see p. 183) Despite the exertions of the famous defense lawyer Edward Broderick, who claimed the confession was beaten out of his client, Lonergan was found guilty of second-degree murder. He was sentenced to thirty-five years to life and was paroled in 1965, whereupon he was immediately deported to his native Canada and ordered never to return to the United States. He died, embroiled in a fight to get some of his wife's fortune, in Toronto on January 2, 1986.

Continue to Second Avenue, take a right, and walk up two blocks. Turn right on 53rd street, and pause at the apartment building at 319 East 53rd Street, once the home of lawyer Steven Romer.

11 Another New York superlative—the largest amount ever stolen by a lawyer from his clients—was some $7 million bagged by Steven Romer, Esq. Romer evidently purloined the money from four clients—one of them an orphaned teenager who lost her entire $741,000 trust fund—to prop up his failing real estate businesses.

On December 31, 1990, just as the story was breaking, the attorney disappeared after mailing letters to several clients describing himself as a legal Robin Hood who "used the money to feed some hungry and poverty-stricken people." Two months later, he appeared in the Manhattan District Attorney's office with a bizarre story. He had been kidnapped, he said, by agents of General Motors, which was out to get him to stop his company from developing a battery for an electric car. Discarding his ill-fitting Robin Hood outfit, he now said that GM took the $7 million. And, he added, he had a brain tumor and had only two months to live. Romer failed to convince prosecutors and was arrested.

On January 6, 1991, Romer was sentenced to 7½ to 22½ years in prison.

Turn around and go back a block on Second Avenue to 52nd Street. Turn right and walk over to Third Avenue. Pause at the southeast corner of Third Avenue and 52nd Street, now a large office building

12 Half a century ago, this site was occupied by a boardinghouse where the infamous Albert Fish lived and where he was arrested in 1934 for the murder of Grace Budd. It is a disturbing landmark, for Albert Fish was, without a doubt, the most repugnant criminal in New York City history. Although he appeared frail, even avuncular when he was finally brought to justice, Fish was a monster: a criminal sadomasochist, a pedophile, and a child murderer who enjoyed torturing, killing, and eating his victims. There are estimates that, in his fifty-year career, he raped hundreds of children and probably killed more than a dozen. Fredric Wertham, the famous psychiatrist whom we met in the Robert Irwin case, spent many hours examining Fish and testified at his murder trial. He later recalled that "Fish's sexual life was of unparalled perversity. I did research in the psychiatric and criminological literature and found no published case that would even nearly compare with his. There was no known perversion that he did not practice and practice frequently." He enjoyed beating himself with a nail-studded paddle, thrusting needles and nails into his body (an x-ray revealed twenty-nine needles permanently lodged in his pelvic region), and inserting alcohol-soaked cotton balls into his rectum and lighting them on fire. He also performed these acts on his victims.

Fish's unsavory crimes went back at least to the turn of the century, and he committed at least three other child murders in the New York area before the Grace Budd killing, but it was the murder of the Budd's young daughter that finally brought the wizened man out of the shadows.

On May 28, 1928, Fish stopped by 406 West 15th Street, the home of Albert and Delia Budd, their teenage son Edward and their ten-year-old daughter Grace. Fish had been attracted by an advertisement that Edward had placed in the *New York World:* "Young man, 18, wishes position in country. Edward Budd, 406 West 15th Street." Fish had no work to offer, of course; he planned to kidnap, rape, and castrate Edward. But as he sat in the kitchen with the Budd family, feeding them imaginary details of his farm on Long Island and his need for a strapping young farmhand, he decided that Edward Budd was somehow not to his liking. He resolved to slake his lust elsewhere. Then daughter Grace walked into the room and Fish changed his mind. Although he preferred young boys, he decided the girl would do, and when he again met with the family a few days later, ostensibly to work out details of Edward's employment, he had already made careful plans.

As he sat again in the Budd kitchen, on June 3, 1928, he let it drop that he was going to a birthday party for a niece on the Upper West Side. Almost as an afterthought, he suggested that perhaps little Grace would enjoy some cake and ice cream and fresh air. The parents looked at each other questioningly, looked at their excited daughter, and looked at the gray-haired farmer. Fish promised to have the girl back by 9:00 that evening. The Budds didn't have the heart to refuse. The pair walked out of the door together, the old man holding Grace by one hand and carrying in his other a canvas bag containing what he called his "instruments of hell": a butcher's knife, a meat cleaver, and a small handsaw. They never returned.

For six years the Budd abduction remained unsolved and her fate a mystery. The case received sensational tabloid treatment, thousands of circulars with her description were distributed, hundreds of leads tracked down. But the trail went cold, and the public, the press, and the police eventually turned to other matters.

Among the many compulsions of Albert Fish was an uncontrollable urge to write obscene letters. In November 1930, he addressed one to the Budd family, a taunting and horrifying screed that described, in chilling detail, how he had killed their daughter. The letter was unsigned, of course, but the envelope provided a clue that eventually solved the case. Detectives discovered on the back flap the inked-over logo and address of an obscure organization, the New York Private Chauffeur's Benevolent Association. Upon questioning the members, they discovered that this group took very good care of its envelopes and that all were accounted for—except for a small stash that a janitor sheepishly admitted he had taken some months previously. And when he recently moved, he had left them in the closet of his boardinghouse room at 200 East 52nd Street. Thither the police rushed, only to find that Fish had checked out of the same room just days before; it appeared that the police had been foiled once again. Then the landlady mentioned that her boarder had promised to return in a week or two to pick up a check sent by one of his sons (Fish was married and was, by all reports, a loving father to his six children). The house was immediately placed under 24-hour surveillance, and on December 13, 1934, Fish sauntered in and was arrested.

His confession, readily offered, was almost too horrifying and fantastic to believe. Fish had taken the young girl by train to an abandoned cottage he was familiar with in a remote area of Westchester County near the town of Worthington. He lured her inside and strangled her. Fish then beheaded the corpse and cut up her body. He sliced off several portions of flesh, wrapped them in newspaper, and took them home on the train. With these pieces he made a stew that he consumed over the following week and a half. During the murder, the dissection, and the cannibalism, Fish was in a constant state of ecstatic sexual delirium. He later said, "I am not insane. I am just queer. I don't understand it myself."

Although most of the jurors at his murder trial conceded that Fish was insane, they figured he deserved the electric chair anyway. Fish was executed in Sing Sing on January 16, 1936.

Turn right on Third Avenue and continue past 55th Street to 922 Third Avenue (on the west side), once Clancy's Bar.

❶❸ For over a hundred years, Irish nationalists have found shelter in New York. Such famous Irish figures as James Stephen, James Conolly, and Jeremiah O'Donovan Rossa spent time in this city; Eamon de Valera was born here. One of the earliest republican organizations, the Fenian Brotherhood, was organized in this city in 1859. Today, the Irish Republican Army finds much of its support, monetary and otherwise, in New York. It's not surprising, then, that Joseph Doherty, a member of the Provisional Irish Republican Army imprisoned in Britain for killing a British soldier, headed for New York when he broke jail.

On May 2, 1980, he and several comrades had been involved in a firefight with British commandos in Belfast that resulted in the death of Herbert Westmacott, a British captain. Doherty was convicted of murder a year later, but was not in court to hear the news: two days before sentencing, he had escaped from Crumlin Road maximum security prison. With the protection of the IRA and its international support system, he made his way to New York, taking the name of Henry J. O'Reilly and eventually ending up behind the brass rail at Clancy's Bar at 922 Third Avenue, an oddly public place for a man on the lam.

At 9:20 AM on June 18, 1983, two FBI agents, dressed as construction workers, entered Clancy's, where, an informer had advised them, Doherty was working. After ordering beers and sizing up their quarry, they took him into custody. Doherty later said he should have known they were agents: construction workers never drink that early. He was taken to the Metropolitan Correctional Facility on Centre Street, where, as he sat in a small cell, his case became a cause célèbre.

Doherty fought extradition, claiming his offense was political and therefore specifically exempted from the extradition treaty between Britain and the United States. A federal judge agreed. But the British government—in the midst of an antiterrorist campaign—was hot to get him and, at their urging, the United States approved a new treaty that retroactively withdrew the "political offense" exception.

Doherty continued his legal fight, and while he sat for years in prison battling a trip over the Atlantic, New York politicians and others rallied behind him. Mayor Dinkins of New York visited him in prison, Cardinal O'Connor of New York rallied to his cause, the president's son called him in his cell. The intersection of Pearl Street and Park Row, just up the street from the lonely cell where the Irish prisoner was languishing, was renamed Joe Doherty Corner in 1990.

The case wended its way through various courts to the U.S. Supreme Court, which ruled in 1992 that Doherty was not entitled to a new hearing and thus cleared the way for his deportation. On February 20, 1992, he returned to the same Belfast prison from which he had broken free nearly a decade before to finish his thirty-year sentence.

Go back now to 55th Street, turn right and stop at the apartment building at 155 East 55th Street.

14 New York has had a long succession of famous madams through its history, from Josephine Woods (see p. 28) to Rosie Hertz (see p. 204) to Sidney Biddle Barrows. Far from being vilified, they have generally been admired for their pluck and enterprise. Some have become celebrities and bestselling authors. East 55th Street has hosted two of the city's most famous members of this sorority, Xaveria Hollander and Polly Adler.

Hollander did business at 155 East 55th Street in the early 1970s with a relatively modest apartment establishment employing a half dozen women. She came to public notice during the Knapp Commission investigation into police corruption. She was paying protection money to policeman William Phillips, who later became a star witness during the Knapp hearings, and the publicity made the fetching European a media star. In true Warholian fashion, she popped up in the newspapers, in *Time* magazine, on TV. She wrote a bestselling autobiography, *The Happy Hooker*, in which she says, "I am happy in my business and love it. Indeed some of the happiest moments of my life have happened in the two years I have been rising in the ranks of New York City prostitution to become the biggest and most important madam in town."

She folded down the sheets for the last time long ago and has since picked up a pen. She has produced over a dozen books ranging from sex guides to torrid novels and writes an advice column for the sexually puzzled for *Penthouse* magazine.

ALSO INFAMOUS

After following a trail of sick and dying folk for four months, doctors finally caught up with Mary Mallon—"Typhoid Mary"—in March 1907 as she was working in a kitchen on Park Avenue just above East 60th Street. She spent nearly three years in prison (though she was never accused of a crime), escaped for five years (leaving another trail of typhus victims), and was recaptured and confined for the next twenty-three years in Riverside Hospital on North Brother Island. A total of 53 cases of typhoid and three deaths were traced to her.

Continue for two more blocks to the corner of 55th Street and Madison Avenue.

15 One of the many brothels of Polly Adler, perhaps the most famous madam in New York history, once stood at 30 East 55th Street. Her place here was a huge twelve-room apartment that included a Louis XVI–style living room, a book-lined library with "a shelf devoted to autographed copies of books written by or about my customers," a dining room that could accommodate fifty guests, a barroom, a fully-equipped kitchen, and four bedrooms, occupied by "the cream of my list: Nora, Rosalie, Kit, and Angelica."

In the glitzy nightclub years of the 1920s and '30s, Adler was the top procuress in town, with a reputation for a high-quality clientele. The *Daily Mirror* called her "the most notorious woman in the history of New York vice." Her clients included businessmen, society fops, theater and movie actors, politicians, policemen, and gangsters, among them Dutch Schultz, Eddie Diamond (Legs's brother), and Ciro "The Artichoke King" Terranova. She was arrested several times, but went to jail only once, in May, 1935, for 24 days. Her connections—and her protection payments—were nearly as legendary as her customers. She retired around 1943.

A guidebook of the mid-1960s laments that "the days of the great madames collapsed with the departure of Polly Adler from the New York scene. Her clientele of famous politicians, actors, millionaires, businessmen, royalty and so on is legendary. There have been a few straggling minor madames since . . . but never one as great."

MUG SHOTS

VELVALEE DICKINSON
World War II Spy

One imagines a spy with the delicious name of Velvalee to be sultry and sophisticated, a habitue of swank nightclubs and diplomats' hotels, an adept at seduction. Velvalee Dickinson though, indeed a spy, in no way resembled any such image. She was a small and slight fifty-year-old widow who owned a doll shop at 718 Madison Avenue. Dubbed "the Doll Woman" by the press, she was tried and convicted in 1944 for sending coded messages to the Japanese with information about the U.S. fleet in the Pacific.

Dickinson had grown up in California. Just before the war she became acquainted with a number of Japanese-American farmers in her work as a real-estate broker and, through them, met several Japanese diplomats from the consulate in San Francisco. She moved to New York in 1937 and it was presumably about that time that she was recruited as an agent.

In early 1942 she took a trip back to California, where she vacationed by loitering around harbors and naval yards. When she returned she sent the information that she picked up regarding the size and condition of ships to a contact in Buenos Aires. Her letters were disguised as gossipy mail. She wrote, for instance, " . . . I went to see MR. SHAW he destroyed YOUR letter, you know he has been ill. His car was damaged but is being repaired now. I saw a few of his family about. They all say Mr. Shaw will be back to work soon." According to the prosecution, this referred to the destroyer U.S.S. *Shaw,* which was damaged during the attack on Pearl Harbor, refitted, and sent to San Francisco at the same time Dickinson was on the West Coast.

Another time she used dolls to describe new ships operating in the Pacific: "The only new dolls I have are three lovely Irish dolls. One of these three dolls is an old Fisherman with a net over his back, another is an old woman with wood on her back and the third is a little boy." These designated an aircraft carrier (which is draped with safety nets), a warship with a wooden superstructure, and a destroyer.

To disguise her missives, Dickinson used the addresses and signed the names of some of her doll-shop customers, and this led to her fall. An undelivered letter was sent back from Buenos Aires to the return address noted on the envelope. This was one of Dickinson's

customers who, completely bewildered by the strange communication
supposedly from herself, turned over the pages to the government.
The trail ended in Velvalee Dickinson's doll shop.

She was indicted for spying for Japan, a capital crime, but managed
to plead guilty to a lesser charge of violating the censorship law. She
maintained, however, that her husband, who died in 1943, was the
spy, and that she had typed his letters without having a clue what
they were all about. On August 14, 1944, she was sentenced to ten
years' imprisonment and a $10,000 fine. She was paroled in 1951
and is thought to have died about ten years later.

Turn left and walk down Madison Avenue two blocks to the northwest
corner of 52nd Street and Madison Avenue, where the Berkshire
Apartments once stood.

16 It is a truth universally acknowledged that an old man in possession
of a good fortune must be very careful. William Rice, an aged and
sickly widower with millions made from cotton, railroads, and real
estate in Texas, was not careful enough, and became the victim of a
murderous plot hatched by his trusted valet, Charles Jones, and a
covetous lawyer, Albert T. Patrick.

Rice and Jones lived alone in the Berkshire Apartments that once
stood here at 500 Madison Avenue. In 1899, lawyer Patrick stopped
by to chat about some litigation that Rice was involved in and evidently hit it off, in some conspiratorial way, with the young Jones.
Over the course of several subsequent meetings, Patrick felt intimate
enough to suggest a strategy to relieve the old man of his money and
Jones, who had served his boss faithfully for many years, agreed with
little hesitation. Jones is usually portrayed in accounts of the case as
a hapless young man who was pressured into participating in fraud
and murder by the nefarious Patrick, but actually he took a very active role in their plan. That he was never punished says more about
the uncertainty of the law than it does about the culpability of the
valet.

For several months the pair worked industriously, forging reams of
documents. First they manufactured a huge correspondence between
Rice and Patrick to create an affectionate relationship between the
millionaire and the lawyer (actually the two had never met). They
forged a letter that transferred Rice's safe deposit box to Patrick;
drew up a document to deliver to Patrick all of Rice's Texas real estate, another for his Louisiana real estate, and a third for all his property in New Jersey; then letters that turned over several savings
account—totaling some $250,000—to the old man's new-found
friend. Then the *pièce de résistance*: they forged a will that gave

Patrick the bulk of the Rice estate and made him executor. This new will also increased the bequests for Rice's relatives. Patrick figured that all men were as grasping as he was, and that the Rice relatives would not challenge a will that enriched them (he was wrong in this calculation).

Now that everything was in place, a problem arose: Rice wouldn't die. The ailing man kept rallying. The pair decided to encourage him, first with mercury pills and then oxalic acid, but Rice seemed to have a Rasputin-like constitution. Finally, on September 23, 1900, they ran out of patience. In later testimony, Jones recounted that Sunday:

> After looking some time for a sponge, I found one that Mr. Rice had used for cleaning his clothes, and I made a cone of a towel, placed the sponge in the small end, and took it and saturated it with chloroform and placed it over my own face. I got a very strong effect from it. I then added a little more and went into Mr. Rice's room. I found he was still sleeping, and placed it over his face and ran out of the room.

With Rice finally dispatched, the two conspirators expected to reap the rewards of their great exertions. Instead, their plans fell apart almost immediately. A forged check to withdraw a large chunk of Rice's bank account was rejected the following day, ostensibly because Jones, in filling it out, had misspelled the payee's name as *Abert* T. Patrick. When relatives were informed by telegram that Rice had requested cremation (another Patrick-Jones forgery), they ordered an autopsy. Upon arrival in New York, they contested the will. The banks then blocked all of Rice's accounts. By early October, the conspirators were in the Tombs, their plans completely unraveled.

The valet became the chief witness against Patrick, whom the state considered the mastermind. After the trial, Jones went free and disappeared in his native Texas.

Patrick not only vehemently declared his innocence, he maintained that no homicide had occurred at all: Rice had died of natural causes. The congestion of the lungs found in the autopsy was, he said, not consistent with chloroform poisoning. He continued his protests after his conviction for first-degree murder, filing appeals and petitions, and his struggle became a cause célèbre. In 1906 his sentence was commuted from death to life imprisonment and in 1912 he was pardoned by the governor of the state. He is said to have gone West and continued his practice of the law. The bulk of William Rice's estate went to the legatee in his authentic will, Rice University in Houston, Texas.

Go right down 52nd Street to Fifth Avenue. Turn left and walk down to
51st Street, then cross Fifth Avenue and continue another block to
Rockefeller Plaza. The Associated Press Building, located just to your
left at 50 Rockefeller Center, once contained the office of political activist
Allard Lowenstein. He was murdered here by his one-time protégé
Dennis Sweeney.

17 The story of Dennis Sweeney's killing of Allard Lowenstein is usually
portrayed as a dramatic signpost of the end of 1960s idealism.
Sweeney is seen as a young man radicalized by the civil rights movement and the war in Vietnam who crashed and burned when that
era's movements and utopianism withered, taking with him the well-
meaning but naive idealist Lowenstein. The two could not, it is said,
survive intact past their time.

Actually the tale is more tragic than such lazy symbolism suggests.
Sweeney was brought down not by political setbacks or the disap-
pointing end of a promising decade, but by a severe mental illness
that produced insistent, hectoring voices in his head, nightmarish
paranoia, and homicidal rage. Lowenstein was not a doomed ghost
of politics past but the victim of a deranged killer.

Although Allard Lowenstein served a term as a Long Island congressman, he was best known as a freelance organizer and a charismatic activist for Democratic party and liberal causes. Crisscrossing
the country, working at a frenetic pace, he seemed to be everywhere,
from Mississippi in 1963 to Chicago in 1968 to Dade County,
Florida in 1980. In the early 1960s he helped rally white students to
the cause of civil rights, in the late '60s, in his greatest moment of
glory, he spearheaded the Dump Johnson movement that successfully foiled Lyndon Johnson's shot at a second presidential term.
During the '70s he served as a member of the Democratic Party National Committee, as president of Americans for Democratic Action,
and as ambassador for special political affairs in the United Nations.
He spoke of running for president of the United States. Among his
circle of friends were Robert Kennedy, Adlai Stevenson, Norman
Thomas, Eleanor Roosevelt, and thousands of college students that
he helped to inspire and politicize in his long years of campus activity. One of these students was Dennis Sweeney.

Sweeney was a sophomore at Stanford University when Lowenstein, then a dean at the school, persuaded him to go to Mississippi in 1963. While working with the Student Nonviolent
Coordinating Committee to organize black residents and champion their right to vote, Sweeney was threatened, run out of town,
beaten, shot at, and bombed. The experience of living through a
summer of reactionary white Mississippi turned him into a radical.

It also sundered him from his mentor, the liberal Lowenstein, whose faith in the system Sweeney came to regard initially as naive and later as pernicious.

Sweeney moved to a commune in Berkeley, California, a hub of student radicalism, and over the next several years, like much of his generation, he fought the good fight against the Vietnam War, a society he saw as immoral, and a government he viewed as repressive. But as early as 1969, Sweeney had begun to show signs of paranoid schizophrenia. He told a visiting friend that the CIA has sprayed poison gas on Berkeley that made everyone sick, but that he had some pills he had pilfered at his job in the post office that would counter the effects of the gas. In the next few years the CIA would get craftier, planting electrodes in his head and using the voices of friends, especially Allard Lowenstein, to persecute him. He pulled a permanent dental bridge out of his mouth with a pair of pliers because he thought it was a transmitter. In 1973 he moved east, withdrawing completely from friends and family, working odd jobs and living in a succession of small, plain, rented rooms in Cambridge, Massachusetts and Mystic, Connecticut. His condition worsened. He believed he was a guinea pig in a huge plot by the CIA and New York Jews. Allard Lowenstein was the mastermind.

On March 3, 1980, Sweeney walked into a sporting goods shop and filled out an application to purchase a handgun. ("Have you ever been adjudicated mentally defective or have you ever been committed to a mental institution?" "No.") Then he called the Rockefeller Center law office of Allard Lowenstein and made an appointment for Friday, March 14. His application was processed without a hitch and he picked up his .38-caliber pistol a week later.

Lowenstein had not seen his ex-protégé in many years, but knew he was troubled. He likely welcomed the chance to counsel the younger man. He had no idea that his voice filled Sweeney's head, or that the troubled man considered him the architect of his torment. The pair spent about ten minutes talking in Lowenstein's office, then Sweeney stood up, shook the hand of his host, and fired all seven rounds of his automatic at Lowenstein. He then walked into the reception room, placed his pistol in the secretary's work tray, and sat down to wait for the police. "He's been controlling my mind for years," Sweeney told the officers. "Now I've put an end to it." He was found not guilty by reason of insanity and placed in the Mid-Hudson Psychiatric Center, a maximum-security facility.

Lowenstein, hit by five of the seven bullets, died that night. He was buried at Arlington Cemetery close to the grave of John Kennedy. A plaza at East 45th Street and First Avenue in front of the United Nations is named for him.

Go back to Fifth Avenue and walk up to Tiffany's jewelry store on the
southeast corner of 57th Street.

18 Tiffany's is one of those institutions, like Fort Knox or the British Museum, that seems so venerable, staid and secure that one is surprised that
anyone would even think of robbing it. Yet when it did happen, the rip-
off of Tiffany's on September 4, 1994, seemed to be just the kind of
heist that this elegant establishment deserved: cool, professional, pulled
off with split-second timing and bravado. Or so it seemed initially.

At 11:40 P.M. that evening, two gunmen gained entry to the world-
renowned jewelry store by sticking a gun in the gut of a security guard
who was entering the store to begin his shift. They tied up the four
employees inside and, while one guarded the hostages, the other
roamed the sales floor picking up loot. The thieves had the whole set-
up sussed: the guard schedules, the location of video cameras and
alarm boxes, the keys needed for the sales floor area. They scooped up
about $1.9 million worth of baubles and fled. No alarms were tripped,
no shots were fired, no one was hurt. A perfect heist, and the costliest
robbery in the one hundred fifty-seven-year history of Tiffany's.

The gunmen acted like savvy professionals, but, according to police, their success was due not to hard-earned expertise but to good
old-fashioned insider information. A week after the robbery, police
arrested Scott Jackson, a security supervisor at Tiffany's and charged
that he had concocted the plot with two cousins, Derrick Jackson
and Mark Klass, who acted as the gunmen. They enlisted three others, including another Tiffany guard, in the plot.

And on closer look, the heist looked a lot less savvy than original
reports had made out. The robbers stole only stock items from the
show cases, rather than the more valuable items that were kept in a
vault. And most tellingly, they had no way of disposing of their loot.
One of the breaks in the case came when police heard from contacts
that someone was selling the Tiffany's jewelry—sometimes for as little as $200 for a $14,000 piece—on the streel level in Harlem. Most
but not all of the loot was recovered.

Perhaps a less ambitious approach would have been more successful. For example, the thieves who simply walked up to the show windows one early morning on August 11, 1958 and battered them in
with sledgehammers may have netted only $163,000 in gems, but
they were never apprehended. A bird in the hand. . . .

Two years later, on June 25, 1960, some copycats tried to pull off
a similar escapade at Cartiers, just down the street. This time the culprits were nabbed, and the incident is interesting because one of
those arrested (though not charged for lack of evidence) was none
other than Patsy Fuca of French Connection fame.

Keep walking up Fifth Avenue for another four blocks, past Grand Army Plaza and the corner of Central Park, to the Pierre Hotel.

19 "It was perfect," Bobby Comfort told his wife just after he and four comrades had robbed the Pierre Hotel. They had grabbed millions in jewelry and cash in a flawless and nonviolent operation that captured both the city's attention and admiration. He was arrested the next week.

Though not quite perfect, the robbery of the Pierre Hotel on January 2, 1972, was certainly impressive. It was the largest hotel heist ever: estimates of the haul range from $3 million to $10 million. Only about $1 million in jewels was recovered, and only two of the robbers served time for the deed.

The criminal partnership of Bobby Comfort and Sorecho "Sammy the Arab" Nalo had enjoyed a long string of success with Manhattan hotel and home robberies throughout 1970. Along with a changing group of freelancers, they robbed the Sherry Netherland, the St. Regis, the Drake, the Carlyle, and the Regency. On October 12, 1970, they held up Sophia Loren in her suite at the Hampshire House on Central Park South, taking $900,000 in jewelry. On June 15, 1971, the pair went to the home of rich socialite Janet Annenberg Neff at One Sutton Place, grabbing jewelry worth $200,000. They were always polite and always well prepared.

But they longed for that one great heist, the huge take that would put them over the top, the best and the last. Comfort and Nalo decided that the Pierre Hotel would be the perfect setting to realize their dream.

As usual, they planned carefully. They chose January 2 not only because it was a quiet night, but also because the safe deposit boxes in the hotel would be stuffed with jewelry from the New Year's Eve parties of the night before. They brought in three friends to help them out, cased the hotel carefully (Comfort took a room there for two weeks), bought tuxedos so they would blend in with the money-eyed patrons, and purchased fourteen pairs of handcuffs.

At 4:00 AM that morning, they pulled up in a limousine to the 61st Street entrance. The night guard, seeing a group of well-dressed gentlemen carrying luggage, opened the door. Only then did he notice that one man was wearing a false nose and carrying a gun. The robbers went to work swiftly, rounding up the other employees and guests—22 in all—and herding them into an office where they were handcuffed and blindfolded. After securing the lobby, they went to work with hammers and chisels on the safe deposit boxes in the vault behind the check-in desk. In two hours, four suitcases were full of gleaming diamond necklaces and bracelets, sapphire brooches and earrings, ruby pins, rings, watches, and bundles of cash. The five robbers left without firing a shot. It had all gone without a hitch.

When the city woke up and learned of the theft, sentiment was all on the side of the suave and audacious bandits. There was little sympathy for the ultrawealthy who had lost their thick strings of diamonds. As one columnist for the *New York Post* wrote:

> In a time when junkies hit old ladies in elevators for fourteen-dollars-and-change or come in the back window looking for the silverware you got one piece at a time at the RKO Prospect in 1951, something this well organized, so minimally violent, and so grand in scale could only be applauded.

It would have been all the more romantic if the perpetrators had gotten clean away, but it was not to be. Nalo, hard up for cash, tried to pawn some of the jewels almost immediately, but the fence he chose was an informer on the FBI payroll. Just a week after the hotel job, the feds moved in, nabbing Comfort in a Manhattan hotel and Nalo in his apartment in the Bronx. They drew four-year sentences each. Their three accomplices were never captured and remain unidentified.

CRIMES OF CENTRAL PARK

Charles Sanfillippo shooting—On August 14, 1938, while three thousand policemen and civilians were attending a memorial service, Charles Sanfillippo, a deranged cop-hater wearing homemade armor, opened fire with two shotguns. He wounded five people before he was killed in a gun battle.

Angel Angelov shooting—Armed with a .45 caliber handgun, Angelov climbed to the roof of a public lavatory near 85th Street and Fifth Avenue on July 3, 1968, and began shooting indiscriminately. He killed two and wounded two before a police sharpshooter felled him. Police found his apartment decorated with pictures of Hitler, Goering, Goebbels, and George Wallace.

The Preppie Murder—One of the most infamous cases of the 1980s, made notorious by its combination of privileged youth and casual sex. Early in the morning of August 26, 1986, Robert Chambers led Jennifer Levin to the park for a sexual tryst and then strangled her. Chambers pleaded guilty to manslaughter in the first degree and was sentenced to five to 15 years.

Central Park jogger—In a case that split the city along racial lines, a 29-year-old white woman (her name was not released) jogging in the park was brutally attacked, raped, and left for dead below the 102nd Street transverse on April 19, 1989. Though she lost eighty percent of her blood, she eventually recovered. Six black youths were charged in the attack; amidst charges of a frame-up, they were all convicted of various charges stemming from the attack.

Rubinstein Found Strangled In His Fifth Ave. Mansion

Draft-Dodger, Financier Was Bound and Gagged —Woman Questioned

By MILTON BRACKER

A mysterious strangler put an end early yesterday to the fantastic career of Serge Rubinstein.

The Russian-born financial wizard and convicted draft-dodger was choked to death in a bedroom of his luxurious five-story home at 814 Fifth Avenue, near Sixty-second Street. His body was discovered at 8:30 A. M., within a few feet of a costume-ball photograph of him garbed as Napoleon.

He wore blue-black silk pajamas. The body was on its back. The hands and feet were tied with cord, and several twists of broad adhesive tape covered the mouth and throat. The nostrils were not covered but there were some bruises and indication of bleeding on the face.

According to an autopsy completed at 6 P. M. by Chief Medical Examiner Milton Helpern, "Rubinstein died of manual strangulation." Dr. Helpern said there were no fingermarks on the

Associated Press
Serge Rubinstein

throat, but that there were abrasions.

Earlier—largely because the victim's nasal passages had not

Continued on Page 10, Column 3

Unmourned financial finagler Serge Rubinstein.

Keep walking up Fifth Avenue past 62nd Street to 814 Fifth Avenue, where the mansion of millionaire Serge Rubinstein once stood.

20 Financier Serge Rubinstein, found trussed and murdered here on January 27, 1955, was so well hated by so many people that the police found themselves in the unusual position of having too many suspects and too many motives. Rubinstein had made a fortune as a master financial manipulator, and he operated absolutely without scruples or mercy. A nearly endless line of betrayed friends, swindled partners, cheated clients, empty-handed creditors, and wronged women seemed to array itself in front of the police.

Rubinstein was born the son of a rich and well-connected banker in prerevolutionary Russia and always assumed that he was born for the life of the moneyed gentry. How he made his fated fortune was of no concern to him. In 1933, in one of his earliest ventures, he wrangled control of the Chosen Corporation, a holding company for several Korean mines. Then, in the words of a later stockholders' lawsuit, he manipulated it by means of "a series of subsidiaries, sub-subsidiaries and affiliates of the subsidiaries and sub-subsidiaries and a series of financial maneuvers in the process of which secret profits, commissions and bonuses were garnered by Rubinstein and his dummy nominees." He was said to have eventually looted $5.9 million from Chosen.

And so on for the next twenty-five years. There were similar episodes with Panhandle Producing and Refining, Brooklyn-Manhattan Transit, Postal Telegraph, and many others. He was sued scores of times. He cheated his own brother of $20,000. The U.S. government put him in prison for draft evasion during World War II and, at the time of his death, was attempting to expel him from the country for entering on a fraudulent Portuguese passport (he never lived a day of his life in Portugal).

On the night of January 26, 1955, Rubinstein had a date with one of the several women with whom he dabbled. After supping they returned here at about 1:30 AM. Rubinstein, drunk, made a pass and the woman left. That was about 2:00 AM.

Six hours later his butler, entering his room to serve breakfast, found him dead. Dressed in black silk pajamas, Rubinstein was tied at the feet and hands, and adhesive tape was wound from his neck to just below his nose. He had died of strangulation, however, not of suffocation; several of the bones in his neck were broken. Strangely though, his hands were tied in front of his body, and the bonds were quite loose. There was no sign of forced entry and nothing had been stolen.

Was Rubinstein the victim of a botched kidnapping or extortion plot? A fumbled burglary? A mob hit? Rough sex gone wrong? The rumors swirled, but never settled. Rubinstein's web of dealing and doubledealing was so tangled that anything was possible. And possibilities are all that remain. Out of the many suspects that police tracked and trailed, not one was ever accused or tried. The death of Serge Rubinstein remains a mystery.

Nearest subway: Fifth Avenue N R; Lexington Avenue B Q
Nearest bus lines: M 1; M 2; M 3; M 4; M 5; M 30; M 66; M 72; Q 32

8

Infamous Eating

A Guide to Restaurants and Bars With Shady Pasts _____

Allstate Cafe
250 West 72nd Street
874-1883

This was once H. M. Tweed's, a singles bar, where on New Year's Day, 1973, Roseann Quinn met John Wayne Wilson and took him home for a one-night stand. She did not survive the evening: Wilson strangled and knifed the young schoolteacher to death. He was apprehended, confessed, and committed suicide in the Tombs while awaiting trial. The murder became an emblem for the dangers of anonymous sex and was made famous in the best-selling novel *Looking for Mr. Goodbar* and in a movie of the same name. American, inexpensive.

Bankers and Brokers Restaurant
301 South End Avenue
432-3250

In 1986, John J. O'Connor, vice president of Local 608 of the United Brotherhood of Carpenters and Joiners, got mad when the owner of this restaurant refused to use his union carpenters in a renovation. He sent in some thugs to trash the place, only to discover that the owner was, reputedly, a member of the Gambino Mafia family and close to boss John Gotti. Later that year, O'Connor was shot and wounded by members of the Westies gang, allegedly at the behest of Gotti. Continental, expensive.

Brewbars
327 West 11th Street
243-5297

For five months in early 1994, the NYPD conducted an under-cover sting operation out of this site. In order to break up a baking industry group they claimed was manipulating bread prices, six cops, dressed in bakers' whites, set up a fake Italian bread bakery here and outfitted the place with hidden cameras and microphones. Coffee house, inexpensive.

Bridge Cafe
279 Water Street
227-3344

In the late nineteenth century, this building housed Tom Norton's saloon and brothel, a low dive catering to the roughs of this very rough neighborhood (see p. 58). American and continental, moderate.

Cafe des Artistes
1 West 67th Street
877-3500

Harry Crosby, poet, publisher, and bohemian, killed his girlfriend, Josephine Bigelow, and himself in an apartment on the ninth floor of the Hotel des Artistes on December 10, 1929. His suicide has been interpreted as a symbol of the death of the idealism of the Lost Generation. Continental, expensive.

Cafe Biondo
141 Mulberry Street
226-9285

Owned by Joseph "Joe Butch" Corrao, allegedly a member of the Gambino Mafia family (see p. 104). It was a favorite of John Gotti. You can watch the comings and goings across the street at the Andrea Doria Social Club (sometimes called the Hawaiian Moonlighters Club), at 140 Mulberry, said to be a Gambino hangout. Italian, moderate.

Casa Bella Restaurant
127 Mulberry Street
431-4080

Owned by Mike Sabella, said to be a captain in the Bonanno Mafia family. Italian, expensive.

Charlton's
922 Third Avenue
688-4646

This was once Clancy's Bar, a neighborhood joint where Joseph Doherty, IRA fugitive, worked and where he was arrested on June 18, 1983. While Doherty battled extradition, claiming that the crime for which he was convicted in Northern Ireland was a political offense, his case became a cause célèbre. He was sent back, however, on February 20, 1992 (see p. 263). American, moderate.

Chumley's
86 Bedford Street
675-4449

The lack of a sign hints at this bar's origin as a speakeasy. It can be entered on Bedford Street or, more thrillingly, through Pamela Court on Barrow Street. The phrase "to 86 someone"—to refuse or eject a customer—probably derives from its address (see p. 138). American, inexpensive.

Cooper Square Restaurant
87 Second Avenue
420-8050

This is where, on July 18, 1981, writer/convict Jack Henry Abbott, on the verge of literary stardom after the success of his prison memoirs, *In the Belly of the Beast*, killed writer/waiter Richard Adan (see p. 207). At that time it was Binibon's Restaurant. American, inexpensive.

Costello's Chinese
18 West 25th Street
633-1373

This little take-out joint is located in the Arlington Hotel, once the headquarters for two of the most powerful and feared racketeers in New York history, Louis "Lepke" Buchalter and Jacob "Gurrah" Shapiro. From here they ran many garment center rackets until the law caught up with them in the late '30s (see p. 167). Chinese, inexpensive.

DiRoberti's Pasticceria
176 First Avenue
674-7137

This venerable pastry shop was headquarters in the late 1980s for John "Handsome Jack" Giordano's bookmaking operation. Giordano, a member of the Gambino Mafia family, was unaware that the New York cops had the place wired. "We had bugs in everything but the cannolis and the espresso machine," said one investigator. Giordano was indicted on August 1, 1991, on state racketeering charges. Italian pastries, inexpensive.

Dorrian's Red Hand
300 East 84th Street
772-6660

A popular watering hole for prep school students on the Upper East Side, and the spot where, on August 25, 1986, Robert Chambers met Jennifer Levin before leading her to Central Park and strangling her. Her murder was one of the most infamous of the 1980s. American, inexpensive.

Elaine's
1703 Second Avenue
534-8103

In the 1960s, Joey Gallo used to hang out here with show business friends. Lately, it's become a favorite with Police Commissioner William Bratton, who spends so much time here that some people have called it Police Plaza North. Italian, expensive.

King Son Cafe
11 Pell Street
608-3366

A hangout for the Flying Dragons gang, an affiliate of the Hip Sing Tong, whose headquarters are across the street at 16 Pell Street. Chinese and American, inexpensive.

El Quijote
226 West 23rd Street
929-1855

Part of the Chelsea Hotel, which has seen a great deal of mischief and misdeeds in its long history. Bank embezzler O. Henry lived here for a time. Literary forger Clifford Irving was a resident in the early 1970s, as was Jerome Johnson, the mysterious assassin who shot Mafia chief Joseph Colombo during an Italian Unity Day rally in Columbus Circle. Punk rocker Sid Vicious murdered his girl-friend, Nancy Spungen, in room 100 on October 12, 1978. Spanish, moderate.

Fat Tuesday's
190 Third Avenue
533-7902

Formerly Joe King's Rathskeller and a speakeasy. Continental, inexpensive.

Fraunces Tavern
54 Pearl Street
269-0144

A bomb attributed to the Puerto Rican nationalist Fuerzas Armadas de Liberación Nacional (FALN) ripped through an annex to the dining room of Fraunces Tavern on January 24, 1975, killing two and injuring fifty-six persons. The FALN have been linked to more than thirty bombings in the metropolitan area. American and continental, expensive.

Giambone's Restaurant
42 Mulberry Street
285-1277

Said to be a great favorite of Mafiosi attending trials, voluntarily or otherwise, across the street in the Criminal Courts Building. Italian, moderate.

John's Restaurant
302 East 12th Street
475-9531

Notable for two pre-mortem meals. Umberto Valenti ate here on August 11, 1922 with Joe "the Boss" Masseria before the latter killed him as they walked out to Second Avenue (see p. 218). Twenty-one years later, notorious anarchist and agitator Carlo Tresca enjoyed dinner here the evening he was assassinated at Fifth Avenue and 15th Street (see p. 48). Italian, expensive.

Judy's Restaurant and Cabaret
49 West 44th Street
764-8930

In the Hotel Iroquois, site of the murder of William Henry Jackson by Paul Geidel on July 27, 1911. Geidel spent 68 years, eight months and two days in prison for the crime, the longest sentence ever served (see p. 190). Continental, moderate.

La Margarita
184 Thompson Street
533-2410

This restaurant is housed in an apartment building that stands on the site of Genovese Trading Co., the junkyard of famous Mafia boss Vito Genovese (see p. 152). Mexican, inexpensive.

La Scala Restaurant
60 West 55th Street
245-1575

On October 21, 1964, just a few hours before an appointment with a grand jury, Joseph Bonanno, boss of one of the five Mafia families, disappeared. He was reported to have been kidnapped at gunpoint on Park Avenue, though many people think it was a ruse to avoid testifying. After he reappeared 19 months later, he hosted a party here to celebrate. During the festivities, trusted lieutenant Joseph Notaro dropped dead of a heart attack. Italian, expensive.

Lanza's Restaurant
168 First Avenue
674-7014

Favorite restaurant of Joe "Piney" Armone, a Gambino Mafia family member and one-time underboss. Armone, whose criminal career began in the '30s, was best friend and advisor to boss Paul Castellano. He died in prison in February 1992. Italian, moderate.

Long Shine Restaurant
53 East Broadway
346-9888

Owned by Cheng Chui "Big Sister" Peng, a well-known figure in Chinatown who is said by law enforcement officials to have made at least $30 million as a smuggler of illegal immigrants. Such activity has long been a staple of organized crime—Mafia boss Salvatore Maranzano made much of his money in the same trade. Cheng was reportedly arrested in China in early 1995. Fujianese Chinese, inexpensive.

L'Oro di Napoli
206 Sullivan Street
598-4952

This restaurant is located right next door to the Triangle Social Club, headquarters for Vincent "The Chin" Gigante, alleged boss of the Genovese Mafia family (see p. 151). The large windows afford a wonderful view of the boss as he shuffles by in slippers and bathrobe. Italian, moderate.

Minetta Tavern
113 MacDougal Street
475-3850

This was once a speakeasy known as the Black Rabbit. Italian, moderate.

P. J. Clarke's
915 Third Avenue
355-9307

The bar here was the favorite in the 1970s of "rogue cop" William Phillips and famous madam Xaviera Hollander, both of whom were prominent figures in the Knapp Commission hearings on police corruption. American, moderate.

Paninoteca
251 Mulberry Street
219-1351

At one time you could sit by the Mulberry Street windows of this pleasant cafe and watch the comings and goings of the Gambino Mafia family members who had business at the Ravenite Club. The club has been quiet since John Gotti's conviction in 1992 (although business is still said to be conducted on Wednesday nights by Peter Gotti, John's brother), but you can still get a sense of the atmosphere of those headier days. Italian, inexpensive.

Pete's Tavern
129 East 18th Street
473-7676

When this was called Healy's Cafe it was a regular hangout of bank embezzler and short story writer O. Henry. It was a speakeasy during Prohibition. American, moderate.

Puffy's Tavern
81 Hudson Street
766-9159

This former speakeasy retains much of the atmosphere of its illicit days.

Ratner's
138 Delancey Street
677-5588

Gangster Meyer Lansky's favorite eatery. Jewish (dairy), moderate.

Rocco Restaurant
181 Thompson Street
677-0590

In early September, 1952, Joseph Valachi, who later became famous as a Mafia informer, met his boss Tony Bender in this restaurant and received a contract to kill Eugenio Giannini, a Lucchese Family member who had become an informant for the Bureau of Narcotics. Valachi subcontracted the assignment to three young thugs. On September 20, 1952, Giannini was found dead on East 107th Street. Italian, moderate.

Second Avenue Deli
156 Second Avenue
677-0606

Mafia boss Paul Castellano liked the corned beef sandwiches here and had a last meal, with FBI officers, on the day of his arrest on racketeering charges in 1985: corned beef on rye and a Cel-Ray celery soda. He was assassinated ten months later. Jewish (fleishig), moderate.

Siam Square Restaurant
92 Second Avenue
505-1240

Eighty years ago this space was a cafe and notorious gangster hangout owned by Abe "The Rabbi" Rabbell. According to contemporary private eye Abe Shoenfeld, regular customers included Harry the Mock, Kid Rags, Curley the Lighthouse, Cock-Eye Weiss, Crazy Itch, Sam the Waiter, Jake the Barber, and Jewback, "gambler and perhaps the best single-handed pinochle player in the country." Thai, inexpensive.

Spark's Steak House
210 East 46th Street
687-4855

The site of the most famous of modern Mafia hits, the killing of Paul Castellano by John Gotti's crew (see p. 251). Continental, very expensive.

SPQR
133 Mulberry Street
925-3120

Once owned by reputed Mafia capo Matty "the Horse" Ianniello, said to have major interests in the construction, concrete and pornography industries. He was in Umberto's Clam House (owned by his brothers) the night Joey Gallo was killed there. Italian, expensive.

Ten Pell Street Restaurant
10 Pell Street
766-2132

This building served as the original headquarters of the Hip Sing Tong when they arrived in the city in the 1890s. It also housed one of the twenty or so opium dens that existed in Chinatown at the time (see p. 94). Hunan and Szechuan Chinese, inexpensive.

Thai Village Restaurant
133 West 3rd Street
254-9513

Located in the building that once housed the brothel of Matilda Hermann, famous as "the French Madam." She was a star witness in the Lexow Committee investigation into police corruption conducted in 1894. Thai, inexpensive.

Top of the Tower
3 Mitchell Place
980-4796

Just six floors beneath this cocktail lounge, Vera Stretz shot and killed her lover Fritz Gephardt in a famous case of the mid-1930s. Although Stretz admitted the deed, she won the sympathy of the jury by claiming that Gephardt tried to force her to commit an unnatural act (fellatio) and that she therefore shot in self-defense. She was acquitted (see p. 256). Cocktail lounge, expensive.

21 Club
21 West 52nd Street
582-7200

This famous restaurant got its start as a speakeasy. Continental, very expensive.

Ukrainian East Village Restaurant
140 Second Avenue
529-5024

Located in the old Stuyvesant Casino, where Jewish gangsters of the 1920s used to hold their parties, and where Big Jack Zelig killed rival gangster "Julie" Morrell (see p. 208). Ukrainian, inexpensive.

Umberto's Clam House
129 Mulberry Street
431-7545

The site of the rubout of brash, charismatic gangster Joey Gallo (see p. 104). Its success is due at least as much to this famous incident as its food. For real authenticity, order the scungilli salad and boiled shrimp. Italian, expensive.

Veselka Restaurant
144 Second Avenue
228-9682

In the 1930s, this was the Boulevard Restaurant. On April 10, 1937, several young thieves tried to pull off a robbery of the late-night restaurant and gambling joint and ended up killing a plain-clothes cop. The incident became celebrated as the case of "the East Side Boys" and resulted in the execution of three of the seven youths involved (see p. 209). American and Ukrainian, inexpensive.

Vincent's Clam Bar
119 Mott Street
226-8133

In the early 1970s, Frank King used to hold court here at a regular table. He was a police officer from the infamous, corrupt Special Investigating Unit and one of the prime suspects—though he was never charged—in the theft of French Connection heroin from the police department's warehouse (see p. 241). Italian, expensive.

Wo Hop Restaurant
17 Mott Street
962-8617

One of the earliest and most celebrated Tong killings took place in this building when young Bo Kum, wife of On Leong member Tchin Len, was murdered on August 15, 1909 by an unknown hitman. Her death unleashed a major Tong war (see p. 92). Chinese, inexpensive.

For Further Reading___

Those wishing to walk further through the pages of New York criminal history have no shortage of trails: there is a large and venerable literature of popular, academic, and scandalous books on the subject. The following selection—personal favorites, classics, and oddities, emphasizing older tomes—is drawn from the books used as sources for *Infamous Manhattan*. Far from comprehensive, it is meant only to provide the traveler with a few compass points.

General histories of New York crime appeared early, reflecting and in turn enhancing the city's fearful reputation. Nineteenth-century works, many of them kept in print for their colorful prose and entertainingly antiquated mores, include Charles Loring Brace's *The Dangerous Classes of New York, and Twenty Years' Work Among Them* (1872), Edward Crapsey's *The Nether Side of New York*, published in the same year, *The New York Tombs* (1874), by warden Charles Sutton, Thomas Byrnes' fascinating *1886 Professional Criminals of America*, a rogues' gallery of mug shots and criminal records, and *Our Police Protectors: A History of the New York Police* (1885) by the overly meticulous chronicler Augustine Costello.

Other general histories that focus on the city's contraband heart include the slapdash three volumes of *American Metropolis* (1897) by Frank Moss, an investigator and lawyer for the Society for the Prevention of Crime. He was no historian, but the third volume, drawn from personal knowledge, is engaging. Edward van Every's anthology, *Sins of New York as "Exposed" by the Police Gazette* (1930), is likewise not necessarily history, but fun to read. Lloyd Morris's *Incredible New York: High Life and Low Life of the Last Hundred Years* (1951) is both accurate and engaging.

One of the great classics of New York criminal history is Herbert Asbury's *The Gangs of New York: An Informal History of the Underworld*, first published in 1927 and still in print. Though not wholly truthful, it is entirely entertaining. Covering much of the same ground with a highbrow bent is *Low Life: Lures and Snares of Old New York* (1991), by Luc Sante.

Another avenue to nineteenth-century New York crime is the distinctive guidebooks and exposés that cropped up in the second half of the century, big, fat books full of minutiae and moralism and quite entertaining to wade through. Many of them have been reprinted. George G. Foster's *New York in Slices* (1849) and *New York by Gas-Light* (1850) are two early examples.

Matthew Hale Smith's *Sunshine and Shadow in New York* (1868) is another. James D. McCabe wrote a pair, *Lights and Shadows of New York* (1872) and *New York by Sunlight and Gaslight* (1882), both of which contain much the same material. Helen Campbell's *Darkness and Daylight, or Lights and Shadows of New York Life*, published in 1897, includes a section by New York Chief of Detectives Thomas Byrnes. Though not quite in the same vein, Jacob Riis's *How the Other Half Lives* (1908) is a classic that must be mentioned.

Specific aspects of the criminal landscape have been mapped as well. Timothy Gilfoyle's incredible *City of Eros: New York City, Prostitution, and the Commercialization of Sex 1790–1920* (1992) seems to be the last word on the subject. Two excellent studies of the Jewish gangs of the Lower East Side exist: Albert Fried's wonderful *The Rise and Fall of the Jewish Gangster in America* (1980; reprinted 1993 by Columbia University Press), and Jenna W. Joselit's academic *Our Gang* (1983). *Crime on the Labor Front* (1950), by Malcolm Johnson, was mentioned in the text. Joel Tyler Headley's *The Great Riots of New York* (1873) is still in print.

The Mafia has bred an extensive literature all its own, books that range from trashy paperbacks to scholarly treatises. Valuable examples of the latter include Alan Block's *East Side—West Side: Organizing Crime in New York 1930–1950* (1983), Thomas Monroe Pitkin and Francesco Cardasco's *The Black Hand: A Chapter in Ethnic Crime* (1977), and Howard Abadinsky's *Organized Crime* (1981). More bracing reading can be found in *Gangland: How the FBI Broke the Mob* (1993) by Howard Blum, an excellent account of the Dapper Don, John Gotti; *Last Days of the Sicilians* (1988) by Ralph Blumenthal; and *Boss of Bosses* (1991) by Joseph F. O'Brien and Andris Kurins. *Donnie Brasco: My Undercover Life in the Mafia* (1987), by Joseph D. Pistone, is absolutely engrossing. There are many, many more.

Casebooks, specific and pithy, are often rewarding. Two recent studies devoted exclusively to the misdeeds of New York are *Rotten Apples* (1991) by Marvin Wolf and Katherine Mader and the flippant *New York Notorious* (1992) by Paul Schwartzmann and Rob Polner. Older but better examples include *Nation-Famous New York Murders* (1914) by Alfred Henry Lewis, *Murder Mysteries of New York* (1932) by Frank O'Brien, *New York Murders* (1944), an anthology edited by Ted Collins, Milton Crane's *Sins of New York* (1950), and St. Clair McKelway's stories from the *New Yorker*, collected in *True Tales from the Annals of Crime and Rascality* (1950).

In the 1920s and early '30s the preeminent American writer of true crime was Edmund Pearson, and his books, including *Studies in Murder* (1924), *Murder at Smutty Nose* (1926), *Instigation of the Devil* (1930), and *More Studies in Murder* (1936), contain several chapters of notorious New York homicides. His cantankerousness gets wearying after a while, though. Other dusty casebooks with New York crimes include *Unsolved Murder Mysteries* (1924) by C. A. Pearce, *Strange and Mysterious Crimes* (1929), which, mysteriously, notes no author or editor, *Murder Won't Out* (1932) by Russel Crouse, and *Murders Not Quite Solved* (1938) by Alvin Harlow.

The reminiscences of policemen and crooks are especially fascinating. A classic is George Walling's *Recollections of a New York Chief of Police*, from

1890, a cornucopia of stories and cases from the golden age of professional crime. Policeman Cornelius Willemse concocted two books, *Behind the Green Lights* (1931) and *A Cop Remembers* (1933), from his escapades with the police department. Michael Fiaschetti, head of the NYPD's Italian Squad, produced *You Gotta Be Rough* (1930). He was. *Memoirs of a Murder Man* (1930) by Homicide Detective Arthur Carey contains fascinating, insider stories of New York dispatchings. Not quite as colorful are Lewis Valentine's *Night Stick* (1947), Harold Danforth's *The D.A.'s Man* (1957), Frederick D. Collin's *Homicide Squad: Adventures of a Headquarters Old Timer* (1944), and Albert Seedman's *Chief!* (1974).

A subset of this genre is lawyer's reminiscences. These include Arthur Train's *True Stories of Crime from the District Attorney's Office* (1908) and *My Day in Court* (1939) and *Luck and Opportunity* (1938) by Francis Wellman. Recollections by reporters, psychologists and even coroners can be had as well.

One of the earliest American criminals to turn literary was George Bidwell, one of the Bank of England forgers, who penned and published the thick confession *Forging His Own Chains* (1891). Stanford White's murderer Harry Thaw wrote one of the strangest books ever put to paper, *The Traitor* (1926). Seemingly clear and yet completely unintelligible. Thief Eddie Guerin, who wrote *I Was A Bandit* (1929), was active only briefly in New York, but he provides a colorful picture of the Tenderloin in its heyday. Madams Polly Adler and Xaviera Hollander both produced autobiographies: Adler's *A House is Not a Home* (1950) is literate and amusing; Hollander's *The Happy Hooker* less so but still absorbing. *Where the Money Was* (1967), the life story of Willie Sutton, is deservedly a classic. Jack Henry Abbott's *In the Belly of the Beast* (1981) is forceful reading.

Accounts of individual crimes and characters begin with the broadsides and penny pamphlets of colonial days and continue strong to this day. There are too many to cite here. Check the bookstores, new and used, of New York. Especially good hunting can be had at New York Bound Bookshop in Rockefeller Center, the Strand Bookstore on Broadway and 12th Street, and the several used bookstores on the new "Bookseller's Row" of West 18th Street. A good mail-order source is Patterson Smith, 23 Prospect Terrace, Montclair, NJ 07042.

Index